An Introduction to Non-Classical Logic

This book is an introduction to non-classical propositional logics. It brings together for the first time in a textbook a range of topics in logic, many of them of relatively recent origin, including modal, conditional, intuitionist, many-valued, paraconsistent, relevant and fuzzy logics. The material is unified by the underlying theme of world semantics. All of the topics are explained clearly and accessibly, using devices such as tableau proofs, and their relation to current philosophical issues and debates is discussed. Students with a basic understanding of classical logic will find this an invaluable introduction to an area that has become of central importance in both logic and philosophy, but which, until now, could be studied only through the research literature. It will interest those studying logic, those who need to know about non-classical logics because of their philosophical importance, and, more widely, those working in mathematics and computer science who wish to know more about the area.

GRAHAM PRIEST is Boyce Gibson Professor of Philosophy at the University of Melbourne and Arché Professorial Fellow in the Department of Logic and Metaphysics, the University of St Andrews. His publications include *In Contradiction* (1987), *Beyond the Limits of Thought* (1995), *Logic: A Very Short Introduction* (2000) and numerous journal articles.

An Introduction to Non-Classical Logic

GRAHAM PRIEST
University of Melbourne

CAMBRIDGE
UNIVERSITY PRESS

PUBLISHED BY THE PRESS SYNDICATE OF THE UNIVERSITY OF CAMBRIDGE
The Pitt Building, Trumpington Street, Cambridge, United Kingdom

CAMBRIDGE UNIVERSITY PRESS
The Edinburgh Building, Cambridge CB2 2RU, UK www.cup.cam.ac.uk
40 West 20th Street, New York, NY 10011–4211, USA www.cup.org
10 Stamford Road, Oakleigh, Melbourne 3166, Australia
Ruiz de Alarcón 13, 28014 Madrid, Spain

First published 2001

Printed in the United Kingdom at the University Press, Cambridge

Typeface 10.5pt/14pt Times *System* 3B2

A catalogue record for this book is available from the British Library

Library of Congress Cataloguing in Publication data

Priest, Graham.
An introduction to non-classical logic / Graham Priest.
p. cm.
Includes bibliographical references and indexes
ISBN 0 521 79098 0 (hardback) – ISBN 0 521 79434 X (paperback)
1. Nonclassical mathematical logic. I. Title.
QA9.4.P75 2000
511.3 – dc21 00-023609

ISBN 0 521 79098 0 hardback
ISBN 0 521 79434 X paperback

To all those from whom I have learned

Contents

Preface

Around the turn of the twentieth century, a major revolution occurred in logic. Mathematical techniques of a quite novel kind were applied to the subject, and a new theory of what is logically correct was developed by Gottlob Frege, Bertrand Russell and others. This theory has now come to be called 'classical logic'. The name is rather inappropriate, since the logic has only a somewhat tenuous connection with logic as it was taught and understood in Ancient Greece or the Roman Empire. But it is classical in another sense of that term, namely standard. It is now the logic that people normally learn when they take a first course in formal logic. They do not learn it in the form that Frege and Russell gave it, of course. Several generations of logicians have polished it up since then; but the logic is the logic of Frege and Russell none the less.

Despite this, many of the most interesting developments in logic in the last forty years, especially in philosophy, have occurred in quite different areas: intuitionism, conditional logics, relevant logics, paraconsistent logics, free logics, quantum logics, fuzzy logics, and so on. These are all logics which are intended either to supplement classical logic, or else to replace it where it goes wrong. The logics are now usually grouped under the title 'non-classical logics'; and this book is an introduction to them.

The subject of non-classical logic is now far too big to permit the writing of a comprehensive textbook, so I have had to place some restrictions on what is covered.[1] For a start, the book is restricted to propositional logic. This is not because there are no non-classical logics that are essentially first-order (there are: free logic), but because the major interest in non-classical logics is *usually* at the propositional level. (Often, the quantifier extensions of these logics are relatively

[1] For a brief introduction and overview of the field, see Priest (1996).

straightforward.) Within propositional logics, I have also restricted the logics considered here to ones which are relevant to the debate about conditionals ('if ... then ...' sentences). Again, this is not because this exhausts non-classical propositional logics (there is quantum logic, for example), but because taking the topic of conditionals as a *leitmotiv* gives the material a coherence that it might otherwise lack. And, of course, conditionals are about as central to logic as one can get.

The major semantical technique in non-classical logics is possible-world semantics. Most non-classical logics have such semantics. This is therefore the major semantical technique that I use in the book. In many ways, the book could be thought of as a set of variations on the theme of possible-world semantics. It should be mentioned that many of the systems discussed in the book have semantics other than possible-world semantics – notably, algebraic semantics of some form or other. Those, however, are an appropriate topic for a different book.

Choosing a kind of proof theory presents more options. Logic is about validity, what follows from what. Hence, the most natural proof theories for logic are natural deduction systems and sequent calculi. Most of the systems we will consider here can, in fact, be formulated in these ways. However, I have chosen not to use these techniques, but to use tableau methods instead (except towards the end of the book, where an axiomatic approach becomes necessary). One reason for this choice is that constructing tableau proofs, and so 'getting a feel' for what is, and what is not, valid in a logic, is very easy (indeed, it is algorithmic). Another is that the soundness and, particularly, completeness proofs for logics are very simple using tableaux. Since these areas are both ones where inexperienced students experience difficulty, tableaux have great pedagogical attractions. I first learned to do tableaux for modal logics, in the way that they are presented in the book, from my colleagues Rod Girle and the now greatly missed Ian Hinckfuss. The myriad variations they take on here are my own.

This book is not meant to provide a first course in logic. I assume that readers are familiar with the classical propositional calculus, though I review this material fairly swiftly in chapter 1. (I do not assume that students are familiar with tableaux, however.) Chapter 2 introduces the basic semantic technique of possible worlds, in the form of semantics for basic modal logic. Chapters 3 and 4 extend the techniques to other modal logics. Chapter 3 looks at other normal systems of modal logic. Chapter 4 looks at non-normal worlds and their uses. Chapter 5 extends the semantic techniques, yet again, to so-called conditional logics. (The material in chapter 5 is significantly harder than anything else before the last couple of chapters of the book.)

The non-classical logics up to this point are all most naturally thought of as extensions of classical logic. In the subsequent chapters, the logics are most naturally seen as rivals to it. Chapter 6 deals with intuitionism. Chapter 7 introduces many-valued logics, and the idea that there might be truth-value gaps (sentences that are *neither* true nor false) and gluts (sentences that are *both* true and false). Chapter 8 then describes first degree entailment, a central system of both relevant and paraconsistent logics. The semantic techniques of the final chapters fuse the techniques of both modal and many-valued logic. Non-normal worlds come into their own in chapter 9, where basic relevant logics are considered. Chapter 10 considers relevant logics more generally; and in chapter 11 fuzzy logic comes under the microscope. The chapters are broken up into sections and subsections. Their numeration is self-explanatory.

The major aim of this book is to explain the basic techniques of non-classical logics. However, these techniques do not float in mid-air: they engage with numerous philosophical issues, especially that of conditionality. The meanings of the techniques themselves also raise important philosophical issues. I therefore thought it important to include some philosophical discussion, usually towards the end of each chapter. The discussions are hardly comprehensive – quite the opposite; but they at least serve to elucidate the technical material, and may be used as a springboard for a more extended consideration for those who are so inclined.

Since proofs of soundness and completeness are such an integral part of modern logic, I have included them for the systems considered here, where possible. This technical material is relatively self-contained, however, and, even though the matter in the book is largely cumulative, can be skipped without prejudice by those who have no need, or taste, for it. For this reason, I have relegated the material to separate sections, marked with an asterisk. These sections also take for granted a little more mathematical sophistication on the part of the reader. Towards the end of each chapter there are also sections containing some historical details and giving suggestions for further reading. At the conclusion of each chapter is a section containing a set of problems, exercises and questions. To understand the material in any but a relatively superficial way, there is no substitute for engaging with these. Questions that pertain to the sections marked with an asterisk are themselves marked with an asterisk, and can be ignored without prejudice.

I have taught a course based on the material in this book, or similar material, a number of times over the last ten years. I am grateful to the generations of students whose feedback has helped to improve both the content and the presentation. I have learned more from their questions than they would ever have been aware of. I am particularly grateful to the class of '99, who laboured under a draft of the book, picking up numerous typos and minor errors. I am grateful, too, to Aislinn Batstone, Stephen Read and some anonymous readers for comments which greatly improved the manuscript. I am sure that it could be improved in many other ways. But if one waited for perfection, one would wait for ever.

Mathematical prolegomenon

In expositions of modern logic, the use of some mathematics is unavoidable. The amount of mathematics used in this text is rather minimal, but it may yet throw a reader who is unfamiliar with it. In this section I will explain briefly two bits of mathematics that will help a reader through the text. The first is some simple set-theoretic notation and its meaning. The second is the notion of proof by induction. It is not necessary to master the following before starting the book; the material can be consulted if and when required.

0.1 Set-theoretic notation

0.1.1 The text makes use of standard set-theoretic notation from time to time (though never in a very essential way). Here is a brief explanation of it.

0.1.2 A set, X, is a collection of objects. If the set comprises the objects $a_1, \ldots, a_n$, this may be written as $\{a_1, \ldots, a_n\}$. If it is the set of objects satisfying some condition, $A(x)$, then it may be written $\{x; A(x)\}$. $a \in X$ means that a is a *member* of the set X, that is, a is one of the objects in X. $a \notin X$ means that a is not a member of X.

0.1.3 *Examples:* The set of (natural) numbers less than 5 is $\{0, 1, 2, 3, 4\}$. Call this F. The set of even numbers is $\{x;\ x \text{ is an even natural number}\}$. Call this E. Then $3 \in F$, and $5 \notin E$.

0.1.4 Sets can have any number of members. In particular, for any a, there is a set whose only member is a, written $\{a\}$. $\{a\}$ is called a *singleton* (and is not to be confused with a itself). There is also a set which has no members, the *empty set*; this is written as ϕ.

0.1.5 *Examples:* $\{3\}$ is the set containing just the number three. It has one member. It is distinct from 3, which is a number, not a set at all, and so has no members.[1] $3 \notin \phi$.

0.1.6 A set, X, is a *subset* of a set, Y, if and only if every member of X is a member of Y. This is written as $X \subseteq Y$. The empty set is a subset of every set (including itself). $X \subset Y$ means that X is a *proper* subset of Y; that is, everything in X is in Y, but there are some things in Y that are not in X. X and Y are identical sets, $X = Y$, if they have the same members, i.e., if $X \subseteq Y$ and $Y \subseteq X$. Hence, if X and Y are not identical, $X \neq Y$, either there are some members of X that are not in Y, or vice versa (or both).

0.1.7 *Examples:* Let N be the set of all natural numbers, and E be the set of even numbers. Then $\phi \subseteq N$ and $E \subseteq N$. Also, $E \subset N$, since $5 \in N$ but $5 \notin E$. If $X \subseteq N$ and $X \neq E$ then either some odd number is in X, or some even number is not in X (or both).

0.1.8 The *union* of two sets, X, Y, is the set containing just those things that are in X or Y (or both). This is written as $X \cup Y$. So $a \in X \cup Y$ if and only if $a \in X$ or $a \in Y$. The *intersection* of two sets, X, Y, is the set containing just those things that are in both X and Y. It is written $X \cap Y$. So $a \in X \cap Y$ if and only if $a \in X$ and $a \in Y$. The *relative complement* of one set, X, with respect to another, Y, is the set of all things in Y but not in X. It is written $Y - X$. Thus, $a \in Y - X$ if and only if $a \in Y$ but $a \notin X$.

0.1.9 *Examples:* Let N, E and O be the set of all numbers, all even numbers, and all odd numbers, respectively. Then $E \cup O = N$, $E \cap O = \phi$. Let $T = \{x;\ x \geq 10\}$. Then $E - T = \{0, 2, 4, 6, 8\}$.

0.1.10 An *ordered pair*, $\langle a, b\rangle$, is a set whose members occur in the order shown, so that we know which is the first and which is the

[1] In some reductions of number theory to set theory, 3 is identified with a certain set, and so may have members. But in the most common reduction, 3 has three members, not one.

second. Similarly for an ordered triple, $\langle a, b, c\rangle$, quadruple, $\langle a, b, c, d\rangle$, and, in general, n-tuple, $\langle x_1, ..., x_n\rangle$. Given n sets $X_1, ..., X_n$, their *cartesian product*, $X_1 \times ... \times X_n$, is the set of all n-tuples, the first member of which is in X_1, the second of which is in X_2, etc. Thus, $\langle x_1, ..., x_n\rangle \in X_1 \times ... \times X_n$ if and only if $x_1 \in X_1$ and ... and $x_n \in X_n$. A *relation*, R, between $X_1, ..., X_n$ is any subset of $X_1 \times ... \times X_n$. $\langle x_1, ..., x_n\rangle \in R$ is usually written as $Rx_1...x_n$. If n is 3, the relation is a *ternary* relation. If n is 2, the relation is a *binary* relation, and Rx_1x_2 is usually written as x_1Rx_2. A *function* from X to Y is a binary relation, f, between X and Y, such that for all $x \in X$ there is a unique $y \in Y$ such that xfy. More usually, in this case, we write: $f(x) = y$.

0.1.11 *Examples:* $\langle 2, 3\rangle \neq \langle 3, 2\rangle$, since these sets have the same members, but in a different order. Let N be the set of numbers. Then $N \times N$ is the set of all pairs of the form $\langle n, m\rangle$, where n and m are in N. If $R = \{\langle 2, 3\rangle, \langle 3, 2\rangle\}$ then $R \subseteq N \times N$ and is a binary relation between N and itself. If $f = \{\langle n, n^2\rangle; n \in N\}$, then f is a function from numbers to numbers, and $f(n) = n^2$.

0.2 Proof by induction

0.2.1 The method of proof by induction (or recursion) on the complexity of sentences is used heavily in the asterisked sections of the book. It is also used occasionally in other sections, though sections where it is employed can be skipped without loss. What this method comes to is this. Suppose that all of the simplest formulas (the propositional parameters) of some formal language have some property, P. (This is called the *basis case*.) And suppose that we know that whenever one constructs more complex formulas out of formulas that have property P, the resulting formulas also have that property. (This is often called the *induction clause*.) Then it follows that all the formulas of that language have the property P. Thus, for example, given that p and q have the property, it follows that $p \wedge q$ has it, as does $\neg p$. But then, so does $\neg p \vee (p \wedge q)$, and so on for any other formula one can construct.

0.2.2 The proof of the induction clause normally breaks down into a number of different cases, one for each of the connectives employed in constructing more complex formulas. Thus, we assume that A has property P and show that $\neg A$ does; we assume that A and B have property P, and show that $A \wedge B$ does; and so on for every connective. The assumption, in each case, is called the *induction hypothesis*.

0.2.3 Here is a simple example of a proof by induction. We show that every formula of the propositional calculus which is grammatical according to the rules of 1.2.2 has an even number of brackets. (This is a bit like cracking a nut with a sledge-hammer; but it illustrates the method clearly.)

Proof:

BASIS CASE: First, we need to establish that this result holds for all of the simplest formulas, the propositional parameters. All such formulas have no (zero) brackets, and 0 is an even number. Hence, the result holds for propositional parameters.

INDUCTION CLAUSE: Next we must establish that if the result holds for some formulas, and we construct other formulas out of those, the result holds for these too. So suppose that A and B have an even number of brackets. (This is the induction hypothesis.) We need to show that each of $\neg A$, $(A \vee B)$, $(A \wedge B)$, $(A \supset B)$ and $(A \equiv B)$ has an even number of brackets too. There is one case for each of the constructions in question.

For $\neg$: the number of brackets in $\neg A$ is the same as the number of brackets in A. Since this is even (by the induction hypothesis), the result follows. (We did not use the induction hypothesis concerning B in this case, but that does not matter.)

For $\vee$: suppose that the number of brackets in A is a, and the number of brackets in B is b. Then the number of brackets in $(A \vee B)$ is $a + b + 2$ (since the construction introduces two new brackets). But a and b are even, and so $a + b + 2$ is even. Hence, the number of brackets in $(A \vee B)$ is even, as required.

For $\wedge$, $\supset$, and $\equiv$: the arguments are exactly the same as for $\vee$.

We have now established thc basis case and the induction clause. It follows from these that the result holds for all formulas; that is, all grammatical formulas have an even number of brackets.

1 Classical logic and the material conditional

1.1 Introduction

1.1.1 The first purpose of this chapter is to review classical propositional logic, including semantic tableaux. The chapter also sets out some basic terminology and notational conventions for the rest of the book.

1.1.2 In the second half of the chapter we also look at the notion of the conditional that classical propositional logic gives, and, specifically, at some of its shortcomings.

1.1.3 The point of logic is to give an account of the notion of validity: what follows from what. Standardly, validity is defined for inferences couched in a formal language, a language with a well-defined vocabulary and grammar, the *object language*. The relationship of the symbols of the formal language to the words of the vernacular, English in this case, is always an important issue.

1.1.4 Accounts of validity themselves are in a language that is normally distinct from the object language. This is called the *metalanguage*. In our case, this is simply mathematical English. Note that 'iff' means 'if and only if'.

1.1.5 It is also standard to define two notions of validity. The first is *semantic*. A valid inference is one that *preserves truth*, in a certain sense. Specifically, every interpretation (that is, crudely, a way of assigning truth values) that makes all the premises true makes the conclusion true. We use the metalinguistic symbol '$\models$' for this. What distinguishes different logics is the different notions of interpretation they employ.

1.1.6 The second notion of validity is *proof-theoretic*. Validity is defined in terms of some purely formal procedure (that is, one that makes reference only to the symbols of the inference). We use the metalinguistic symbol '$\vdash$' for this notion of validity. In our case, this procedure will (mainly) be one employing tableaux. What distinguishes different logics here are the different tableau procedures employed.

1.1.7 Most contemporary logicians would take the semantic notion of validity to be more fundamental than the proof-theoretic one, though the matter is certainly debatable. However, given a semantic notion of validity, it is always useful to have a proof-theoretic notion that corresponds to it, in the sense that the two definitions always give the same answers. If every proof-theoretically valid inference is semantically valid (so that $\vdash$ entails $\models$) the proof-theory is said to be *sound*. If every semantically valid inference is proof-theoretically valid (so that $\models$ entails $\vdash$) the proof-theory is said to be *complete*.

1.2 The syntax of the object language

1.2.1 The symbols of the object language of the propositional calculus are an infinite number of propositional parameters:[1] $p_0, p_1, p_2, \ldots$; the connectives: $\neg$ (negation), $\wedge$ (conjunction), $\vee$ (disjunction), $\supset$ (material conditional), $\equiv$ (material equivalence); and the punctuation marks: (,).

1.2.2 The (well-formed) formulas of the language comprise all, and only, the strings of symbols that can be generated recursively from the propositional parameters by the following rule:

If A and B are formulas, so are $\neg A$, $(A \vee B)$, $(A \wedge B)$, $(A \supset B)$, $(A \equiv B)$.

1 These are often called 'propositional variables'.

1.2.3 I will explain a number of important notational conventions here. I use capital Roman letters, A, B, C, ..., to represent arbitrary formulas of the object language. Lower-case Roman letters, p, q, r, ..., represent arbitrary, but distinct, propositional parameters. I will always omit outermost parentheses of formulas if there are any. So, for example, I write $(A \supset (B \vee \neg C))$ simply as $A \supset (B \vee \neg C)$. Upper-case Greek letters, Σ, Π, ..., represent arbitrary sets of formulas; the empty set, however, is denoted by the (lower case) ϕ, in the standard way. I often write a finite set, $\{A_1, A_2, \ldots, A_n\}$, simply as $A_1, A_2, \ldots, A_n$.

1.3 Semantic validity

1.3.1 An *interpretation* of the language is a function, ν, which assigns to each propositional parameter either 1 (true), or 0 (false). Thus, we write things such as $\nu(p) = 1$ and $\nu(q) = 0$.

1.3.2 Given an interpretation of the language, ν, this is extended to a function that assigns every formula a truth value, by the following recursive clauses, which mirror the syntactic recursive clauses:[2]

$\nu(\neg A) = 1$ if $\nu(A) = 0$, and 0 otherwise.

$\nu(A \wedge B) = 1$ if $\nu(A) = \nu(B) = 1$, and 0 otherwise.

$\nu(A \vee B) = 1$ if $\nu(A) = 1$ or $\nu(B) = 1$, and 0 otherwise.

$\nu(A \supset B) = 1$ if $\nu(A) = 0$ or $\nu(B) = 1$, and 0 otherwise.

$\nu(A \equiv B) = 1$ if $\nu(A) = \nu(B)$, and 0 otherwise.

1.3.3 Let Σ be any set of formulas (the premises); then A (the conclusion) is a *semantic consequence* of Σ ($\Sigma \models A$) iff there is no interpreta-

2 The reader might be more familiar with the information contained in these clauses when it is depicted in the form of a table, usually called a *truth table*, such as the following one for *conjunction*:

$\wedge$	**1**	**0**
1	1	0
0	0	0

tion that makes all the members of Σ true and A false, that is, every interpretation that makes all the members of Σ true makes A true. '$\Sigma \not\models A$' means that it is not the case that $\Sigma \models A$.

1.3.4 A is a *logical truth* (*tautology*) ($\models A$) iff it is a semantic consequence of the empty set of premises ($\phi \models A$), that is, every interpretation makes A true.

1.4 Tableaux

1.4.1 A *tree* is a structure that looks, generally, like this:[3]

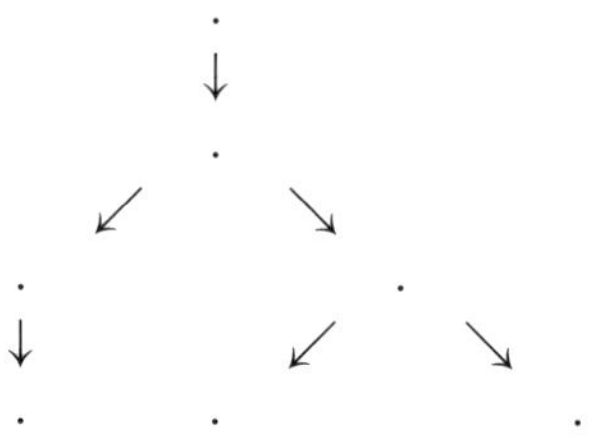

The dots are called *nodes*. The node at the top is called the *root*. The nodes at the bottom are called *tips*. Any path from the root down a series of arrows as far as you can go is called a *branch*. (Later on we will have trees with infinite branches, but not yet.)

1.4.2 To test an inference for validity, we construct a tableau which begins with a single branch at whose nodes occur the premises (if there are any) and the negation of the conclusion. We will call this the *initial list*. We then apply rules which allow us to extend this branch. The rules for the conditional are as follows:

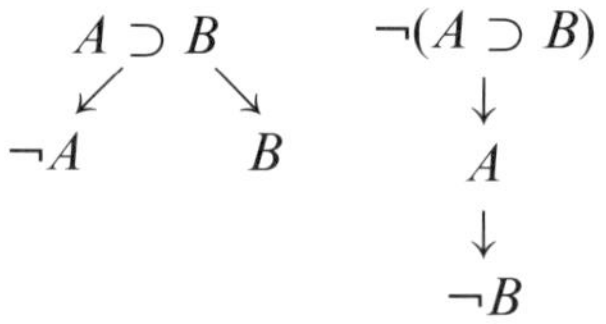

[3] Strictly speaking, for those who want the precise mathematical definition, it is a partial order with a unique maximum element, x_0, such that for any element, x_n, there is a unique finite chain of elements $x_n \leq x_{n-1} \leq \ldots \leq x_1 \leq x_0$.

The rule on the right is to be interpreted as follows. If we have a formula $\neg(A \supset B)$ at a node, then every branch that goes through that node is extended with two further nodes, one for A and one for $\neg B$. The rule on the left is interpreted similarly: if we have a formula $A \supset B$ at a node, then every branch that goes through that node is split at its tip into two branches; one contains a node for $\neg A$; the other contains a node for B.

1.4.3 For example, to test the inference whose premises are $A \supset B$, $B \supset C$, and whose conclusion is $A \supset C$, we construct the following tree:

$$
\begin{array}{ccccccccc}
 & & & & A \supset B & & & & \\
 & & & & \downarrow & & & & \\
 & & & & B \supset C & & & & \\
 & & & & \downarrow & & & & \\
 & & & & \neg(A \supset C) & & & & \\
 & & & & \downarrow & & & & \\
 & & & & A & & & & \\
 & & & & \downarrow & & & & \\
 & & & & \neg C & & & & \\
 & & & \swarrow & & \searrow & & & \\
 & & \neg A & & & & B & & \\
 & \swarrow & \downarrow & & & & \downarrow & \searrow & \\
\neg B & & C & & & & \neg B & & C \\
\times & & \times & & & & \times & & \times
\end{array}
$$

The first three formulas are the premises and negated conclusion. The next two formulas are produced by the rule for the negated conditional applied to the negated conclusion; the first split on the branch is produced by applying the rule for the conditional to the first premise; the next splits are produced by applying the same rule to the second premise. (Ignore the '$\times$'s: we will come back to those in a moment.)

1.4.4 The other connectives also have rules, which are as follows.

$$
\begin{array}{c}
\neg\neg A \\
\downarrow \\
A
\end{array}
$$

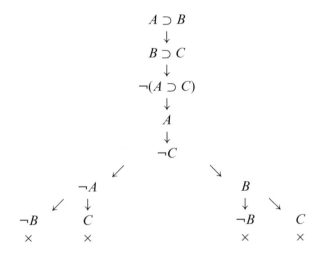

$$
\begin{array}{ccc} & A \vee B & \\ \swarrow & & \searrow \\ A & & B \end{array}
\qquad\qquad
\begin{array}{c} \neg(A \vee B) \\ \downarrow \\ \neg A \\ \downarrow \\ \neg B \end{array}
$$

$$
\begin{array}{ccc} & \neg(A \wedge B) & \\ \swarrow & & \searrow \\ \neg A & & \neg B \end{array}
\qquad\qquad
\begin{array}{c} A \wedge B \\ \downarrow \\ A \\ \downarrow \\ B \end{array}
$$

$$
\begin{array}{ccc} & A \equiv B & \\ \swarrow & & \searrow \\ A & & \neg A \\ \downarrow & & \downarrow \\ B & & \neg B \end{array}
\qquad
\begin{array}{ccc} & \neg(A \equiv B) & \\ \swarrow & & \searrow \\ A & & \neg A \\ \downarrow & & \downarrow \\ \neg B & & B \end{array}
$$

Intuitively, what a tableau means is the following. If we apply a rule to a formula, then if that formula is true in an interpretation, so are the formulas below on at least one of the branches that the rule generates. (Of course, there may be only one such branch.) This is a useful mnemonic for remembering the rules. It must be stressed, though, that officially the rules are purely formal.

1.4.5 A tableau is *complete* iff every rule that can be applied has been applied. By applying the rules over and over, we may always construct a complete tableau. In the present case, the branches of a completed tableau are always finite,[4] but in the tableaux of some subsequent chapters they may be infinite.

1.4.6 A branch is *closed* iff there are formulas of the form A and $\neg A$ on two of its nodes; otherwise it is *open*. A closed branch is indicated by writing an $\times$ at the bottom. A *tableau* itself is closed iff every branch is closed; otherwise it is open. Thus the tableau of 1.4.3 is closed: the leftmost branch contains A and $\neg A$; the next contains A

[4] This is not entirely obvious, though it is not difficult to prove.

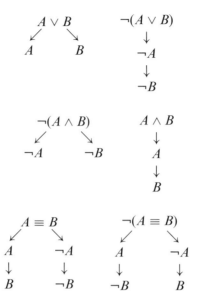

and $\neg A$ (and C and $\neg C$); the next contains B and $\neg B$; the rightmost contains C and $\neg C$.

1.4.7 A is a proof-theoretic consequence of the set of formulas Σ ($\Sigma \vdash A$) iff there is a complete tree whose initial list comprises the members of Σ and the negation of A, and which is closed. We write $\vdash A$ to mean that $\phi \vdash A$, that is, where the initial list of the tableau comprises just $\neg A$. '$\Sigma \nvdash A$' means that it is not the case that $\Sigma \vdash A$.[5]

1.4.8 Thus, the tree of 1.4.3 shows that $A \supset B, B \supset C \vdash A \supset C$. Here is another, to show that $\vdash ((A \supset B) \wedge (A \supset C)) \supset (A \supset (B \wedge C))$. To save space, we omit arrows where a branch does not divide.

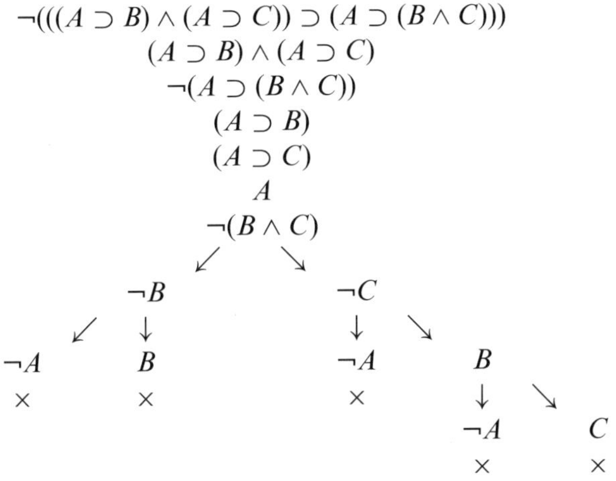

Note that when we find a contradiction on a branch, there is no point in continuing it further. We know that the branch is going to close, whatever else is added to it. Hence, we need not bother to extend a branch as soon as it is found to close. Notice also that, wherever possible, we apply rules that do not split branches before

[5] There may, in fact, be several completed trees for an inference, depending upon the order of the premises in the initial list and the order in which rules are applied. Fortunately, they all give the same result, though this is not entirely obvious. See 1.14, problem 5.

rules that split branches. Though this is not essential, it keeps the tableau simpler, and is therefore useful practically.

1.4.9 In practice, it is also a useful idea to put a tick at the side of a formula once one has applied a rule to it. Then one knows that one can forget about it.

1.5 Counter-models

1.5.1 Here is another example, to show that $(p \supset q) \vee (r \supset q) \nvdash (p \vee r) \supset q$.

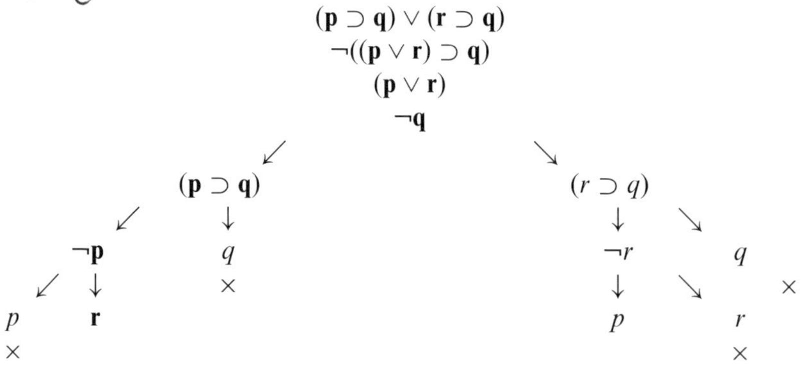

The tableau has two open branches. The leftmost one is emphasised in bold for future reference.

1.5.2 The tableau procedure is, in effect, a systematic search for an interpretation that makes all the formulas on the initial list true. Given an open branch of a tableau, such an interpretation can, in fact, be read off from the branch.

1.5.3 The recipe is simple. If the propositional parameter, p, occurs at a node on the branch, assign it 1; if $\neg p$ occurs at a node on the branch, assign it 0. (If neither p nor $\neg p$ occurs in this way, it may be assigned anything one likes.)

1.5.4 For example, consider the tableau of 1.5.1 and its (bolded) leftmost open branch. Applying the recipe gives the interpretation, ν, such that $\nu(r) = 1$, and $\nu(p) = \nu(q) = 0$. It is simple to check directly that $\nu((p \supset q) \vee (r \supset q)) = 1$ and $\nu((p \vee r) \supset q) = 0$. Since p is false, $p \supset q$ is true, as is $(p \supset q) \vee (r \supset q)$. Since r is true, $p \vee r$ is true; but q is false; hence, $(p \vee r) \supset q$ is false.

1.5.5 As one would hope, the tableau procedure we have been looking at is sound and complete with respect to the semantic notion of consequence, i.e., if Σ is a finite set of sentences, $\Sigma \vdash A$ iff $\Sigma \models A$. That is, the search procedure really works. If there is an interpretation that makes all the formulas on the initial list true, the tableau will have an open branch which, in effect, specifies one. And if there is no such interpretation, every branch will close. These facts are not obvious. The proof is in 1.11.[6]

1.6 Conditionals

1.6.1 In the remainder of this chapter, we look at the notion of conditionality that the above, classical, semantics give us, and at its inadequacy. But first, what is a conditional?

1.6.2 Conditionals relate some proposition (the *consequent*) to some other proposition (the *antecedent*) on which, in some sense, it depends. They are expressed in English by 'if' or cognate constructions:

If the bough breaks (then) the cradle will fall.

The cradle will fall if the bough breaks.

The bough breaks only if the cradle falls.

[6] The restriction to finite Σ is due to the fact that tableaux have been defined only for finite sets of premises. It is possible to define tableaux for infinite sets of premises as well (not putting all the premises at the start, but introducing them, one by one, at regular intervals down the branches). If one does this, the soundness and completeness results generalise to arbitrary sets of premises, but we will not go into this here.

If the bough were to break the cradle would fall.

Were the bough to break the cradle would fall.

1.6.3 Note that the grammar of conditionals imposes certain requirements on the tense (past, present, future) and mood (indicative, subjunctive) of the sentences expressing the antecedent and consequent within it. These may be different when the antecedent and consequent stand alone. To see this, just consider the following applications of *modus ponens* (if A then B; A; hence B):

If he *takes* a plane he will get there quicker.
He *will take* a plane.
Hence, he will get there quicker.

If he *had come* in the window there *would have been* foot-marks.
He *did come* in the window.
So, there *are* foot-marks.

1.6.4 Note, also, that not all sentences using 'if' are conditionals; consider, for example, 'If I may say so, you have a nice ear-ring', '(Even) if he was plump, he could still run fast', or 'If you want a banana, there is one in the kitchen.' A rough and ready test for 'if A, B' to be a conditional is that it can be rewritten equivalently as 'that A implies that B'.

1.7 The material conditional

1.7.1 The connective $\supset$ is usually called the *material conditional* (or *material implication*). As its truth conditions show, $A \supset B$ is logically equivalent to $\neg A \vee B$. It is true iff A is false or B is true. Thus, we have:

$$B \models A \supset B$$

$$\neg A \models A \supset B$$

These are sometimes called the 'paradoxes of material implication'.

1.7.2 People taking a first course in logic are often told that English conditionals may be represented as $\supset$. There is an obvious objection to this claim, though. If it were correct, then the truth conditions of $\supset$ would ensure the truth of the following, which appear to be false:

If New York is in New Zealand then $2+2=4$.

If New York is in the United States then World War II ended in 1945.

If World War II ended in 1941 then gold is an acid.

1.7.3 It is possible to reply to this objection as follows. These examples are, indeed, true. They strike us as counterintuitive, though, for the following reason. Communication between people is governed by many pragmatic rules of conversation, for example 'be relevant', 'assert the strongest claim you are in a position to make'. We often use the fact that these rules are in place to draw conclusions. Consider, for example, what you would infer from the following questions and replies: 'How do you use this drill?', 'There's a book over there.' (It is a drill manual. *Relevance*.) 'Who won the 3.30 at Ascot?', 'It was a horse named either Blue Grass or Red Grass.' (The speaker does not know which. *Assert the strongest information*.) These inferences are inferences, not from the *content* of what has been said, but from the fact that *it has been said*. The process is often dubbed 'conversational implicature'. Now, the claim goes, the examples of 1.7.2 strike us as odd since anyone who asserted them would be violating the rule *assert the strongest*, since, in each case, we are in a position to assert either the consequent or the negation of the antecedent (or both).

1.8 Subjunctive and counterfactual conditionals

1.8.1 A harder objection to the correctness of the material conditional is to the effect that there are pairs of conditionals which appear to have the same antecedent and consequent, but which clearly have different truth values. They cannot both, therefore, be material conditionals. Consider the examples:

(1) If Oswald didn't shoot Kennedy someone else did. (True)

(2) If Oswald hadn't shot Kennedy someone else would have. (False)

1.8.2 In response to this kind of example, it is not uncommon for philosophers to distinguish between two sorts of conditionals: conditionals in which the consequent is expressed using the word 'would' (called 'subjunctive' or 'counterfactual'), and others (called 'indicative'). Subjunctive conditionals, like (2), cannot be material: after all, (2) is false, though its antecedent is false (assuming the results of the Warren Commission!). But indicative conditionals may still be material.

1.8.3 The claim that the English conditional is ambiguous between subjunctive and indicative is somewhat dubious, though. There appears to be no grammatical justification for it, for a start. In (1) and (2) the 'if's are grammatically identical; it is the tenses and/or moods of the verbs involved which make the difference.

1.8.4 What these differences seem to do is to get us to evaluate the truth values of conditionals from different points in time. Thus, we evaluate (1) as true from the present, where Kennedy has, in fact, been shot. The difference of tense and mood of (2) asks us to evaluate the conditional 'If Oswald doesn't shoot Kennedy, someone else will' from the perspective of a time just before Kennedy was shot. It is, in a certain sense, the past tense of that conditional. Notice that no difference of the kind between (1) and (2) arises in the case of present-tense conditionals. There is no major difference between 'If I shoot you, you will die' and 'If I were to shoot you, you would die.'

1.9 More counter-examples

1.9.1 There are more fundamental objections against the claim that the indicative English conditional (even if it is distinct from the subjunctive) is material. It is easy to check that the following inferences are valid.

$$(A \wedge B) \supset C \vdash (A \supset C) \vee (B \supset C)$$

$$(A \supset B) \wedge (C \supset D) \vdash (A \supset D) \vee (C \supset B)$$

$$\neg(A \supset B) \vdash A$$

If the English indicative conditional were material, the following inferences would, respectively, be instances of the above, and therefore valid, which they are clearly not.

(1) If you close switch x and switch y the light will go on. Hence, it is the case either that if you close switch x the light will go on, or that if you close switch y the light will go on. (Imagine an electrical circuit where switches x and y are in series, so that both are required for the light to go on, and both switches are open.)

(2) If John is in Paris he is in France, and if John is in London he is in England. Hence, it is the case either that if John is in Paris he is in England, or that if he is in London he is in France.

(3) It is not the case that if there is a good god the prayers of evil people will be answered. Hence, there is a god.

1.9.2 Notice that all these conditionals are indicative. Note, also, that appealing to conversational rules cannot explain why the conclusions appear odd, as in 1.7.3. For example, in the first, it is not the case that we already know which disjunct of the conclusion is true: *both* appear to be false.

1.9.3 It might be pointed out that the above arguments are valid if 'if' is understood as $\supset$. However, this just concedes the point: 'if' in English is not understood as $\supset$.

1.10 Arguments for $\supset$

1.10.1 The claim that the English conditional (or even the indicative conditional) is material is therefore hard to sustain. In the light of this it is worth asking why anyone ever thought this. At least in the modern period, a large part of the answer is that, until the 1960s, standard truth-table semantics were the only ones that there were, and $\supset$ is the only truth function that looks an even remotely plausible candidate for 'if'.

1.10.2 Some arguments have been offered, however. Here is one, to the effect that 'If A then B' is true iff '$A \supset B$' is true.

1.10.3 First, suppose that 'If A then B' is true. Either $\neg A$ is true or A is. In this first case, $\neg A \vee B$ is true. In the second case, B is true by *modus ponens*. Hence, again, $\neg A \vee B$ is true. Thus, in either case, $\neg A \vee B$ is true.

1.10.4 The converse argument appeals to the following plausible claim:

> (*) 'If A then B' is true if there is some true statement, C, such that from C and A together we can deduce B.

Thus, we agree that the conditional 'If Oswald didn't kill Kennedy, someone else did' is true because we can deduce that someone other than Oswald killed Kennedy from the fact that Kennedy was murdered and Oswald did not do it.

1.10.5 Now, suppose that $\neg A \vee B$ is true. Then from this and A we can deduce B, by the *disjunctive syllogism*: $A, \neg A \vee B \vdash B$. Hence, by (*), 'If A then B' is true.

1.10.6 We will come back to this argument in a later chapter. For now, just note the fact that it uses the disjunctive syllogism.

1.11 *Proofs of theorems

1.11.1 DEFINITION: Let ν be any propositional interpretation. Let b be any branch of a tableau. Say that ν is *faithful* to b iff for every formula, A, on the branch, $\nu(A) = 1$.

1.11.2 SOUNDNESS LEMMA: If ν is faithful to a branch of a tableau, b, and a tableau rule is applied to b, then ν is faithful to at least one of the branches generated.

Proof:

The proof is by a case-by-case examination of the tableau rules. Here are the cases for the rules for $\supset$. The other cases are left as exercises. Suppose that ν is faithful to b, that $\neg(A \supset B)$ occurs on b, and that we apply a rule to it. Then only one branch eventuates, that obtained by adding A and $\neg B$ to b. Since ν is faithful to b, it makes every formula on b true. In particular, $\nu(\neg(A \supset B)) = 1$. Hence, $\nu(A \supset B) = 0$, $\nu(A) = 1$, $\nu(B) = 0$, and so $\nu(\neg B) = 1$. Hence, ν makes every formula on b true. Next, suppose that ν is faithful to b, that $A \supset B$ occurs on b, and that we apply a rule to it. Then two branches eventuate, one extending b with $\neg A$ (the left branch); the other extending b with B (the right branch). Since ν is faithful to b, it makes every formula on b true. In particular, $\nu(A \supset B) = 1$. Hence, $\nu(A) = 0$, and so $\nu(\neg A) = 1$, or $\nu(B) = 1$. In the first case, ν is faithful to the left branch; in the second, it is faithful to the right.

1.11.3 SOUNDNESS THEOREM: For finite Σ, if $\Sigma \vdash A$ then $\Sigma \models A$.

Proof:

We prove the contrapositive. Suppose that $\Sigma \not\models A$. Then there is an interpretation, ν, which makes every member of Σ true, and A false – and hence makes $\neg A$ true. Now consider a completed tableau for the inference. ν is faithful to the initial list. When we apply a rule to the list, we can, by the Soundness Lemma, find at least one of its extensions to which ν is faithful. Similarly, when we apply a rule to this, we can find at least one of *its* extensions to which ν is faithful; and so on. By repeatedly applying the Soundness Lemma in this way, we can find a whole branch, b, such that ν is faithful to every initial section of it. (It follows that ν is faithful to b itself, but we do not need this fact to make the proof work.) Now, if b were closed, it would have to contain some formulas of the form B and $\neg B$, and these must occur in some initial section of b. But this is impossible since ν is faithful to this section, and so it would follow that $\nu(B) = \nu(\neg B) = 1$, which cannot be the case. Hence, the tableau is open, i.e., $\Sigma \nvdash A$.

1.11.4 DEFINITION: Let b be an open branch of a tableau. The interpretation *induced* by b is any interpretation, ν, such that for every propositional parameter, p, if p is at a node on b, $\nu(p) = 1$, and if $\neg p$ is at a node on b, $\nu(p) = 0$. (And if neither, $\nu(p)$ can be anything one likes.) This is well defined, since b is open, and so we cannot have both p and $\neg p$ on b.

1.11.5 COMPLETENESS LEMMA: Let b be an open complete branch of a tableau. Let ν be the interpretation induced by b. Then:

if A is on b, $\nu(A) = 1$

if $\neg A$ is on b, $\nu(A) = 0$

Proof:

The proof is by induction on the complexity of A. If A is a propositional parameter, the result is true by definition. If A is complex, it is of the form $B \wedge C$, $B \vee C$, $B \supset C$, $B \equiv C$, or $\neg B$. Consider the first case, and suppose that $B \wedge C$ is on b. Since b is complete, the rule for conjunction has been applied to it. Hence, both B and C are on the branch. By induction hypothesis, $\nu(B) = \nu(C) = 1$. Hence, $\nu(B \wedge C) = 1$, as required. Next, suppose that $\neg(B \wedge C)$ is on b. Since the rule for negated conjunction has been applied to it, either $\neg B$ or $\neg C$ is on the branch. By induction hypothesis, either $\nu(B) = 0$ or $\nu(C) = 0$. In either case,

$\nu(B \wedge C) = 0$, as required. The cases for the other binary connectives are similar. For $\neg$: suppose that $\neg B$ is on b. Then, since the result holds for B, $\nu(B) = 0$. Hence, $\nu(\neg B) = 1$. If $\neg\neg B$ is on b, then so is B, by the rule for double negation. By induction hypothesis, $\nu(B) = 1$, so $\nu(\neg B) = 0$.

1.11.6 COMPLETENESS THEOREM: For finite Σ, if $\Sigma \models A$ then $\Sigma \vdash A$.

Proof:

We prove the contrapositive. Suppose that $\Sigma \nvdash A$. Consider a completed open tableau for the inference, and choose an open branch. The interpretation that the branch induces makes all the members of Σ true, and A false, by the Completeness Lemma. Hence, $\Sigma \not\models A$.

1.12 History

The propositional logic described in this chapter was first formulated by Frege in his *Begriffsschrift* (translated in Bynum, 1972) and Russell (1903). Semantic tableaux in the form described here were first given in Smullyan (1968). The issue of how to understand the conditional is an old one. Disputes about it can be found in the Stoics and in the Middle Ages. Some logicians at each of these times endorsed the material conditional. For an account of the history, see Sanford (1989). The defence of the material conditional in terms of conversational rules is due to Grice (1989, chs. 1–4). The argument for distinguishing between the indicative and subjunctive conditionals was first given by Adams (1970). The examples of 1.9 are taken from a much longer list given by Cooper (1968). The argument of 1.10 was given by Faris (1968).

1.13 Further reading

For an introduction to classical logic based on tableaux, see Jeffrey (1991), Howson (1997) or Restall (2000a). For a number of good papers discussing the connection between material, indicative and subjunctive conditionals, see Jackson (1991). For further discussion of the examples of 1.9, see Routley, Plumwood, Meyer and Brady (1982, ch. 1).

1.14 Problems

1. Check the truth of each of the following, using tableaux. If the inference is invalid, read off a counter-model from the tree, and check directly that it makes the premises true and the conclusion false, as in 1.5.4.

   (*a*) $p \supset q, r \supset q \vdash (p \vee r) \supset q$

   (*b*) $p \supset (q \wedge r), \neg r \vdash \neg p$

   (*c*) $\vdash ((p \supset q) \supset q) \supset q$

   (*d*) $\vdash ((p \supset q) \wedge (\neg p \supset q)) \supset \neg p$

   (*e*) $p \equiv (q \equiv r) \vdash (p \equiv q) \equiv r$

   (*f*) $\neg(p \supset q) \wedge \neg(p \supset r) \vdash \neg q \vee \neg r$

   (*g*) $p \wedge (\neg r \vee s), \neg(q \supset s) \vdash r$

   (*h*) $\vdash (p \supset (q \supset r)) \supset (q \supset (p \supset r))$

   (*i*) $\neg(p \wedge \neg q) \vee r, p \supset (r \equiv s) \vdash \ p \equiv q$

   (*j*) $p \equiv \neg\neg q, \neg q \supset (r \wedge \neg s), s \supset (p \vee q) \vdash (s \wedge q) \supset p$

2. Give an argument to show that $A \models B$ iff $\models A \supset B$. (*Hint*: split the argument into two parts: left to right, and right to left. Then just apply the definition of $\models$. You may find it easier to prove the contrapositives. That is, assume that $\not\models A \supset B$, and deduce that $A \not\models B$; then vice versa.)

3. How, if at all, could one defend or attack the arguments of 1.7, 1.8 and 1.9?

4. *Check the details omitted in 1.11.2 and 1.11.5.

5. *Use the Soundness and Completeness Lemmas to show that if one completed tableau for an inference is open, they all are. Infer that the result of a tableau test is indifferent to the order in which one lists the premises of the argument and applies the tableau rules.

2 Basic modal logic

K

2.1 Introduction

2.1.1 In this chapter, we look at the basic technique – possible-world semantics – variations on which will occupy us for most of the following chapters. (We will return to the subject of the conditional in chapter 4.)

2.1.2 This will take us into an area called *modal logic*. This chapter concerns the most basic modal logic, *K* (after Kripke).

2.2 Necessity and possibility

2.2.1 Modal logic concerns itself with the *modes* in which things may be true/false, particularly their possibility, necessity and impossibility. These notions are highly ambiguous, a subject to which we will return in the next chapter.

2.2.2 The modal semantics that we will examine employ the notion of a *possible world*. Exactly what possible worlds are, we will return to later in this chapter. For the present, the following will suffice. We can all imagine that things might have been different. For example, you can imagine that things are exactly the same, except that you are a centimetre taller. What you are imagining here is a different situation, or possible world. Of course, the actual world is a possible world too, and there are indefinitely many others as well, where you are two centimetres taller, three centimetres taller, where you have a different colour hair, where you were born in another country, and so on.

2.2.3 The other intuitive notion that the semantics employs is that of *relative possibility*. Given how things are now, it is possible for me to be in New York in a week's time, 26 January. Given how things will be in six days and twenty-three hours, it will no longer be possible. (I am writing in Brisbane.) Or, even if one countenances the possibility of some futuristic and exceptionally fast form of travel, assuming that I do not leave Brisbane in the next eight days, it will then be impossible for me to be in New York on 26 January. Hence, certain states of affairs are possible relative to some situations (worlds), but not others.

2.3 Modal semantics

2.3.1 A propositional modal language augments the language of the propositional calculus with two monadic operators, $\Box$ and $\Diamond$.[1] Intuitively, $\Box A$ is read as 'It is necessarily the case that A'; $\Diamond A$ as 'It is possibly the case that A'.

2.3.2 Thus, the grammar of 1.2.2 is augmented with the rule:

If A is a formula, so are $\Box A$ and $\Diamond A$.

2.3.3 An *interpretation* for this language is a triple $\langle W, R, \nu\rangle$. W is a non-empty set. Formally, W is an arbitrary set of objects. Intuitively, its members are possible worlds. R is a binary relation on W (so that, technically, $R \subseteq W \times W$). Thus, if u and v are in W, R may or may not relate them to each other. If it does, we will write uRv, and say that v is *accessible* from u. Intuitively, R is a relation of relative possibility, so that uRv means that, relative to u, situation v is possible. ν is a function that assigns a truth value (1 or 0) to each pair comprising a world, w, and a propositional parameter, p. We write this as $\nu_w(p) = 1$ (or $\nu_w(p) = 0$). Intuitively, this is read as 'at world w, p is true (or false)'.

[1] Some logicians use L and M, respectively.

2.3.4 Given an interpretation, ν, this is extended to assign a truth value to every formula at every world by a recursive set of conditions. The conditions for the truth functions ($\neg$, $\wedge$, $\vee$, etc.) are the same as those for propositional logic (1.3.2), except that things are relativised to worlds. Thus, for $\neg$, $\wedge$ and $\vee$, the conditions go as follows. For any world $w \in W$:

$\nu_w(\neg A) = 1$ if $\nu_w(A) = 0$, and 0 otherwise.

$\nu_w(A \wedge B) = 1$ if $\nu_w(A) = \nu_w(B) = 1$, and 0 otherwise.

$\nu_w(A \vee B) = 1$ if $\nu_w(A) = 1$ or $\nu_w(B) = 1$, and 0 otherwise.

In other words, worlds play no essential role in the truth conditions for the non-modal operators.

2.3.5 They play an essential role in the truth conditions for the modal operators. For any world $w \in W$:

$\nu_w(\Diamond A) = 1$ if, for some $w' \in W$ such that wRw', $\nu_{w'}(A) = 1$; and 0 otherwise.

$\nu_w(\Box A) = 1$ if, for all $w' \in W$ such that wRw', $\nu_{w'}(A) = 1$; and 0 otherwise.

In other words, 'It is possibly the case that A' is true at a world, w, if A is true at *some* world, possible relative to w. And 'It is necessarily the case that A' is true at a world, w, if A is true at *every* world, possible relative to w.

2.3.6 Note that if w accesses no worlds, everything of the form $\Diamond A$ is false at w – if w accesses no worlds, it accesses no worlds at which A is true. And if w accesses no worlds, everything of the form $\Box A$ is true at w – if w accesses no worlds, then (vacuously) at all worlds that w accesses A is true.[2]

[2] Recall that 'all Xs are Ys' is logically equivalent to 'there are no Xs that are not Ys'.

2.3.7 A finite interpretation (that is, where W is a finite set) can be perspicuously represented diagrammatically. For example, let $W = \{w_1, w_2, w_3\}$; $w_1 R w_2$, $w_1 R w_3$, $w_3 R w_3$ (and no other worlds are related by R); $v_{w_1}(p) = 0$, $v_{w_1}(q) = 0$; $v_{w_2}(p) = 1$, $v_{w_2}(q) = 1$; $v_{w_3}(p) = 1$, $v_{w_3}(q) = 0$. This interpretation can be represented as follows:

$$
\begin{array}{ccc}
 & & w_2 \quad p \quad q \\
 & \nearrow & \\
\neg p \quad \neg q \quad w_1 & & \\
 & \searrow & \curvearrowright \\
 & & w_3 \quad p \quad \neg q
\end{array}
$$

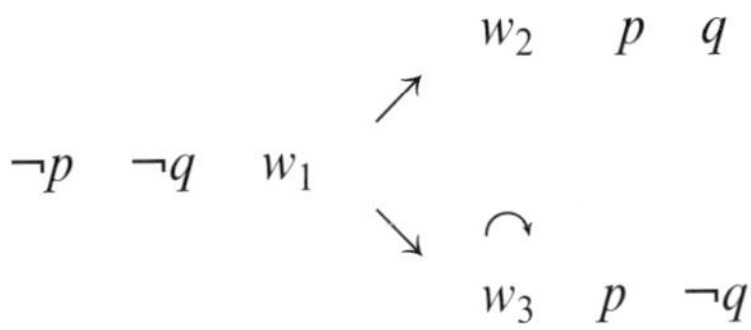

The arrows represent accessibility. In particular,

$$
\begin{array}{c}
\curvearrowright \\
w_3
\end{array}
$$

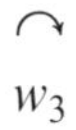

means that w_3 accesses itself.

2.3.8 The truth conditions of 2.3.4 and 2.3.5 can be used to work out the truth values of compound sentences, and these can be marked on the diagram in the same way. For example, since p and q are true at w_2, so is $p \wedge q$. But $w_1 R w_2$; hence, $\Diamond(p \wedge q)$ is true at w_1. At the only world that w_3 accesses (namely itself), p is true. Hence, $\Box p$ is true at w_3. But w_1 accesses w_3, hence, $\Diamond \Box p$ is true at w_1. w_2 accesses no world; hence, $\Diamond q$ is false at w_2, so $\neg \Diamond q$ is true there. We can add these facts to the diagram in the obvious way:

$$
\begin{array}{ccc}
 & & w_2 \quad \begin{array}{cc} p & q \\ p \wedge q & \neg \Diamond q \end{array} \\
 & \nearrow & \\
\begin{array}{cc} \neg p & \neg q \\ \Diamond(p \wedge q) & \Diamond \Box p \end{array} \quad w_1 & & \\
 & \searrow & \curvearrowright \\
 & & w_3 \quad \begin{array}{cc} p & \neg q \\ \Box p & \end{array}
\end{array}
$$

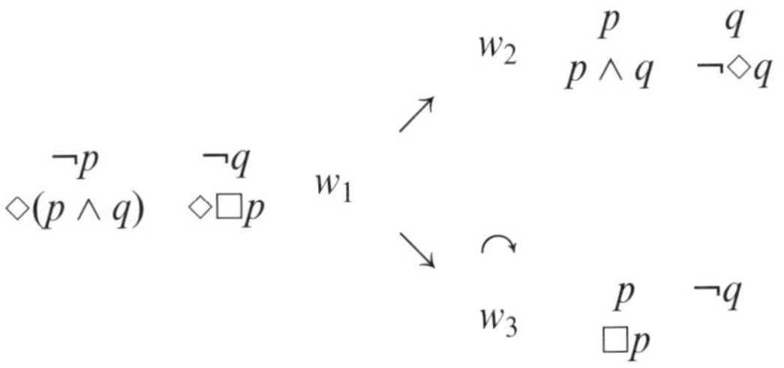

2.3.9 Observe that the truth value of $\neg \Diamond A$ at any world, w, is the same as that of $\Box \neg A$. For:

$$\begin{aligned} \nu_w(\neg\Diamond A) = 1 \quad & \text{iff} \quad \nu_w(\Diamond A) = 0 \\ & \text{iff} \quad \text{for all } w' \text{ such that } wRw',\ \nu_{w'}(A) = 0 \\ & \text{iff} \quad \text{for all } w' \text{ such that } wRw',\ \nu_{w'}(\neg A) = 1 \\ & \text{iff} \quad \nu_w(\Box\neg A) = 1 \end{aligned}$$

2.3.10 Similarly, the truth value of $\neg\Box A$ at a world is the same as that of $\Diamond\neg A$. The proof is left as an exercise.

2.3.11 An inference is valid if it is truth-preserving at all worlds of all interpretations. Thus, if Σ is a set of formulas and A is a formula, then semantic consequence and logical truth are defined as follows:

$\Sigma \models A$ iff for all interpretations $\langle W, R, \nu\rangle$ and all $w \in W$: if $\nu_w(B) = 1$ for all $B \in \Sigma$, then $\nu_w(A) = 1$.

$\models A$ iff $\phi \models A$, i.e., for all interpretations $\langle W, R, \nu\rangle$ and all $w \in W$, $\nu_w(A) = 1$.

2.4 Modal tableaux

2.4.1 Tableaux for modal logic are similar to those for propositional logic (1.4), except for the following modifications. At every node of the tree there is either a formula and a natural number (0, 1, 2, ...), thus: A, i; or something of the form irj, where i and j are natural numbers. Intuitively, different numbers indicate different possible worlds; A, i means that A is true at world i; and irj means that world i accesses world j.[3]

2.4.2 Second, the initial list for the tableau comprises $A, 0$, for every premise, A (if there are any), and $\neg B, 0$, where B is the conclusion.

2.4.3 Third, the rules for the truth-functional connectives are the same as in non-modal logic, except that the number associated with any

[3] I will avoid using r as a propositional parameter where this might lead to confusion.

formula is also associated with its immediate descendant(s). Thus, the rule for disjunction, for example, is:

$$A \vee B, i$$
$$\swarrow \qquad \searrow$$
$$A, i \qquad B, i$$

2.4.4 There are four new rules for the modal operators:

$$\neg \Box A, i \qquad \neg \Diamond A, i$$
$$\downarrow \qquad \downarrow$$
$$\Diamond \neg A, i \qquad \Box \neg A, i$$

$$\Box A, i \qquad \Diamond A, i$$
$$irj \qquad \downarrow$$
$$\downarrow \qquad irj \quad new \; index$$
$$every \, j \quad A, j \qquad A, j$$

In the rule for $\Box$ (bottom left), both of the formulas above the arrow must be present for the rule to be triggered, and it is applied for *every* such j. In the rule for $\Diamond$ (bottom right), the number j must be *new*. That is, it must not occur on the branch anywhere above.

2.4.5 Finally, a branch is closed iff for some formula, A, and number, i, A, i and $\neg A, i$ both occur on the branch. (It must be the same i in both cases.)[4]

2.4.6 Here are some examples of tableaux:

(i) $\Box(A \supset B) \wedge \Box(B \supset C) \vdash \Box(A \supset C)$.

---

[4] It is not obvious, but, as in the propositional case, every tableau of the kind we are dealing with here is finite.

$$
\begin{array}{ccc}
 & \Box(A \supset B) \wedge \Box(B \supset C), 0 & \\
 & \neg\Box(A \supset C), 0 & \\
 & \Box(A \supset B), 0 & \\
 & \Box(B \supset C), 0 & \\
 & \Diamond\neg(A \supset C), 0 & \\
 & 0r1 & (1) \\
 & \neg(A \supset C), 1 & (1) \\
 & A, 1 & \\
 & \neg C, 1 & \\
 & A \supset B, 1 & (2) \\
 & B \supset C, 1 & (2) \\
 & \swarrow \quad \searrow & \\
\neg A, 1 & & B, 1 \\
\times & & \downarrow \quad \searrow \\
 & & \neg B, 1 \qquad C, 1 \\
 & & \times \qquad\quad \times
\end{array}
$$

The lines marked (1) are obtained by applying the rule for $\Diamond$ to the line immediately above them. The lines marked (2) are the results of two applications of the rule for $\Box$ to the conjuncts of the premise.

(ii) $\vdash \Diamond(A \wedge B) \supset (\Diamond A \wedge \Diamond B)$.

$$
\begin{array}{ccc}
\multicolumn{2}{c}{\neg(\Diamond(A \wedge B) \supset (\Diamond A \wedge \Diamond B)), 0} & \\
\multicolumn{2}{c}{\Diamond(A \wedge B), 0} & \\
\multicolumn{2}{c}{\neg(\Diamond A \wedge \Diamond B), 0} & \\
\swarrow & \searrow & \\
\neg\Diamond A, 0 & \neg\Diamond B, 0 & \\
\Box\neg A, 0 & \Box\neg B, 0 & \\
0r1 & 0r1 & (1) \\
A \wedge B, 1 & A \wedge B, 1 & (1) \\
A, 1 & A, 1 & \\
B, 1 & B, 1 & \\
\neg A, 1 & \neg B, 1 & (2) \\
\times & \times &
\end{array}
$$

The lines marked (1) result from an application of the rule for $\Diamond$ to the formula at the second node of the tableau. The line marked (2) results from applications of the rule for $\Box$ to $\Box\neg A, 0$ (left branch) and $\Box\neg B, 0$ (right branch).

(iii) $\nvdash (\Diamond p \wedge \Diamond\neg q) \supset \Diamond\Box\Diamond p$

$$\begin{array}{ll}
\neg((\Diamond p \wedge \Diamond\neg q) \supset \Diamond\Box\Diamond p), 0 & \\
\Diamond p \wedge \Diamond\neg q, 0 & \\
\neg\Diamond\Box\Diamond p, 0 & \\
\Diamond p, 0 \checkmark & \\
\Diamond\neg q, 0 \checkmark & \\
\Box\neg\Box\Diamond p, 0 & (1) \\
0r1 & (2) \\
p, 1 & (2) \\
\neg\Box\Diamond p, 1 \checkmark & (3) \\
\Diamond\neg\Diamond p, 1 \checkmark & \\
1r2 & \\
\neg\Diamond p, 2 \checkmark & \\
\Box\neg p, 2 & \\
0r3 & (4) \\
\neg q, 3 & (4) \\
\neg\Box\Diamond p, 3 \checkmark & (5) \\
\Diamond\neg\Diamond p, 3 \checkmark & \\
3r4 & \\
\neg\Diamond p, 4 \checkmark & \\
\Box\neg p, 4 &
\end{array}$$

The lines marked (2) result from an application of the rule for $\Diamond$ to the fourth line of the tableau. The lines marked (4) result from an application of the same rule to the fifth line of the tableau. Note that, as the example shows, when we apply the rule for $\Diamond$, we may have to go back and apply the rule for $\Box$ again, to the new world (number) that has been introduced. Thus, the line marked (3) results from a first application of the rule to line (1). Line (5) results from a second application. For this reason, if one is ticking nodes to show that one has finished with them, one should never tick a node of the form $\Box A$, since one may have to come back and use it again.

2.4.7 Counter-models can be read off from an open branch of a tableau in a natural way. For each number, i, that occurs on the branch, there is a world, w_i; $w_i R w_j$ iff irj occurs on the branch; for every propositional parameter, p, if p, i occurs on the branch, $v_{w_i}(p) = 1$, if $\neg p, i$ occurs on the branch, $v_{w_i}(p) = 0$ (and if neither, $v_{w_i}(p)$ can be anything one wishes).

2.4.8 Thus, the counter-model given by the open (and only) branch of the last example of 2.4.6 is as follows: $W = \{w_0, w_1, w_2, w_3, w_4\}$.

w_0Rw_1, w_1Rw_2, w_0Rw_3, w_3Rw_4. There are no other worlds related by R. $\nu_{w_1}(p) = 1$, $\nu_{w_3}(q) = 0$; otherwise, ν is arbitrary. The interpretation can be depicted thus:

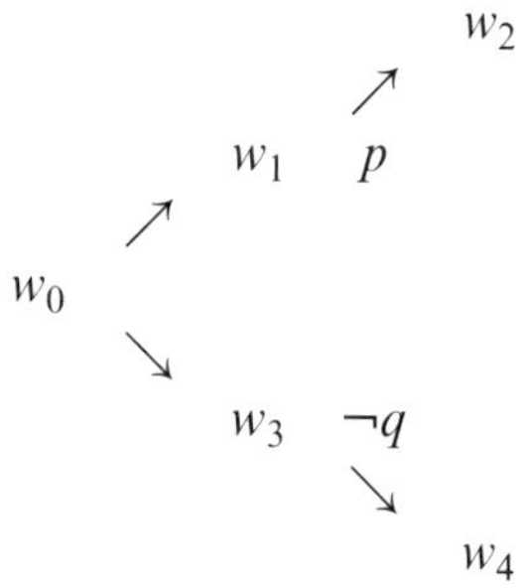

Using the truth conditions, one can check directly that the interpretation works. Since p is true at w_1, $\Diamond p$ is true at w_0. Similarly, $\Diamond\neg q$ is true at w_0. Hence, the antecedent is true at w_0. w_2 accesses no worlds; so $\Diamond p$ is false at w_2, and $\Box\Diamond p$ is false at w_1. Similarly, $\Box\Diamond p$ is false at w_3. Hence, there is no world which w_0 can access at which $\Box\Diamond p$ is true. Thus, $\Diamond\Box\Diamond p$ is false at w_0. It follows, then, that $(\Diamond p \wedge \Diamond\neg q) \supset \Diamond\Box\Diamond p$ is false at w_0.

2.4.9 The tableaux just described are sound and complete with respect to the semantics. The proof is given in 2.9.

2.5 Possible worlds: representation

2.5.1 In the rest of this chapter we look at the major philosophical question that modal semantics generate: what do they *mean*?

2.5.2 One might suggest that they do not mean anything. They are simply a mathematical apparatus – interpretations comprise just bunches of objects (W) furnished with some properties and relations – to be thought of purely instrumentally as delivering an appropriate notion of validity.

2.5.3 But there is something very unsatisfactory about this, as there is about all instrumentalisms. If a mathematical 'black box' gives what seem to be the right answers, one wants to know why. There must be some relationship between how it works and reality which explains why it gets things right.

2.5.4 The most obvious explanation in this context is that the mathematical structures that are employed in interpretations *represent* something or other which underlies the correctness of the notion of validity.

2.5.5 In the same way, no one supposes that truth is simply the number 1. But that number, and the way that it behaves in truth-functional semantics, are able to represent truth, because the structure of their machinations corresponds to the structure of truth's own machinations. This explains why truth-functional validity works (when it does).

2.5.6 So, the question arises: what exactly, in reality, does the mathematical machinery of possible worlds represent? Possible worlds, of course (what else?). But what are they?

2.6 Modal realism

2.6.1 The simplest suggestion (usually termed 'modal realism') is that possible worlds are things exactly like the actual world. They are composed of physical objects like people, chairs and stars (if any exist in those worlds), in their own space and time (if there are such things in those worlds). These objects exist just as much as you and I do, just in a different place/time – though not ones in this world.

2.6.2 The thought is, no doubt, a little mind-boggling. But so are many of the developments in modern physics. And why should metaphysics not have the right to boggle the mind just as much as physics?

2.6.3 Many arguments may be put both for and against this proposal – as they may be for all the views that I will mention. Here is one argument against. What makes such a world a *different* possible world, and not simply part of this one? The natural answer is that the space, time and causation of that world are unconnected with the space, time and causation of this world. One cannot travel from here to there in space or time; nor can causal processes from here reach there, or vice versa.

2.6.4 But why should that make it a *different* world? Suppose that because of the spatial geometry of the inside of a black hole, one could travel thence down a worm hole into a part of the cosmos with its own space and time; and suppose, then, that the worm hole closed up. We would not think of that region, now causally isolated from the rest, as a different possible world: merely an inaccessible part of this one.

2.6.5 The point may be put in a different way. Why should we think that something is possible in *this* world merely because it is actually happening at another place/time? I do not, after all, think that it is possible to see kangaroos in Antarctica merely because they are seen in Australia.

2.7 Modal actualism

2.7.1 Another possibility (frequently termed 'modal actualism') is that, though possible worlds exist, they are not the physical entities that the modal realist takes them to be. They are entities of a different kind: specifically, abstract entities (like numbers, assuming there to be such things).

2.7.2 What kind of abstract entities? There are several possible candidates here. A natural one is to take them to be sets of propositions, or other language-like entities. Crudely, a possible world is individuated by the set of things true at it, which is just the set of propositions it contains.

2.7.3 But a problem arises with this suggestion when one asks which sets are worlds? Clearly not all sets are possible worlds. For example, a set that contains two propositions but not their conjunction could not be a possible world.

2.7.4 For a set of propositions to form a world, it must at least be closed under valid inference. (If a proposition is true at a world, and it entails another, then so is that.) But there's the rub. The machinery of worlds was meant to explain why certain inferences, and not others, are valid. But it now seems that the notion of validity is required to explain the notion of world – not the other way around.

2.7.5 A variation of actualism which avoids this problem is known as 'combinatorialism'. A possible world is merely the set of things in *this* world, rearranged in a different way. So in this world, my house is in Australia, and not China; but rearrange things, and it could be in China, and not Australia.

2.7.6 Combinatorialism is still a version of actualism, because an arrangement is, in fact, an abstract object. It is a *set* of objects with a certain structure. But it avoids the previous objection, since one may explain what combinations there are without invoking the notion of validity.

2.7.7 But combinatorialism has its own problems. For example, it would seem to be entirely possible that there is an object such that neither it nor any of its parts exist in this world. It is clear, though, that such an object could not exist in any world obtained simply by rearranging the objects in this world. Hence, there are possible worlds which cannot be delivered by combinatorialism.

2.8 Meinongianism

2.8.1 Both realism and actualism take possible worlds and their denizens, whatever they are, to exist, either as concrete objects or as abstract objects. Another possibility is to take them to be non-existent objects. (We know, after all, that such things do not really exist!)

2.8.2. We are all, after all, familiar with the thought that there are non-existent things, like fairies, Father Christmas (sorry) and phlogiston. Possible worlds are things of this kind.

2.8.3 The view that there are non-existent objects was espoused, famously, by Meinong. It had a very bad press for a long time in English-speaking philosophy, but it is fair to say that many of the old arguments against the possibility of there being non-existent objects are not especially cogent.

2.8.4 For example, one argument against such objects is that, since they cannot interact with us causally, we would have no way of knowing anything about them. But exactly the same is true, of course, of possible worlds as both the realist and the actualist conceive them, so this can hardly count to their advantage against Meinongianism about worlds.

2.8.5 Moreover, it is very clear how we know facts about at least some non-existent objects: they are simply stipulated. Holmes lived in Baker Street – and not Oxford Street – because Conan Doyle decided it was so.

2.8.6 The preceding considerations hardly settle the matter of the nature of possible worlds. There are many other suggested answers (most of which are some variation on one or other of the themes that I have mentioned); and there are many objections to the suggestions I have raised, other than the ones that I have given, as well as possible replies to the objections I have raised; philosophers can have hours of fun with possible worlds. This will do for the present, though.

2.9 *Proofs of theorems

2.9.1 The soundness and completeness proofs for K are essentially variations and extensions of the soundness and completeness proofs for propositional logic. We redefine faithfulness and the induced interpretation. The proofs are then much as in 1.11.

2.9.2 DEFINITION: Let $\mathcal{I} = \langle W, R, \nu \rangle$ be any modal interpretation, and b be any branch of a tableau. Then $\mathcal{I}$ is *faithful* to b iff there is a map, f, from the natural numbers to W such that:

For every node A, i on b, A is true at $f(i)$ in $\mathcal{I}$.

If irj is on b, $f(i)Rf(j)$ in $\mathcal{I}$.

We say that f *shows* $\mathcal{I}$ to be faithful to b.

2.9.3 SOUNDNESS LEMMA: Let b be any branch of a tableau, and $\mathcal{I} = \langle W, R, \nu \rangle$ be any interpretation. If $\mathcal{I}$ is faithful to b, and a tableau rule is applied to it, then it produces at least one extension, b', such that $\mathcal{I}$ is faithful to b'.

Proof:

Let f be a function which shows $\mathcal{I}$ to be faithful to b. The proof proceeds by a case-by-case consideration of the tableau rules. The cases for the propositional rules are essentially as in 1.11.2. Suppose, for example, that $A \wedge B, i$ is on b, and that we apply the rule for conjunction to give an extended branch containing A, i and B, i. Since $\mathcal{I}$ is faithful to b, $A \wedge B$ is true at $f(i)$. Hence, A and B are true at $f(i)$. Hence, $\mathcal{I}$ is faithful to the extension of b. We will therefore consider only the modal rules in detail. Consider the rule for negated $\Diamond$. Suppose that $\neg\Diamond A, i$ occurs on b, and that we apply the rule to extend the branch with $\Box\neg A, i$. Since $\mathcal{I}$ is faithful to b, $\neg\Diamond A$ is true at $f(i)$. Hence, $\Box\neg A$ is true at $f(i)$ (by 2.3.9). Hence, $\mathcal{I}$ is faithful to the extension of b. The rule for negated $\Box$ is similar (invoking 2.3.10).

This leaves the rules for $\Box$ and $\Diamond$. Suppose that $\Box A, i$ is on b, and that we apply the rule for $\Box$. Since $\mathcal{I}$ is faithful to b, $\Box A$ is true at $f(i)$. Moreover, for any i and j such that irj is on b, $f(i)Rf(j)$. Hence, by the truth conditions for $\Box$, A is true at $f(j)$, and so $\mathcal{I}$ is faithful to the extension of the branch. Finally, suppose that $\Diamond A, i$ is on b and we apply the rule for $\Diamond$ to get nodes of the form irj and A, j. Since $\mathcal{I}$ is faithful to b, $\Diamond A$ is true at $f(i)$. Hence, for some $w \in W$, $f(i)Rw$ and A is true at w. Let f' be the same as f except that $f'(j) = w$. Note that f' also shows that $\mathcal{I}$ is faithful to b, since f and f' differ only at j; this does not occur on b. Moreover, by definition, $f'(i)Rf'(j)$, and A is true at $f'(j)$. Hence, f' shows $\mathcal{I}$ to be faithful to the extended branch.

2.9.4 SOUNDNESS THEOREM FOR *K*: For finite Σ, if $\Sigma \vdash A$ then $\Sigma \models A$.

Proof:

Suppose that $\Sigma \not\models A$. Then there is an interpretation, $\mathcal{I} = \langle W, R, v \rangle$, that makes every premise true, and A false, at some world, w. Let f be any function such that $f(0) = w$. This shows $\mathcal{I}$ to be faithful to the initial list. The proof is now exactly the same as in the non-modal case (1.11.3).

2.9.5 DEFINITION: Let b be an open branch of a tableau. The interpretation, $\mathcal{I} = \langle W, R, v \rangle$, induced by b, is defined as in 2.4.7. $W = \{w_i; i$ occurs on $b\}$. $w_i R w_j$ iff irj occurs on b. If p, i occurs on b, then $v_{w_i}(p) = 1$; if $\neg p, i$ occurs on b, then $v_{w_i}(p) = 0$ (and otherwise $v_{w_i}(p)$ can be anything one likes).

2.9.6 COMPLETENESS LEMMA: Let b be any open complete branch of a tableau. Let $\mathcal{I} = \langle W, R, v \rangle$ be the interpretation induced by b. Then:

if A, i is on b then A is true at w_i

if $\neg A, i$ is on b then A is false at w_i

Proof:

The proof is by recursion on the complexity of A. If A is atomic, the result is true by definition. If A occurs on b, and is of the form $B \vee C$, then the rule for disjunction has been applied to $B \vee C, i$. Thus, either B, i or C, i is on b. By induction hypothesis, either B or C is true at w_i. Hence, $B \vee C$ is true at w_i, as required. The case for $\neg(B \vee C)$ is similar, as are the cases for the other truth functions. Next, suppose that A is of the form $\Box B$. If $\Box B, i$ is on b, then for all j such that irj is on b, B, j is on b. By construction and the induction hypothesis, for all w_j such that $w_i R w_j$, B is true at w_j. Hence, $\Box B$ is true at w_i, as required. If $\neg\Box A, i$ is on b, then $\Diamond\neg A, i$ is on b; so, for some j, irj and $\neg A, j$ are on b. By induction hypothesis, $w_i R w_j$ and A is false at w_j. Hence, $\Box A$ is false at w_i as required. The case for $\Diamond$ is similar.

2.9.7 COMPLETENESS THEOREM: For finite Σ, if $\Sigma \models A$ then $\Sigma \vdash A$.

Proof:

Suppose that $\Sigma \nvdash A$. Given an open branch of the tableau, the interpretation that this induces makes all the premises true at w_0 and A false at w_0 by the Completeness Lemma. Hence, $\Sigma \not\models A$.

2.10 History

Modal logic is as old as logic. Aristotle himself gave an account of which modal syllogisms he took to be valid (see Kneale and Kneale, 1975, ch. 2, sect. 8). Modal logic and semantics were also discussed widely in the Middle Ages (see Knuuttila, 1982). In the modern period, the subject of modal logic was initiated by C. I. Lewis just before the First World War (see Lewis and Langford, 1931). Initially, it received a bad press, largely as a result of the criticisms of Quine – whose work also produced much of the unpopularity of Meinongianism. (On both, see the papers in Quine, 1963.) Things changed with the invention of possible-world semantics in the early 1960s. These are due to the work of a number of people, most notably that of Kripke (1963). (For a history, see Copeland, 1996, pp. 8–15.)

The notion of a possible world is to be found in Leibniz (e.g., *Monadology*, sect. 53). Modal realism has been espoused most famously by D. Lewis (1986). Notable proponents of actualism include Plantinga and Stalnaker. Combinatorialism is espoused by Cresswell. See the papers by all three in Loux (1979). One of the stoutest defences of non-existent objects, and an advocate of possible worlds as non-existent objects is Routley (1980). Kripke's own views on the nature of possible worlds can be found in Kripke (1977).

2.11 Further reading

Perhaps the best introduction to modal logic is still Hughes and Cresswell (1996). The semantics of K are given in chapter 2. (Hughes and Cresswell use axiom systems rather than tableaux for their proof theory.) Chellas (1980) is also excellent, though a little more demanding mathematically. Modal tableaux for propositional logics can be found in chapters 2 and 3 of Girle (2000). A somewhat different form can be found in chapter 2 of Fitting and Mendelsohn (1999). A useful collection of essays on the nature of possible worlds is Loux (1979); chapter 15, 'The Trouble with Possible Worlds', by Lycan, is a good orientational survey. Read (1994, ch. 4) is also an excellent discussion.

2.12 Problems

1. Check the details of 2.3.10.

2. Show the following. Where the tableau does not close, use it to define a counter-model, and draw this, as in 2.4.8.

   (*a*) $\vdash (\Box A \wedge \Box B) \supset \Box(A \wedge B)$

   (*b*) $\vdash (\Box A \vee \Box B) \supset \Box(A \vee B)$

   (*c*) $\vdash \Box A \equiv \neg\Diamond\neg A$

(*d*) $\vdash \Diamond A \equiv \neg\Box\neg A$

(*e*) $\vdash \Diamond(A \wedge B) \supset (\Diamond A \wedge \Diamond B)$

(*f*) $\vdash \Diamond(A \vee B) \supset (\Diamond A \vee \Diamond B)$

(*g*) $\Box(A \supset B) \vdash \Diamond A \supset \Diamond B$

(*h*) $\Box A, \Diamond B \vdash \Diamond(A \wedge B)$

(*i*) $\vdash \Box A \equiv \Box(\neg A \supset A)$

(*j*) $\vdash \Box A \supset \Box(B \supset A)$

(*k*) $\vdash \neg\Diamond B \supset \Box(B \supset A)$

(*l*) $\nvdash \Box(p \vee q) \supset (\Box p \vee \Box q)$

(*m*) $\Box p, \Box\neg q \nvdash \Box(p \supset q)$

(*n*) $\Diamond p, \Diamond q \nvdash \Diamond(p \wedge q)$

(*o*) $\nvdash \Box p \supset p$

(*p*) $\nvdash \Box p \supset \Diamond p$

(*q*) $p \nvdash \Box p$

(*r*) $\nvdash \Box p \supset \Box\Box p$

(*s*) $\nvdash \Diamond p \supset \Diamond\Diamond p$

(*t*) $\nvdash p \supset \Box\Diamond p$

(*u*) $\nvdash \Diamond p \supset \Box\Diamond p$

(*v*) $\nvdash \Diamond(p \vee \neg p)$

3. How might one reply to the objections of 2.5–2.8, and what other objections are there to the views on the nature of possible worlds explained there? What other views could there be?

4. *Check the details omitted in 2.9.3 and 2.9.6.

3 Normal modal logics

3.1 Introduction

3.1.1 In this chapter we look at some well-known extensions of K, the system of modal logic that we considered in the last chapter.

3.1.2 We then look at the question of which systems of modal logic are appropriate for which notions of necessity.

3.2 Semantics for normal modal logics

3.2.1 There are many systems of modal logic. If there is any doubt as to which one is being considered in what follows, we subscript the turnstile ($\models$ or $\vdash$) used. Thus, the consequence relation of K is written as $\models_K$.

3.2.2 The most important class of modal logics is the class of *normal* logics. The basic normal logic is the logic K.

3.2.3 Other normal modal logics are obtained by defining validity in terms of truth preservation in some special class of interpretations. Typically, the special class of interpretations is one containing all and only those interpretations whose accessibility relation, R, satisfies some constraint or other. Some important constraints are as follows:

> ρ (rho), reflexivity: for all w, wRw.
>
> σ (sigma), symmetry: for all w_1, w_2, if w_1Rw_2, then w_2Rw_1.
>
> τ (tau), transitivity: for all w_1, w_2, w_3, if w_1Rw_2 and w_2Rw_3, then w_1Rw_3.

η (eta), extendability: for all w_1, there is a w_2 such that $w_1 R w_2$.

3.2.4 We term any interpretation in which R satisfies condition ρ a ρ-*interpretation*. We denote the logic defined in terms of truth preservation over all worlds of all ρ-interpretations, $K\rho$, and write its consequence relation as $\models_{K\rho}$. Thus, $\Sigma \models_{K\rho} A$ iff, for all ρ-interpretations $\langle W, R, \nu\rangle$, and all $w \in W$, if $\nu_w(B) = 1$ for all $B \in \Sigma$, then $\nu_w(A) = 1$. Similarly for σ, τ and η.

3.2.5 The conditions on R can be combined. Thus, for example, a $\rho\sigma$-interpretation is one in which R is reflexive and symmetric; and the logic $K\sigma\tau$ is the consequence relation defined over all $\sigma\tau$-interpretations. Historically, the systems $K\rho$, $K\eta$, $K\rho\sigma$, $K\rho\tau$ and $K\rho\sigma\tau$ are known as *T*, *D*, *B*, *S4* and *S5*, respectively.

3.2.6 Note that if R is reflexive, it is extendable. (If a world accesses itself, it certainly accesses something.) But otherwise, with one exception, all the conditions on R are independent: one can mix and match at will. For example, here is a relation that is symmetric and reflexive, but not transitive:

$$\overset{\curvearrowright}{w_1} \rightleftarrows \overset{\curvearrowright}{w_2} \rightleftarrows \overset{\curvearrowright}{w_3}$$

The other combinations are left as an exercise (see 3.10, problem 1). The exception is that σ, τ and η, together, give ρ.[1]

3.2.7 Every normal modal logic, L, is an extension of K, in the sense that if $\Sigma \models_K A$ then $\Sigma \models_L A$. For if truth is preserved at all worlds of *all* interpretations, *a fortiori* it is preserved at all worlds of any restricted class of interpretations.

3.2.8 This is an important kind of argument that we use a number of times, so let us pause over it for a moment. Consider the following diagram:

---

[1] Consider any world, w. By η, wRw' for some w'. So, by σ, $w'Rw$, and, by τ, wRw.

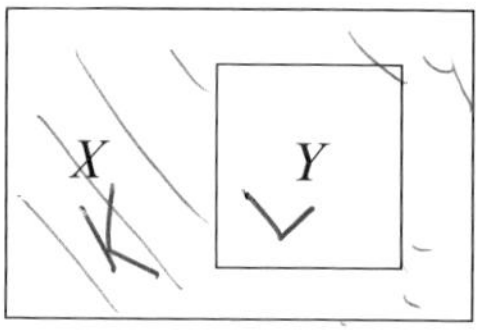

Suppose that the outer box contains all interpretations of a certain kind (in our case, all K interpretations), and that the inner box contains some more restricted class of interpretations (in our case, those appropriate for the logic L). Then if truth (from premise to conclusion) is preserved in all worlds of all interpretations in X, then it is preserved in all worlds of all interpretations in Y. Hence, the logic determined by the class of interpretations Y is an extension of that determined by the class X.

3.2.9 For exactly this reason, $K\rho\sigma$ is an extension of $K\rho$; $K\rho\sigma\tau$ is an extension of $K\rho\sigma$, and so on.

3.3 Tableaux for normal modal logics

3.3.1 The tableau rules for K can be extended to work for other normal systems as well. Essentially, this is done by adding rules which introduce further information about r on branches. Since this information comes into play when the rule for $\Box$ is applied, the effect of this is to increase the number of applications of that rule.

3.3.2 The rules for ρ, σ and τ are, respectively:

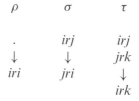

ρ	σ	τ
.	irj	irj
$\downarrow$	$\downarrow$	jrk
iri	jri	$\downarrow$
		irk

(We come to the rule for η in the next section.) The rule for ρ means that if i is any integer on the tableau, we introduce iri. It can therefore be applied to world 0 after the initial list, and, thereafter, after the introduction of any new integer. The other two rules are self-explanatory. Note that if the application of a rule would result in just repeating lines already on the tableau, it is not applied. Thus, for example, if we apply the σ-rule to irj to get jri, we do not then apply it again to jri to get irj. The following three subsections give examples of tableaux for $K\rho$, $K\sigma$ and $K\tau$, respectively.

3.3.3 $\vdash_{K\rho} \Box p \supset p$:

$$\neg(\Box p \supset p), 0$$
$$0r0$$
$$\Box p, 0$$
$$\neg p, 0$$
$$p, 0$$
$$\times$$

The last line is obtained from $\Box p, 0$, since $0r0$. Since $\Box p \supset p$ is not valid in K (2.12, problem 2(o)), this shows that $K\rho$ is a *proper* extension of K. (That is, $K\rho$ is not exactly the same as K.)

3.3.4 $\vdash_{K\sigma} p \supset \Box\Diamond p$:

$$\neg(p \supset \Box\Diamond p), 0$$
$$p, 0$$
$$\neg\Box\Diamond p, 0$$
$$\Diamond\neg\Diamond p, 0$$
$$0r1$$
$$\neg\Diamond p, 1$$
$$1r0$$
$$\Box\neg p, 1$$
$$\neg p, 0$$
$$\times$$

The last line follows from the fact that $\Box\neg p, 1$, since $1r0$. Since $p \supset \Box\Diamond p$ is not valid in K (2.12, problem 2(t)), this shows that $K\sigma$ is a proper extension of K.

3.3.5 $\vdash_{K\tau} \Box p \supset \Box\Box p$:

$$\neg(\Box p \supset \Box\Box p), 0$$
$$\Box p, 0$$
$$\neg\Box\Box p, 0$$
$$\Diamond\neg\Box p, 0$$
$$0r1$$
$$\neg\Box p, 1$$
$$\Diamond\neg p, 1$$
$$1r2$$
$$\neg p, 2$$
$$0r2$$
$$p, 2$$
$$\times$$

When we add $1r2$ to the tableau because of the $\Diamond$-rule, we already have $0r1$; hence, we add $0r2$. Since $\Box p$ holds at 0, an application of the rule for $\Box$ immediately closes the tableau. Since $\Box p \supset \Box\Box p$ is not valid in K (2.12, problem 2(r)), this shows that $K\tau$ is a proper extension of K.

3.3.6 For 'compound' systems, all the relevant rules must be applied. There may be some interplay between them. To keep track of this, adopt the following procedure. New worlds are normally introduced by the $\Diamond$-rule. Apply this first. Then compute all the new facts about r that need to be added, and add them. Finally, backtrack if necessary and apply the $\Box$-rule wherever the new r facts require it. The procedure is illustrated in the following tableau, demonstrating that $\vdash_{K\sigma\tau} \Diamond p \supset \Box\Diamond p$. For brevity's sake, we write more than one piece of information about r on the same line.

$$\neg(\Diamond p \supset \Box\Diamond p), 0$$
$$\Diamond p, 0$$
$$\neg\Box\Diamond p, 0$$
$$0r1$$
$$p, 1$$
$$1r0, 1r1, 0r0$$
$$\Diamond\neg\Diamond p, 0$$
$$0r2$$
$$\neg\Diamond p, 2$$
$$2r0, 2r2, 1r2, 2r1$$
$$\Box\neg p, 2$$
$$\neg p, 2$$
$$\neg p, 1$$
$$\neg p, 0$$
$$\times$$

The line $\Diamond\neg\Diamond p, 0$ requires the construction of a new world, 2, with an application of the $\Diamond$-rule. This is done on the next two lines. We then add all the new information about r that the creation of world 2 requires. $2r0$ is added because of symmetry; $2r2$ is added because of transitivity and the fact that we have $2r0$ and $0r2$; $1r2$ is added because of transitivity and the fact that we have $1r0$ and $0r2$; similarly, $2r1$ is added because of transitivity. Symmetry and transitivity require no other facts about r. In constructing a tableau, it may help to keep track of things if one draws a diagram of the world structure, as it emerges.

3.3.7 Counter-models read off from an open branch of a tableau incorporate the information about r in the obvious way. Thus, consider the following tableau, which shows that $\nvdash_{K\rho\sigma} \Box p \supset \Box\Box p$.

$$\neg(\Box p \supset \Box\Box p), 0$$
$$0r0$$
$$\Box p, 0$$
$$\neg\Box\Box p, 0$$
$$p, 0$$
$$\Diamond\neg\Box p, 0$$
$$0r1$$
$$\neg\Box p, 1$$
$$1r1, 1r0$$
$$p, 1$$
$$\Diamond\neg p, 1$$
$$1r2$$
$$\neg p, 2$$
$$2r2, 2r1$$

The counter-model is $\langle W, R, v \rangle$, where $W = \{w_0, w_1, w_2\}$, R is such that $w_0 R w_0$, $w_1 R w_1$, $w_2 R w_2$, $w_0 R w_1$, $w_1 R w_0$, $w_1 R w_2$ and $w_2 R w_1$, and v is such that $v_{w_0}(p) = v_{w_1}(p) = 1$, $v_{w_2}(p) = 0$. In pictures:

$$w_0 \quad \rightleftarrows \quad w_1 \quad \rightleftarrows \quad w_2$$
$$p \qquad\qquad p \qquad\qquad \neg p$$

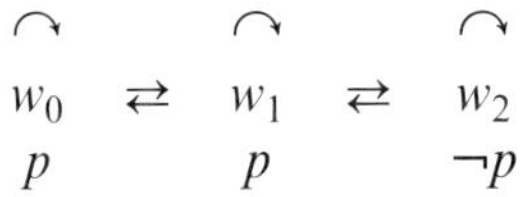

3.3.8 The tableau systems above are all sound and complete with respect to their respective semantics. The proof of this can be found in 3.7.

3.4 Infinite tableaux

3.4.1 The tableau rule for η is as follows:

$$\eta$$

$$\cdot$$
$$\downarrow$$
$$irj$$

It is applied to any integer, i, on a branch, provided that there is not already something of the form irj on the branch, and the j in question must then be *new*.

3.4.2 Care must be taken in applying this rule. If it is applied every time as soon as it is possible to do so, we go off into an infinite regress from which we never return. For when we introduce j, we have (since j is new) to introduce a new k and add jrk, and then a new l, and add krl, and so on.

3.4.3 The rule is alright, however, provided that one does not apply it immediately, where to do so would prevent other rules from being applied. It must still be applied at some time, of course (unless the tableau closes first). Soundness and completeness for the rule are proved in 3.7.

3.4.4 The following tableau demonstrates that $\vdash_{K\eta} \Box p \supset \Diamond p$.

$$\begin{array}{c} \neg(\Box p \supset \Diamond p), 0 \\ \Box p, 0 \\ \neg\Diamond p, 0 \\ \Box\neg p, 0 \\ 0r1 \\ p, 1 \\ \neg p, 1 \\ \times \end{array}$$

This inference is not valid in K (2.12, problem 2(p)). Hence, $K\eta$ is a proper extension of K.

3.4.5 Even with the rule applied in this way, though, if the tableau fails to close, it will be infinite, as the following tableau, demonstrating that $\nvdash_{K\eta} \Box p$, illustrates:

$$\begin{array}{c} \neg\Box p, 0 \\ \Diamond\neg p, 0 \\ 0r1 \\ \neg p, 1 \\ 1r2 \\ 2r3 \\ \vdots \end{array}$$

The tableau is infinite, but the (only) branch is still open. Hence, the inference is still invalid. The branch also specifies a counter-model, though this, too, is infinite. It may be depicted thus:

$$\begin{array}{ccccccc} & & \neg p & & & & \\ w_0 & \rightarrow & w_1 & \rightarrow & w_2 & \rightarrow & \cdots \end{array}$$

3.4.6 This does not mean that the only counter-models to $\Box p$ in $K\eta$ are infinite. For example, the following will do, as may easily be checked:

$$\begin{array}{c} \curvearrowright \\ w_0 \\ \neg p \end{array}$$

If an inference is not valid in η, however, and it has a finite counter-model, the tableau procedure will not find it. Such models can be found by trial and error: make a guess; see if it works; if it does not, try making an appropriate change; see if it works; if it does not, try making an appropriate change; etc.

3.4.7 It is not only the system $K\eta$ that may give rise to infinite tableaux; even $K\tau$ may give rise to them. Consider the tableau showing that $\nvdash_{K\tau} \neg(\Diamond p \wedge \Box\Diamond p)$:

$$\begin{array}{c} \neg\neg(\Diamond p \wedge \Box\Diamond p), 0 \\ \Diamond p \wedge \Box\Diamond p, 0 \\ \Diamond p, 0 \\ \Box\Diamond p, 0 \\ 0r1 \\ p, 1 \\ \Diamond p, 1 \\ 1r2 \\ p, 2 \\ 0r2 \\ \Diamond p, 2 \\ 2r3 \\ p, 3 \\ \vdots \end{array}$$

Every time we open a new world, i, transitivity gives us $0ri$. And since $\Box\Diamond p$ holds at 0, the $\Box$-rule requires us to write $\Diamond p, i$, which requires us to open a new world …

3.4.8 Again, though, an infinite counter-model can be read off the open branch:

$$\begin{array}{ccccccccc} & & p & & p & & p & & \\ w_0 & \rightarrow & w_1 & \rightarrow & w_2 & \rightarrow & w_3 & \rightarrow & \cdots \end{array}$$

This is a very simple example, however. In general, it is often very difficult to establish that a tableau is infinite and open, and an even more difficult task to read off the counter-model when it is.

3.4.9 It is usually much easier to find a simpler counter-model by trial and error. Thus, it is easy enough to establish that the following interpretation is a counter-model for the inference of 3.4.7:

$$\begin{array}{c} \curvearrowright \\ w_0 \\ p \end{array}$$

3.4.10 We conclude this section by noting the following. I did not choose the examples of 3.3.3, 3.3.4, 3.3.5 and 3.4.4 at random. The principles shown to hold in each case are, in a sense, the *characteristic* principles of the logics $K\rho$, $K\sigma$, $K\tau$ and $K\eta$.[2]

3.5 *S5*

3.5.1 The system *S5* is special. To see how, let an υ-interpretation – 'υ' (upsilon) for universal – be an interpretation in which R satisfies the following condition: for all w_1 and w_2, $w_1 R w_2$ – everything relates to everything.

3.5.2 In an υ-interpretation, R drops out of the picture altogether, in effect. We can just as well define an υ-interpretation to be a pair $\langle W, \nu\rangle$, where the truth conditions for $\Box$ are simply: $\nu_w(\Box A) = 1$ iff for all $w' \in W$, $\nu_{w'}(A) = 1$; and similarly for $\Diamond$.

[2] And, technically, each, when added to some axiom system for K, gives a complete axiomatisation of the logic.

3.5.3 Tableaux for $K\upsilon$ can also be formulated very simply: r is never mentioned. Applying the $\Diamond$-rule to $\Diamond A, i$ gives a new line of the form A, j (new j); and in applying the $\Box$-rule to $\Box A$, i, we add A, j for every j. For example, $\vdash_{K\upsilon} \Diamond A \supset \Box\Diamond A$:

$$\neg(\Diamond A \supset \Box\Diamond A), 0$$
$$\Diamond A, 0$$
$$\neg\Box\Diamond A, 0$$
$$\Diamond\neg\Diamond A, 0$$
$$A, 1$$
$$\neg\Diamond A, 2$$
$$\Box\neg A, 2$$
$$\neg A, 0$$
$$\neg A, 1$$
$$\neg A, 2$$
$$\times$$

3.5.4 Now, $K\rho\sigma\tau$ and $K\upsilon$ are, in fact, equivalent, in the sense that $\Sigma \models_{K\rho\sigma\tau} A$ iff $\Sigma \models_{K\upsilon} A$. Half of this fact is obvious. It is easy to check that if a relationship satisfies the condition υ it satisfies the conditions ρ, σ and τ. Hence, if truth is preserved at all worlds of all $\rho\sigma\tau$-interpretations, it is preserved at all worlds of all υ-interpretations. Hence, if $\Sigma \models_{K\rho\sigma\tau} A$, then $\Sigma \models_{K\upsilon} A$. The converse is not so obvious. (A proof can be found in 3.7.5.)

3.5.5 Because of the equivalence between $K\upsilon$ and $K\rho\sigma\tau$, the name *S5* tends to be used, indifferently, for either of these systems.

3.5.6 There are many other normal modal logics. Some of these glorify in names such as *S4.2*. The number indicates that the system is between *S4* and *S5* in strength, but otherwise is not to be taken too seriously.

3.6 Which system represents necessity?

3.6.1 Let us now turn to a philosophical issue raised by the multiplicity of normal modal logics. Which system is correct? There is, in fact, no single answer to this question, since there are many different notions of necessity (and, correlatively, possibility and impossibility) and the first thing that one needs to do is distinguish among them.

3.6.2 Among the many notions, we can distinguish at least the following: logical, metaphysical, physical, epistemic and moral. How, exactly, to characterise each of these notions is a moot point; however, a rough characterisation will do for our purposes.

3.6.3 A standard way of defining logical necessity is in terms of analyticity. That is, A is logically necessary if its truth is determined solely by the meanings of the words it contains. We might argue about which sentences are analytic in this sense, but it would standardly be assumed that the following examples are: 'If it rains today then it rains today', '$2 + 2 = 4$'.

3.6.4 It is plausible to suppose that the appropriate system of modal logic for logical necessity is *S5*. Certainly, it would appear that logical truths satisfy the principles characteristic of $K\rho$, $K\sigma$ and $K\tau$. If A's truth is analytic, A is certainly true ($\Box A \supset A$). If A's truth is determined simply from the meanings of the words it contains, then so is the truth of the claim that A is analytic ($\Box A \supset \Box\Box A$). And if A is true (e.g., 'snow is white'), then $\neg A$ ('snow isn't white') is not analytically true, so $\neg\Box\neg A$ ('it is not analytically true that snow isn't white'), and this is so simply in virtue of the meanings of the words involved ($A \supset \Box\Diamond A$) (though one certainly might have one's doubts about this last claim).

3.6.5 Let us turn now to physical necessity and its cognates. Something is physically necessary if it is determined by the laws of nature, and physically possible if it is compatible with the laws of nature. Thus, it is physically impossible for me to jump thirty metres into the air (though this is not a logical impossibility).

3.6.6 Some also hold that there is a distinct notion of metaphysical necessity/possibility. Something is metaphysically necessary if it is determined by the laws of metaphysics. What are such laws like?

According to Aristotle, at least, some of my properties are *essential*. That is, I could not lose them and continue to exist. Thus, I could lose the property of being 80kg and still exist, but I could not lose the property of being human and still exist. That is part of my essence. Hence, it is a metaphysical law that I am human. Note that given the laws of physics (and biology), it might well be physically impossible for me to grow another three metres taller, but this is not a metaphysical impossibility: height is not an essential property.

3.6.7 The modal logics of physical and metaphysical necessity are certainly at least as strong as $K\rho$: if A's truth is determined by the laws of physics/metaphysics, then A is true. But it is not clear that they are stronger. For example, it is determined by the laws of physics that I do not accelerate through the speed of light. But why should this fact itself be determined by the laws of physics (as required by $K\tau$ and its extensions)? Similarly, I am not a frog, and so it is metaphysically possible that I am not a frog. But is *that* fact true because of the essence of something (as required by $K\sigma$ and its extensions)? The essence of possibility?

3.6.8 The fourth notion of necessity and its cognates is epistemic.[3] Something is epistemically necessary if it is known to be true, and possible if it could be true for all we know. Thus, it is presently epistemically possible that the cosmos will start to contract in the future. But if there is not sufficient matter in the universe, this is, in fact, a physical impossibility.

3.6.9 If something is known to be true, it is certainly true. Hence, the principle $\Box A \supset A$ holds for epistemic necessity. The principles for $K\sigma$ and $K\tau$ are almost certainly false, however (though they are frequently assumed in the literature). For example, you can know something without believing that you know it. ('I didn't believe that I had

[3] When applied in this way, '□' is usually written as 'K', and the logic is called *epistemic logic*. Though it hardly corresponds to a standard notion of necessity, one may also interpret '□' as 'it is believed that'. When applied in this way, '□' is usually written as 'B', and the logic is called *doxastic logic*.

really absorbed all that information, but when it came to the exam, I found that I had.') *A fortiori*, you can know something without knowing that you know it (assuming, as is standardly done, that knowledge entails belief).

3.6.10 For epistemic necessity, moreover, there is a real doubt about the adequacy of any extension of K. It is a feature of all normal logics that if $A \models B$ then $\Box A \models \Box B$. For if A is true at all worlds accessible from w, and A entails B, then B is true at all worlds accessible from w. But things that we know may well have all kinds of complex and recondite consequences of which we are unaware, and so do not know.

3.6.11 Finally, moral necessity: something is morally necessary if it is required by the laws of morality (and again we might well disagree about what is morally obligatory).[4] Notoriously, $\Box A \supset A$ fails for this. Often, people do not bring about what they morally ought to. The principles of $K\sigma$ and $K\tau$ are also dubious. Suppose, for example, that you murder someone; then (arguably) you ought to be punished. But you ought not to have murdered them in the first place, so it ought not to be the case that you ought to be punished ($\Box A \supset \Box\Box A$ fails).

3.6.12 It is standardly assumed that the correct modal logic for moral necessity is $K\eta$, whose characteristic principle is the Kantian one that 'ought implies can' ($\Box A \supset \Diamond A$). One may doubt this too, though. It would appear that people sometimes face moral dilemmas, where they ought to bring it about that A, and they ought to bring about that $\neg A$ too. Maybe they give a solemn promise to each of two different parties. They are then obliged to bring about A, but they are also obliged to bring about $\neg A$. So $\Box A \supset \neg\Box\neg A$ fails.

3.6.13 Nearly all the claims of this section are disputable (and have been disputed). But these considerations will serve to illustrate some

[4] When interpreted in this way, '$\Box$' is usually written as 'O' (and '$\Diamond$' as 'P'), and the logic is called *deontic logic*.

of the things at issue concerning disputes over the correct modal logic.[5]

3.7 *Proofs of theorems

3.7.1 THEOREM: The tableaux for $K\rho$, $K\sigma$, $K\tau$ and $K\eta$ are sound with respect to their semantics.

Proof:

The proof is as for K (2.9.2–2.9.4). All we need to do is check that the Soundness Lemma still works given the new rules. So suppose that f shows $\mathcal{I}$ to be faithful to b and that we then apply one of the rules. For ρ: we get iri, but $f(i)Rf(i)$ since R is reflexive. For σ: since irj is on b, $f(i)Rf(j)$, but then $f(j)Rf(i)$ since R is symmetric, as required. For τ: since irj and jrk are on b, $f(i)Rf(j)$ and $f(j)Rf(k)$. Hence $f(i)Rf(k)$ since R is transitive, as required. For η: i occurs on b, and we apply the rule to get irj, where j is new. We know that for some $w \in W, f(i)Rw$. Let f' be the same as f except that $f'(j) = w$. Since j does not occur on b, f' shows that $\mathcal{I}$ is faithful to b. Moreover, $f'(i)Rf'(j)$ by construction. Hence, f' shows that $\mathcal{I}$ is faithful to the extended branch.

3.7.2 THEOREM: The tableaux for systems with any combination of ρ, σ, τ and η are sound with respect to their semantics.

Proof:

We just combine each of the individual arguments.

3.7.3 THEOREM: The tableaux for $K\rho$, $K\sigma$, $K\tau$ and $K\eta$ are complete with respect to their semantics.

[5] One may also interpret the operator $\Box$ as 'it will always be the case that', a sort of temporal necessity. The properties it has will then depend on the properties one takes time itself to have. This is explored in *tense logic*, where $\Box$ is usually written as G, and a symmetric operator, H ('it has always been the case that'), is added. The interplay between these operators is also very important.

Proof:

The proof is as for K (2.9.6–2.9.7). All we have to do, in addition, is check that the interpretation induced by the open branch, b, is of the required kind. For ρ: for every $w_i \in W$, iri occurs on b (by the ρ-rule), hence, by definition of R, $w_i R w_i$. For σ: for $w_i, w_j \in W$, suppose that $w_i R w_j$. Then irj occurs on b; but then jri occurs on b (by the σ-rule). Hence, $w_j R w_i$, as required. For τ: for $w_i, w_j, w_k \in W$, suppose that $w_i R w_j$ and $w_j R w_k$. Then irj and jrk occur on b; but then irk occurs on b (by the τ-rule). Hence, $w_i R w_k$, as required. For η: if $w_i \in W$ then for some j, irj is on b. Hence, for some j, $w_i R w_j$, as required.

3.7.4 THEOREM: The tableaux for systems with any combination of ρ, σ, τ and η are complete with respect to their semantics.

Proof:

We just combine each of the individual arguments.

3.7.5 THEOREM: $\Sigma \models_{K\rho\sigma\tau} A$ iff $\Sigma \models_{K\upsilon} A$.

Proof:

The proof from left to right is as stated in 3.5.4. From right to left: suppose that $\Sigma \not\models_{K\rho\sigma\tau} A$. Let $\mathcal{I} = \langle W, R, \nu \rangle$, be a $\rho\sigma\tau$-interpretation, such that for some $w \in W$, all members of Σ are true at w, but A is not. Let $W' = \{w'; wRw'\}$.[6] Let $\mathcal{I}' = \langle W', R', \nu' \rangle$, where R' and ν' are the restrictions of R and ν, respectively, to W'. Then $\mathcal{I}'$ is an υ-interpretation. For if $x, y \in W'$, $wR'x$ and $wR'y$. Thus $xR'w$, by symmetry, and $xR'y$, by transitivity. A further crucial fact is that if $x \in W'$ and xRy then $y \in W'$. For wRx and xRy entail wRy. Hence, if $x \in W'$, R and R' relate x to exactly the same worlds (*).

Now, if it can be established that for all $x \in W'$, and for all A, the truth values of A in $\mathcal{I}$ and $\mathcal{I}'$ are the same, we will have what we want. This fact is established by induction over the construc-

[6] R is an equivalence relation, and W' is just the equivalence class of w.

tion of A. For parameters, it is true by definition. For truth-functional connectives, the result is straightforward. The case for $\Box$ is as follows; that for $\Diamond$ is similar. Suppose that $x \in W'$.

$$\begin{array}{lll} v'_x(\Box A) = 1 & \text{iff} & \text{for all } y \in W'\text{, such that } xR'y,\ v'_x(A) = 1 \\ & \text{iff} & \text{for all } y \in W'\text{, such that } xR'y,\ v_x(A) = 1 \\ & \text{iff} & \text{for all } y \in W\text{, such that } xRy,\ v_x(A) = 1 \\ & \text{iff} & v_x(\Box A) = 1 \end{array}$$

The first and last lines hold in virtue of the truth conditions of $\Box$. The second line holds by induction hypothesis. The third line holds by (*).

3.8 History

C. I. Lewis proposed five systems of modal logic, which he labelled *S1*–*S5* (see Lewis and Langford, 1931). We look at *S1*–*S3* in the next chapter. The system T was proposed by Feys. For its history, see Hughes and Cresswell (1996, p.50, n.7). The name B stands for 'Brouwer', the founder of intuitionism, because of a (somewhat tenuous) connection between the characteristic principle of B, $A \supset \Box\Diamond A$, and intuitionist logic (for details, see Hughes and Cresswell, 1996, p.70, n.5). D stands for 'deontic', a name given to the system by Lemmon and Scott (see Hughes and Cresswell, 1996, p.50, n.8).

The possibility of interpreting a modal logic as an epistemic logic or a deontic logic, was suggested by Von Wright (1951, 1957). The person who realised the similarity between tense and modality, and invented tense logic, was Prior (1957).

3.9 Further reading

Hughes and Cresswell (1996, chs. 2–4) survey a number of systems of modal logic, including those discussed in this chapter. Girle (2000, chs. 2–3) contains tableau systems for the modal logics of this chapter.

Various notions of necessity are discussed in Lemmon (1959). The most famous defence of the notion of metaphysical necessity in contemporary philosophy is Kripke (1980). A standard exposition of epistemic logic is to be found in Hintikka (1962). A good introductory collection of essays on deontic logic is Hilpinen (1981). On the possibility of moral dilemmas, see Gowans (1987).

3.10 Problems

1. This exercise concerns combinations of relations.

   (*a*) For each of ρ, σ, τ and η, produce a relation which satisfies one of these but none of the others (except that ρ implies η, so this case is impossible).

   (*b*) There are six pairs of these conditions: $\rho\sigma$, $\rho\tau$, $(\rho\eta)$, $\sigma\tau$, $\sigma\eta$ and $\tau\eta$. Since ρ entails η, the third of these is simply ρ. For each of the five genuine compound pairs, produce a relation that satisfies this condition, but none of the others (except that any relation that is ρ must also be η).

   (*c*) There are four triples of these conditions: $\rho\sigma\tau$, $(\rho\sigma\eta)$, $(\rho\tau\eta)$, $(\sigma\tau\eta)$. Because ρ entails η, the middle two are simply $\rho\sigma$ and $\rho\tau$. Moreover, for the same reason, and because $\sigma\tau\eta$ entails ρ (as we noted in 3.2.6), the first and last are identical. (And for good measure, $\rho\sigma\tau\eta$ is simply $\rho\sigma\tau$ as well.) Hence, there is only one genuine triple.

2. Which of the inferences of 2.12, problems 2(l)–(v) hold in $K\rho$, $K\sigma$, $K\tau$ and $K\eta$. Check with appropriate tableaux. If a tableau does not close, define and draw a counter-model.

3. Show the following in $K\rho$:

   (*a*) $\vdash (\Box(A \supset B) \wedge \Box(B \supset C)) \supset \Box(A \supset C)$

   (*b*) $\vdash (\Box(A \supset B) \wedge \Diamond(A \wedge C)) \supset \Diamond(B \wedge C)$

   (*c*) $\vdash (\Box A \wedge \Box B) \supset \Box(A \equiv B)$

(*d*) $\vdash \Diamond(A \supset B) \equiv (\Box A \supset \Diamond B)$

(*e*) $\vdash (\Diamond\neg A \vee \Diamond\neg B) \vee \Diamond(A \vee B)$

(*f*) $\vdash \Diamond(A \supset (B \wedge C)) \supset ((\Box A \supset \Diamond B) \wedge (\Box A \supset \Diamond C))$

4. Show the following in $K\rho\tau$:

(*a*) $\vdash (\Box A \vee \Box B) \equiv \Box(\Box A \vee \Box B)$

(*b*) $\vdash \Box(\Box(A \equiv B) \supset C) \supset (\Box(A \equiv B) \supset \Box C)$

5. Show the following in $K\upsilon$:

(*a*) $\vdash \Diamond A \supset \Diamond\Diamond A$

(*b*) $\vdash \Diamond A \supset \Box\Diamond A$

(*c*) $\vdash \Box(\Box A \supset \Box B) \vee \Box(\Box B \supset \Box A)$

(*d*) $\vdash \Box(\Diamond A \supset B) \equiv \Box(A \supset \Box B)$

6. Which of the following hold in $K\rho\tau$?

(*a*) $\vdash \Diamond\Box p \supset \Box\Diamond p$

(*b*) $\vdash \Box(\Box p \supset q) \vee \Box(\Box q \supset p)$

(*c*) $\vdash \Box(p \equiv q) \supset \Box(\Box p \equiv \Box q)$

(*d*) $\vdash \Diamond\Box p \equiv \Box\Diamond p$

7. The following exercises concern the relationships between various normal modal logics.

(*a*) If R is reflexive (ρ), it is extendable (η). Hence, if truth is preserved at all worlds of all η-interpretations, it is preserved at all worlds of all ρ-interpretations. Consequently, the system $K\rho$ is an extension of the system $K\eta$. Find an inference demonstrating that it is a proper extension.

(*b*) Show that none of the systems $K\rho$, $K\sigma$ and $K\tau$ is an extension of any of the others (i.e., for each pair, find an inference that is valid in one but not the other, and then vice versa).

(*c*) By combining the individual conditions, we obtain the systems $K\rho\sigma$, $K\rho\tau$, $K\sigma\tau$, $K\sigma\eta$ and $K\tau\eta$ (see problem 1(b)). $K\rho\sigma$ is an extension of $K\rho$ and $K\sigma$. Show that it is a proper extension of each of these. Do the same for the other four binary systems. Show that none of the five binary systems is an extension of any other.

(*d*) Combining three (or four) of the conditions, we obtain only the system $K\rho\sigma\tau$ (see problem 1(c)). Show that this is a proper extension of each of the binary systems of the last question.

8. Object to some of the arguments of 3.6.

9. *Show that the tableaux for $K\upsilon$, as described in 3.5.3, are sound and complete with respect to the semantics, as described in 3.5.2.

10. *Let α (anti-reflexivity) be the condition: for all w, it is not the case that wRw. Show that the logic $K\alpha$ is the same as the logic K. (*Hint*: think about the interpretations produced by K-tableaux.)

11. *A relation, R, is *Euclidean* iff, if wRu, and wRv then uRv (and also, of course, vRu). An ε-interpretation is one in which R is Euclidean. What tableau rules are sound and complete for $K\varepsilon$? Show that $K\varepsilon$ is distinct from K, $K\rho$, $K\sigma$, $K\tau$ and $K\eta$. (*Hint*: consider the formula $\Diamond A \supset \Box\Diamond A$.)

12. *Show that if a relation is reflexive and Euclidean then it is (*a*) symmetric and (*b*) transitive. Infer that $K\rho\varepsilon$, $K\rho\sigma\varepsilon$, $K\rho\varepsilon\tau$ and $K\varepsilon\rho\sigma\tau$ are all the same. Infer also that $K\rho\tau$ is a sub-system of $K\rho\varepsilon$. Show that the converse is false.

4 Non-normal worlds; strict conditionals

4.1 Introduction

4.1.1 In this chapter we look at some systems of modal logic weaker than K (and so non-normal). These involve so-called non-normal worlds. Non-normal worlds are worlds where the truth conditions of modal operators are different.

4.1.2 We are then in a position to return to the issue of the conditional, and have a look at an account of a modal conditional called the *strict* conditional.

4.2 Non-normal worlds

4.2.1 Let us start by looking at the technicalities concerning non-normality. In due course we will be able to discuss what they mean.

4.2.2 A non-normal interpretation of a modal propositional language is a structure, $\langle W, N, R, \nu\rangle$, where W, R and ν are as in previous chapters, and $N \subseteq W$. Worlds in N are called *normal.* Worlds in $W - N$ (the worlds that are not normal) are called *non-normal.*

4.2.3 The truth conditions for the truth functions, $\wedge$, $\vee$, $\neg$, etc. are the same as before (2.3.4). The truth conditions for $\Box$ and $\Diamond$ at normal worlds are also as before (2.3.5). But if w is non-normal:

$$\nu_w(\Box A) = 0$$

$$\nu_w(\Diamond A) = 1$$

In a sense, at non-normal worlds, everything is possible, and nothing is necessary.

4.2.4 Note that at every world, w, $\neg\Box A$ and $\Diamond\neg A$ still have the same truth value, as do $\neg\Diamond A$ and $\Box\neg A$. We saw this to be the case for normal worlds in 2.3.9 and 2.3.10. It is easy to see that this is also true if w is non-normal.

4.2.5 Logical validity is defined in terms of truth preservation at *normal* worlds, thus:

$\Sigma \models A$ iff for all interpretations $\langle W, N, R, \nu\rangle$ and all $w \in N$: if $\nu_w(B) = 1$ for all $B \in \Sigma$ then $\nu_w(A) = 1$.

$\models A$ iff $\phi \models A$, i.e., iff for all $\langle W, N, R, \nu\rangle$ and all $w \in N$, $\nu_w(A) = 1$.

4.2.6 If the accessibility relation, R, may be any binary relation on W, the logic this construction gives will be called N.[1] As with normal modal logics, additional logics can be formed by placing constraints on R, such as reflexivity, transitivity, symmetry, etc. (as in 3.2). In fact, of course, how R behaves at non-normal worlds is irrelevant, since this plays no role in determining truth values. We use $N\rho$ to refer to the non-normal logic determined by the class of all interpretations where R is reflexive; $N\sigma\tau$, to refer to the non-normal logic determined by the class of all interpretations where R is symmetric and transitive, and so on. As for normal logics, $N\rho\tau$ is an extension of $N\rho$, which is an extension of N, etc.

4.2.7 Historically, $N\rho$ and $N\rho\tau$ are the Lewis systems *S2* and *S3* respectively. $N\rho\sigma\tau$ is the non-Lewis system *S3.5*.

4.2.8 Non-normal worlds were originally invented purely as a technical device to give a possible-world semantics for the Lewis systems

[1] The name is not standard, but is sensible enough. Note that N is also used for the normal worlds in an interpretation. Context, however, will disambiguate.

weaker than *S4*. As we shall see in due course, though, they have a perfectly good philosophical meaning. For the record, Lewis thought that the correct system of modal logic for logical necessity was *S2*.

4.3 Tableaux for non-normal modal logics

4.3.1 A tableau technique for N is obtained by modifying the technique for K as follows. If world i occurs on a branch of a tableau, call it $\Box$-*inhabited* if there is some node of the form $\Box B, i$ on the branch. The rule for $\Diamond A, i$ (2.4.4) is activated only when $i = 0$ or i is $\Box$-inhabited. Otherwise, details are the same as for K.

4.3.2 The rationale for the new $\Diamond$-rule is, roughly, as follows. If $i = 0$, i must be a normal world (since the tableau is a search for a normal world where the premises are true and the conclusion is false), and so the $\Diamond$-rule is applied in the usual way. If $i > 0$, it can be assumed to be non-normal as long as the branch of the tableau is not $\Box$-inhabited. Nothing, then, needs to be done. But as soon as i is $\Box$-inhabited, it can no longer be non-normal (since nothing of the form $\Box A$ is true at a non-normal world), and so the standard rule for $\Diamond$ must be applied. The next two subsections give example tableaux for N.

4.3.3 $\vdash_N \Box(A \supset B) \supset (\Box A \supset \Box B)$:

$$\neg(\Box(A \supset B) \supset (\Box A \supset \Box B)), 0$$
$$\Box(A \supset B), 0$$
$$\neg(\Box A \supset \Box B), 0$$
$$\Box A, 0$$
$$\neg\Box B, 0$$
$$\Diamond\neg B, 0$$
$$0r1$$
$$\neg B, 1$$
$$A \supset B, 1$$
$$A, 1$$
$$\swarrow \quad \searrow$$
$$\neg A, 1 \qquad B, 1$$
$$\times \qquad\quad \times$$

The $\Diamond$-rule is applied to $\Diamond\neg B, 0$, because we are dealing with world 0.

4.3.4 $\nvdash_N \Box(p \supset \Box(q \supset q))$:

$$\begin{array}{c}
\neg\Box(p \supset \Box(q \supset q)), 0 \\
\Diamond\neg(p \supset \Box(q \supset q)), 0 \\
0r1 \\
\neg(p \supset \Box(q \supset q)), 1 \\
p, 1 \\
\neg\Box(q \supset q), 1 \\
\Diamond\neg(q \supset q), 1
\end{array}$$

On the (only) branch of the tableau, world 1 is not $\Box$-inhabited. Consequently, the $\Diamond$-rule is not applied to the last line, and the tableau ends open.

4.3.5 Bearing in mind the comments of 4.3.2, it is easy to see how a counter-model for an inference can be read off from an open tableau branch. The method is exactly the same as for K, except that world 0 is always normal, and all other worlds are non-normal, unless they are $\Box$-inhabited.

4.3.6 Thus, in the counter-model determined by the tableau of 4.3.4, $W = \{w_0, w_1\}$; $N = \{w_0\}$; $w_0 R w_1$; and ν is such that $\nu_{w_1}(p) = 1$. If we indicate that a world is non-normal by putting it in a box, the interpretation can be depicted thus:

$$\begin{array}{ccc}
 & & p \\
w_0 & \rightarrow & \boxed{w_1}
\end{array}$$

4.3.7 Tableaux for $N\rho$, $N\rho\tau$, etc. are obtained by adding the extra tableau rules for ρ, $\rho\tau$, etc., as for K (3.3).

4.3.8 The tableaux for N and its extensions are sound and complete with respect to their respective semantics. The proof can be found in 4.10.

4.4 The properties of non-normal logics

4.4.1 A K-interpretation is simply a special case of an N-interpretation, namely, one where $W = N$. Hence, if truth is preserved at all worlds of all N-interpretations, it is preserved at all worlds of all K-interpretations. Hence, the logic K is an extension of N. (Another way of seeing this is to note that any tableau that closes under the rules for N must also close under the rules for K.)

4.4.2 The same is true for the corresponding extensions of K and N: $K\rho$ and $N\rho$, $K\rho\tau$ and $N\rho\tau$, etc.

4.4.3 But each K-logic is a proper extension of the corresponding N-logic. It is easy enough to check that $\vdash_K \Box(p \supset \Box(q \supset q))$ (and *a fortiori* any of K's extensions), but as the tableau of 4.3.4 shows, it is not valid in N. Moreover, adding any of the rules for r to this tableau does not close it, either. None of the rules makes world 1 $\Box$-inhabited; hence, it remains open. Hence, this inference is not valid in any of the extensions of N either.

4.4.4 Note that $K\rho\sigma\tau$ ($K\upsilon$) is the strongest of all the logics we have looked at: every normal system that we looked at is contained in $K\rho\sigma\tau$ (3.2.9), and every non-normal system that we looked at is contained in the corresponding normal system (4.4.1, 4.4.2). N is the weakest system we have met. It is contained in every non-normal system, and also in K, and so in every normal system.

4.4.5 It might be wondered what happens if we define a logic with non-normal semantics, and validity defined in terms of truth preservation at all worlds (normal *and* non-normal). This gives a sub-logic of the corresponding non-normal logic. (If truth is preserved at *all* worlds of an interpretation, it is preserved at all normal worlds.) In fact, it is a proper sub-logic. In any non-normal modal logic, for example, $\models \Box(A \vee \neg A)$. But since $\Box(A \vee \neg A)$ is not true at non-normal worlds, $\Box(A \vee \neg A)$ is not valid if logical truth is defined with reference to all worlds. Hence, this definition can be used to create logics weaker than N.[2]

4.4.6 Let us finally, now, return to the question of the meaning of non-normal worlds. For any normal system, L, if $\models_L A$ then $\models_L \Box A$. (This is sometimes called the *Rule of Necessitation*.) For if $\models_L A$ then A is true at all worlds of all L-interpretations. Hence, if w is any such world, A is true at all worlds accessible from w. Hence, $\Box A$ is true at w. Thus, $\models_L \Box A$.

4.4.7 The Rule of Necessitation fails in every non-normal logic, L, however. Consider, for example, $A \vee \neg A$. This holds at all worlds, normal or non-normal. Hence, $\Box(A \vee \neg A)$ holds at all normal worlds, i.e., $\models_L \Box(A \vee \neg A)$. But at any non-normal world, $\Box(A \vee \neg A)$ is false. Hence, if there are any non-normal worlds in an interpretation, $\Box\Box(A \vee \neg A)$ is false at all normal worlds of that interpretation, i.e., $\not\models_L \Box\Box(A \vee \neg A)$.[3]

4.4.8 The failure of the Rule of Necessitation is, perhaps, the most distinctive feature of non-normal systems. And it fails, as we have just seen, because logical truths may fail to hold at non-normal worlds. Non-normal worlds are, thus, worlds where 'logic is not guaranteed to hold'. We come back to this insight in a later chapter.

4.5 Strict conditionals

4.5.1 Now that we have covered material on modal logic, we can return to the question of the conditional.

---

[2] The logics which are the same as *S2* and *S3*, except that validity is defined in terms of truth preservation at all worlds, are sometimes called *E2* and *E3*.

[3] Similarly, the principle that if $A \models B$ then $\Box A \models \Box B$, which holds in all normal logics, as we saw in 3.6.10, also fails in non-normal logics. If $\Box A$ is true at a normal world of an interpretation, it follows that A is true at all worlds in it; but it does not follow from this and $A \models B$ that B is true at all the worlds in it – only that it is true at all *normal* worlds in it.

4.5.2 Consider a true material conditional, such as 'The sun is shining $\supset$ Canberra is the federal capital of Australia'. One is inclined to reject this as a true conditional just because the truth of the material conditional is too contingent an affair. Things could have been quite otherwise, in which case the material conditional would have been false. This suggests defining the conditional, 'if A then B' as $\Box(A \supset B)$, where $\Box$ expresses an appropriate notion of necessity.

4.5.3 When Lewis created modern modal logic, he was not, in fact, concerned with modality as such. He was dissatisfied with the material conditional. He defined $A \dashv B$ as $\Box(A \supset B)$, and suggested this as a correct account of the conditional. $\dashv$ is usually called the *strict conditional*.

4.5.4 It is easy enough to check that all the following are false in $K\rho\sigma\tau$, and so in all the normal and non-normal logics we have looked at.

$$B \models A \dashv B$$

$$\neg A \models A \dashv B$$

$$(A \wedge B) \dashv C \models (A \dashv C) \vee (B \dashv C)$$

$$(A \dashv B) \wedge (C \dashv D) \models (A \dashv D) \vee (C \dashv B),$$

$$\neg(A \dashv B) \models A$$

But these inferences are the basis of all the objections to the material account of the conditional that we looked at in 1.7–1.9. Hence, the strict conditional is not subject to any of the objections to which the material conditional is.

4.6 The paradoxes of strict implication

4.6.1 Does it provide an adequate account of the conditional? Each system of modal logic gives $\dashv$ different properties. Hence, before we can answer that question, we need to address the question of which system of modal logic it is that is at issue. Let me make two comments on this.

4.6.2 First, it is natural to suppose that any notion of necessity that is to be employed in defining a notion of conditionality must be at least as strong as $K\rho$ (or $N\rho$ if one is countenancing non-normal systems). This is because, without ρ, *modus ponens* fails: $A, A \multimap B \not\models B$. With it, it holds, as simple tableau tests verify.

4.6.3 Second, a further determination of this question is not very important for what follows. This is because the major objections to the claim that English conditionals are strict hinge on a feature that the strict conditional possesses in all systems of modal logic. In all systems of modal logic the following hold:

$$\Box B \models A \multimap B$$

$$\neg\Diamond A \models A \multimap B$$

These facts are sometimes called the 'paradoxes of strict implication'. A tableau test verifies that these hold in N, and so in all the normal and non-normal systems that we have looked at. Since, in all systems, we also have $\models \Box(B \vee \neg B)$ and $\models \neg\Diamond(A \wedge \neg A)$, this gives us as special cases:

$$\models A \multimap (B \vee \neg B)$$

$$\models (A \wedge \neg A) \multimap B$$

4.7 ... and their problems

4.7.1 If we read $\multimap$ as the conditional, the paradoxes of strict implication are highly counterintuitive. For example, 'There is an infinitude of prime numbers' is a logical truth; yet:

If Brisbane is in Australia, there is an infinitude of prime numbers

If there is not an infinitude of prime numbers, Brisbane is in Germany

do not appear to be true.

4.7.2 This point is inconclusive, at least as far as indicative conditionals go, since one might just accept the paradoxes, and try to explain why the two preceding statements, and their kind, appear counterintuitive, by using Grice's notion of conversational implicature (1.7.3). The conditionals are true enough, but simply unassertable, since we are in a position, in each case, to assert stronger information: necessarily there is an infinitude of prime numbers; it is impossible that there is not.

4.7.3 It will not help for subjunctive conditionals, however. For asserting such a conditional does *not* conversationally imply that we do not know the status of the antecedent and consequent. (On the contrary, it often implies that we do.) It is not, therefore, linguistically odd. For example, it is logically impossible to square the circle (that is, construct a square with an area equal to that of a given circle by means of ruler and compasses). But even though we know this, it is not at all odd to assert that, none the less, if Hobbes (who thought he had succeeded in squaring the circle) had done so, he would have become a very famous mathematician. Moreover, there are clearly *false* subjunctive conditionals with impossible antecedents. For example, I can assure you that it is not the case that if you were to square the circle I would give you my life's savings.

4.7.4 Here is another objection against $\dashv$ being the indicative conditional. Let A be 'There is an infinite number of prime numbers'. Since A is a necessary truth, $(A \vee \neg A) \dashv A$ is true. If the conditional were strict implication, the following would therefore be a sound argument: If $A \vee \neg A$ then A; but $A \vee \neg A$; hence A. Now, imagine someone offering this as a proof for the infinitude of primes in a class on number theory. It is clear that it would not be acceptable.

4.7.5 This objection may also be challenged. For an argument to be acceptable, it must be more than just sound. In particular, it must not beg the question (assume what is at issue). And the only reason we have for supposing the conditional premise to be true is that the consequent is necessarily true. The proof at issue would therefore beg the question.

4.8 The explosion of contradictions

4.8.1 The toughest objections to a strict conditional, at least as an account of the indicative conditional, come from the fact that $\models (A \wedge \neg A) \dashv B$. If this were the case, then, by *modus ponens*, we would have $(A \wedge \neg A) \models B$. Contradictions would entail everything. Not only is this highly counterintuitive, there would seem to be definite counter-examples to it. There appear to be a number of situations or theories which are inconsistent, yet in which it is manifestly incorrect to infer that everything holds. Here are three very different examples.

4.8.2 The first is a theory in the history of science: Bohr's theory of the atom (the 'solar system' model). This was internally inconsistent. To determine the behaviour of the atom, Bohr assumed the standard Maxwell electromagnetic equations. But he also assumed that energy could come only in discrete packets (quanta). These two things are inconsistent (as Bohr knew); yet both were integrally required for the account to work. The account was therefore essentially inconsistent. Yet many of its observable predictions were spectacularly verified. It is clear though that not everything was taken to follow from the account. Bohr did not infer, for example, that electronic orbits are rectangles.

4.8.3 Another example: pieces of legislation are often inconsistent. To avoid irrelevant historical details, here is an hypothetical example. Suppose that an (absent-minded) state legislator passes the following traffic laws. At an unmarked junction, the priority regulations are:

(1) Any woman has priority over any man.

(2) Any older person has priority over any younger person.

(We may suppose that clause 2 was meant to resolve the case where two men or two women arrive together, but the legislator forgot to make it subordinate to clause 1.) The legislation will work perfectly happily in three out of four combinations of sex and age. But suppose that Ms X, of age 30, approaches the junction at the same time as Mr Y, of age 40. Ms X has priority (by 1), but has not got priority (by 2 and the meaning of 'priority'). Hence, the situation is inconsistent. But, again, it would be stupid to infer from this that, for example, the traffic laws are *consistent*.

4.8.4 Third example: it is possible to have visual illusions where things appear contradictory. For example, in the 'waterfall effect', one's visual system is conditioned by constant motion of a certain kind, say a rotating spiral. If one then looks at a stationary situation, say a white wall, it appears to move in the opposite direction. But, a point in the visual field, say at the top, does not appear to move, for example, to revolve around to the bottom. Thus, things appear to move without changing place: the perceived situation is inconsistent. But not everything perceivable holds in this situation. For example, it is not the case that the situation is red all over.[4]

4.9 Lewis' argument for explosion

4.9.1 Let us end by considering a final objection to $\prec$ as providing a correct account of the conditional. It is natural to object that this account cannot be correct, since a conditional requires some kind of connection between antecedent and consequent; yet a strict conditional requires no such connection. There is no connection in general, for example, between $A \wedge \neg A$ and B.

[4] A fourth kind of example is provided by certain fictional situations, in which contradictory states of affairs hold. This may well be the case without everything holding in the fictional situation.

4.9.2 C. I. Lewis, who did accept $⥽$ as an adequate account of the conditional, thought that there was a connection, at least in this case. The connection is shown in the following argument:

$$\dfrac{\dfrac{A \wedge \neg A}{A} \qquad \dfrac{\dfrac{A \wedge \neg A}{\neg A}}{\neg A \vee B}}{B}$$

Premises are above lines; conclusions are below. The only ultimate premise is $A \wedge \neg A$; the only ultimate conclusion is B. The inferences that the argument uses are: inferring a conjunct from a conjunction; inferring a disjunction from a disjunct; and the disjunctive syllogism: $A, \neg A \vee B \vdash B$. Of course, all these are valid in the modal logics we have looked at. If contradictions do not entail everything, then one of these must be wrong. We will return to this point in a later chapter.

4.9.3 Lewis also argued that there is a connection in the case of the conditional $A⥽(B \vee \neg B)$ as well. The connection is provided by the following argument:

$$\dfrac{\dfrac{\dfrac{A}{(A \wedge B) \vee (A \wedge \neg B)}}{A \wedge (B \vee \neg B)}}{(B \vee \neg B)}$$

This argument is less convincing than that of 4.9.2, however, since the first step seems evidently to smuggle in the conclusion.

4.10 *Proofs of theorems

4.10.1 THEOREM: The tableaux for N are sound with respect to their semantics.

Proof:

The proof is as for K (2.9.2–2.9.4) with a couple of minor amendments. First, we add a new clause to the definition of faithfulness, namely:

$f(0) \in N$

The proof of the Soundness Lemma proceeds as before, except for the cases for the modal rules. The negated rules are taken care of by 4.2.4. For the $\Diamond$-rule: Suppose that f shows $\mathcal{I}$ to be faithful to b, and that we apply the rule to $\Diamond A, i$ to get A, j for a new j; then either $i = 0$ or i is $\Box$-inhabited. In either case, $f(i)$ is normal. (In the first case, this is obvious; in the second case, there is some node of the form $\Box B, i$ on b; and since f shows $\mathcal{I}$ to be faithful to b, $\Box B$ is true at $f(i)$; but $\Box B$ is false at every non-normal world.) Hence there is a world, w, such that B is true at w. Let f' be the same as f, except that $f'(j) = w$. Then f' shows $\mathcal{I}$ to be faithful to the extended branch, as in the corresponding case for K. For the $\Box$-rule: suppose that f shows $\mathcal{I}$ to be faithful to b, and that we apply the rule to $\Box A, i$ and irj to get A, j. Since $\Box A$ is true at $f(i)$, $f(i)$ must be normal; and since $f(i)Rf(j)$, it follows that A is true at $f(j)$.

In the proof of the Soundness Theorem proper, suppose that $\Sigma \not\models A$. Let $\mathcal{I} = \langle W, N, R, \nu \rangle$ and $w \in N$ be such that at w every member of Σ is true and A is false. Let $f(0) = w$. Then f shows $\mathcal{I}$ to be faithful to the initial list. The argument then goes as for K.

4.10.2 THEOREM: The tableaux for extensions of N with ρ, τ, etc., and their various combinations, are sound with respect to their respective semantics.

Proof:

The argument is as for K (3.7.1–3.7.2).

4.10.3 THEOREM: The tableaux for N are complete with respect to their semantics.

Proof:

The proof is as for K (2.9.5–2.9.7) with a couple of minor amendments. First, given an open branch, b, we define the induced interpretation as for K, except that $i \in N$ iff $i = 0$ or i is $\Box$-inhabited on b.

The argument for the Completeness Lemma is the same as that for K, except the cases for the modal operators, which go as follows. Suppose that $\Diamond A, i$ is on b. If $i \notin N$ then $\Diamond A$ is true at w_i by definition. If $i \in N$ then the $\Diamond$-rule has been applied to it. Hence, for some new j, irj and A, j occur on b. By induction hypothesis, $w_i R w_j$, and A is true at w_j. Since w_i is normal, $\Diamond A$ is true at w_i, as required. If $\neg\Diamond A, i$ is on b then $\Box\neg A, i$ is on b. By definition, i is $\Box$-inhabited. Hence, for every j such that irj is on b, $\neg A, j$ is on b. By induction hypothesis, A is false at every w_j such that $w_i R w_j$; and since i is normal, $\Diamond A$ is false at w_j. The case for $\Box$ is similar.

The proof of the Completeness Theorem proper is the same as that for K.

4.10.4 THEOREM: The tableaux for extensions of N with ρ, τ, etc., and their various combinations, are complete with respect to their respective semantics.

Proof:

The argument is as for K (3.7.3–3.7.4).

4.11 History

The notion of a non-normal world, and the semantics for *S2* and *S3*, were invented by Kripke (1965a). The Lewis system *S1* proved recalcitrant to a semantical modelling. A suitable one was eventually given by Cresswell (1995). The semantics has non-normal worlds, but the behaviour of modal formulas at these requires more complex machinery. The logics *E2* and *E3* were proposed by Lemmon (1957). *S6* and *S7* (see 4.13, problem 8) were produced in the 1940s. For their history, see Hughes and Cresswell (1996, p. 207, n. 24).

The argument of 4.7.4 is due to Anderson and Belnap (1975, p. 17), the founders of relevant logic, which we will come to in later chapters. The Lewis argument that everything follows from a contradiction was known in the Middle Ages, for example, by Scotus. Its earliest known appearance in logic appears to be in the work of William of Soissons in the twelfth century. See Martin (1985).

4.12 Further reading

For a good discussion of some of the history of Lewis' investigations of modal logic, and of non-normal systems, see Hughes and Cresswell (1996, ch. 11). For some philosophical discussion of non-normal worlds, see Cresswell (1967). Tableaux for non-normal logics can be found in Girle (2000, ch. 5).

For papers on either side of the debate about the adequacy of the strict conditional, see Bennett (1969) and Meyer (1971). For a discussion of whether contradictions entail everything, see Priest and Routley (1989b, pp. 483–98). Historical details of Bohr's theory of the atom and its inconsistency can be found in Brown (1993); and the waterfall effect is discussed in most psychology textbooks on perception, for example, Robinson (1972). For an essentially inconsistent fictional situation, see Priest (1997a).

4.13 Problems

1. Check the details of 4.4.3, 4.5.4, 4.6.2 and 4.6.3.

2. Show the following for N:

   (*a*) $\vdash A \prec A$

   (*b*) $\vdash ((A \prec B) \wedge (B \prec C)) \prec (A \prec C)$

   (*c*) $\vdash (A \prec B) \prec (\neg B \prec \neg A)$

   (*d*) $\vdash \Box\neg A \supset \Box\neg(A \wedge B)$

3. Show the following for N. Specify a counter-model and draw a picture of it.

   (*a*) $\nvdash \Box p \supset p$

   (*b*) $\nvdash \Box p \supset \Box\Box p$

   (*c*) $\nvdash \neg(p \prec p) \prec q$

   (*d*) $\nvdash \Box(p \prec p)$

(*e*) $\nvdash (p \prec q) \prec (\Box p \prec \Box q)$

(*f*) $\nvdash \Box\Box p \prec (\Box q \prec \Box\Box q)$

(*g*) $\nvdash \Diamond\Diamond p$

(*h*) $\nvdash \Box\Box(p \vee \neg p)$

4. Which of the above (in problem 3) hold in *S2* ($N\rho$)? Which hold in *S3* ($N\rho\tau$)?

5. Repeat 3.10, problem 7, with *N* instead of *K*. (Beware: in $N\tau$, $\Box p \supset \Box\Box p$ is *not* valid. A little ingenuity is required here.)

6. How might one object to the arguments of 4.7 and 4.8?

7. Show that $\vdash \Diamond\Diamond(p \wedge \neg p) \vee \Box(q \prec q)$, in both *S2* and *S3*, but that neither disjunct is valid in either *S2* or *S3*. (Note that there is nothing odd, in general, about having a logically valid disjunction, each disjunct of which is not logically valid – just consider $p \vee \neg p$. But it is odd for this to arise if the disjuncts have no propositional parameter in common.)

8. *Call a world *standard* if it is both normal and accesses a non-normal world. A new notion of validity is obtained if we define it in terms of truth preservation at standard worlds. Show that according to this definition of validity, $\Diamond\Diamond A$ is valid. If, in addition, we insist that *R* be reflexive, or reflexive and transitive, we obtain the non-Lewis systems *S6* and *S7*, respectively. These are extensions of *S2* and *S3*, respectively, but, despite the numerology, they are not extensions of *S5*. Design tableau systems for *S6* and *S7* and prove them sound and complete.

EXTENSIONS OF CLASSICAL LOGIC UP TO HERE

5 Conditional logics

5.1 Introduction

5.1.1 In this chapter we look at what have come to be called ‘conditional logics’. These are a type of modal logic where there is a multiplicity of accessibility relations of a certain kind.

5.1.2 The logics also introduce us to some more problematic inferences concerning the conditional, and we discuss what to make of these.

5.2 Some more problematic inferences

5.2.1 Let us start with the inferences. It is easy enough to check that the following are all valid in classical logic:

Antecedent strengthening: $A \supset B \models (A \wedge C) \supset B$

Transitivity: $A \supset B, B \supset C \models A \supset C$

Contraposition: $A \supset B \models \neg B \supset \neg A$

It is also easy to check that the same is true if ‘$\supset$’ is replaced by ‘⥽’. (The inferences all hold in N, and so in all modal systems.)

5.2.2 But now consider the three following arguments of the same respective forms:

(1) If it does not rain tomorrow we will go to the cricket. Hence, if it does not rain tomorrow and I am killed in a car accident tonight then we will go to the cricket.

(2) If the other candidates pull out, John will get the job. If John gets the job, the other candidates will be disappointed. Hence, if the other candidates pull out, they will be disappointed.

(3) If we take the car then it won't break down *en route*. Hence, if the car does break down *en route*, we didn't take it.

If the conditional were either material or strict, then these inferences would be valid, which they certainly do not appear to be, since they may have true premises and a false conclusion. Hence, we have a new set of objections against the conditional being either material or strict. (And since the conditionals are indicative, they tell just as much against one who claims only that English indicative conditionals are material.)

5.2.3 What is one to say about these objections? It is often the case that, when one gives an argument, one does not mention explicitly some of the premises, perhaps because they are pretty obvious. Thus, I might say: this plane lands in Rome; therefore, this plane lands in Italy. Here I omit the fact that Rome is in Italy. Arguments where premises are omitted in this way are traditionally called *enthymemes*. Just as arguments can be enthymematic, so can conditionals. Thus, suppose that I say: if this plane lands in Rome, it lands in Italy. Strictly speaking, one may say, the conditional is false. It is an enthymeme of the true conditional: if this plane lands in Rome, and Rome is in Italy, then this plane lands in Italy.

5.2.4 Now consider the first argument of 5.2.2. A natural thing to say is that the inference *is* valid. It is just that the premise is not, strictly speaking, true. What we are assenting to, when we assent to the premise, is really the conditional: if it does not rain tomorrow *and* I am not killed in a car accident tonight, then we will go to the cricket tomorrow. The premise is an enthymematic form of that. Similar comments can be made about the other arguments of 5.2.2. Thus, the second premise of the second argument is, strictly speaking, false. What is true is that if John gets the job *and* the other candidates do not pull out, they will be disappointed. Thus, one may defuse these counter-examples.

5.2.5 This move is essentially right, but it is a bit too swift, though. Come back to the premise of the first argument. If the conditional 'if it does not rain tomorrow, we will go to the cricket' is not true, then neither is the conditional 'if it does not rain tomorrow and I am not killed in a car accident tonight, we will go to the cricket'. I might be killed in a domestic accident, all means of transport may break down tomorrow, we might be invaded by Martians, etc. The list of conditions is, arguably, open-ended and indefinite. So no conditional of this kind that we could formulate explicitly is true!

5.2.6 Fortunately, though, we can capture all the open-ended conditions in a catch-all clause. We can say: 'if it does not rain tomorrow then, other things being equal, we will go to the cricket' or 'if it does not rain tomorrow and everything else relevant remains unchanged, we will go to the cricket'. The Latin for 'other things being equal' is *ceteris paribus*, so we can call this a *ceteris paribus* clause. It is the conditional with the *ceteris paribus* clause that we are really assenting to when we assent to the premise of the first argument. Similarly for the other arguments.

5.2.7 A conditional of this kind is of the form 'if A and C_A then B', where C_A is the *ceteris paribus* clause. How does this clause function? It is no ordinary conjunct. For a start, as we have seen, it captures an open-ended set of conditions. It also depends very much on A. (That is what the subscript A is there to remind you of.) If A is 'it does not rain tomorrow', then C_A includes the condition that we are not invaded by Martians. If A is 'flying saucers arrive from Mars', it does not. Finally, it is indexical; that is, what it comprises depends very much on what is already the case: it depends on the world at which we are evaluating the conditional. Thus, for example, if A is 'it does not rain tomorrow', then, for our world, C_A entails that we are not invaded by Martians; but in a world where Martians have already landed, it does not.

5.2.8 Let us write $A > B$ for a conditional with a *ceteris paribus* clause. Suppose one accepts a strict account of the conditional. Then a conditional $A \dashv B$ is true (at a world) if $A \supset B$ is true at every (accessible) world; that is, if B is true at every (accessible) world at which A is true. Thus, the conditional $A > B$ is true (at a world) if B is true at every (accessible) world at which $A \wedge C_A$ is true. How do we spell out this idea more precisely?

5.3 Conditional semantics

5.3.1 First, we extend our formal language with the connective $>$. Thus, if A and B are formulas, so is $A > B$. Let the set of formulas of the language be $\mathcal{F}$.

5.3.2 To keep things simple, we assume that the logic of the modal operators is $K\upsilon$. In this way, we need not worry about an accessibility relation for the modal operators in an interpretation.

5.3.3 An interpretation for the extended language is a structure of the form $\langle W, \{R_A; A \in \mathcal{F}\}, \nu\rangle$. W and ν are as for $K\upsilon$. The middle component, $\{R_A; A \in \mathcal{F}\}$, is a collection of binary relations on W, R_A, one for every formula, A. Intuitively, $w_1 R_A w_2$ means that A is true at w_2, which is, *ceteris paribus*, the same as w_1.

5.3.4 Given an interpretation, ν is extended to give a truth value to every formula at every world. The conditions for the truth functions, and for $\Box$ and $\Diamond$, are as for the modal logic $K\upsilon$. For $>$ the condition is:

$$\nu_w(A > B) = 1 \text{ iff for all } w' \text{ such that } wR_Aw',\ \nu_{w'}(B) = 1$$

One may look at the situation like this: every formula, A, gives rise to a corresponding necessity operator, $\boxed{A}$. $A > B$ is then just $\boxed{A}B$.

5.3.5 A little bit of notation will make many of the following details easier to follow. Let us write the set of worlds accessible to w under R_A as $f_A(w)$. Thus, $f_A(w) = \{x \in W; wR_Ax\}$. R and f are, in fact, interdefinable, since wR_Aw' iff $w' \in f_A(w)$. Thus, we may couch any discussion in terms of R or f indifferently. Next, let $[A]$ be the class of worlds where A is true, $\{w; \nu_w(A) = 1\}$. With these conventions, the truth conditions of $A > B$ can be stated very simply: $A > B$ is true at w iff $f_A(w) \subseteq [B]$. Note also that $A \dashv B$ is true at w iff $[A] \subseteq [B]$. (Since we are operating in K_υ, the truth value of $A \dashv B$ does not depend on w.)

5.3.6 Validity is defined as truth preservation over all worlds of all interpretations, as in normal modal logics. We will call this conditional logic C.[1] Since no constraints are placed on the relations R_A, C is the analogue for conditional logics of the modal logic K.

5.4 Tableaux for C

5.4.1 Tableaux for C are obtained simply by modifying those for K. Nodes may now be of the form A, i or ir_Aj. The rules for the truth-functional and modal connectives are as in $K\upsilon$. The rules for $>$ are as follows:

$$\begin{array}{c} A > B, i \\ ir_Aj \\ \downarrow \\ B, j \end{array} \qquad \begin{array}{c} \neg(A > B), i \\ \downarrow \\ ir_Aj \\ \neg B, j \end{array}$$

In the first rule, this is applied for every ir_Aj on the branch. In the second, j has to be new. (The first rule is just like the rule for $\Box$; the second rule is just like the rule for $\Diamond$, given that $\neg\Box C$ is equivalent to $\Diamond\neg C$.)

[1] In the notation we are employing, C is also used as a variable for formulas. But the context will always disambiguate.

5.4.2 Here is an example tableau, demonstrating that $A > B \vdash_C A > (B \vee C)$:

$$
\begin{array}{c}
A > B, 0 \\
\neg(A > (B \vee C)), 0 \\
0r_A 1 \\
\neg(B \vee C), 1 \\
\neg B, 1 \\
\neg C, 1 \\
B, 1 \\
\times
\end{array}
$$

The third and fourth lines are obtained from the second by the rule for negated $>$. The last line is obtained from the first and third by the rule for $>$.

5.4.3 Here is another to show that $p > r \nvdash_C (p \wedge q) > r$:

$$
\begin{array}{c}
p > r, 0 \\
\neg((p \wedge q) > r), 0 \\
0r_{p\wedge q} 1 \\
\neg r, 1
\end{array}
$$

Note that we cannot apply the rule for $>$ to the first line, to close off the tableau. For this, we would need $0r_p 1$, which we do not have. It is easy enough to check that the other inferences corresponding to the arguments of 5.2.2 are invalid, as is to be expected: $p > q, q > r \nvdash_C p > r$; $p > q \nvdash_C \neg q > \neg p$. Details are left as an exercise.

5.4.4 Counter-models are read off from the tableau in a natural way. If there is something of the form $A > B$ or $\neg(A > B)$ on the branch, then R_A is as the information about r_A on the branch specifies. Otherwise, R_A may be arbitrary. Thus, in the counter-model given by 5.4.3, $W = \{w_0, w_1\}$; $w_0 R_{p\wedge q} w_1$ (and those are the only things that $R_{p\wedge q}$ relates); R_p relates nothing to anything; for every other formula, A, R_A can be anything one likes; and ν is such that $\nu_{w_1}(r) = 0$. In pictures:

$$
\begin{array}{ccc}
w_0 & \xrightarrow{p\wedge q} & w_1 \\
 & & \neg r
\end{array}
$$

It is easy to check directly that this makes the premise true and the conclusion false at w_0. r is true at every world accessible to w_0 via r_p. (There are none.) Hence, $p > r$ is true at w_0. And at some world accessible to w_0 via $R_{p \wedge q}$, r is false. Hence, $(p \wedge q) > r$ is false at w_0.

5.4.5 The tableaux are sound and complete with respect to C. The proof of this can be found in 5.9.

5.5 Extensions of *C*

5.5.1 Just as with K, one can extend C by adding constraints on the accessibility relations. A couple of these are mandated by the very intuition explained in 5.2.8. No doubt, the reader will have been wanting to point out for some time now that there is nothing in the semantics, so far, that requires A to be true at w' if wR_Aw'. Thus the following condition is very natural:

(1) $f_A(w) \subseteq [A]$

Moreover, if the world, w, is already such that A is true there, then, presumably, the worlds that are essentially the same as w, except that A is true there, must include w itself. This motivates the condition:

(2) If $w \in [A]$, then $w \in f_A(w)$

It is difficult to get any other conditions uncontentiously out of the motivating conditions of 5.2.8.

5.5.2 We call the logic in which validity is defined in terms of truth preservation at all worlds of all interpretations where, for every formula A, R_A satisfies conditions (1) and (2), C^+. For the usual reasons, C^+ is an extension of C.

5.5.3 Tableaux for C^+ are obtained by modifying the rule for negated $>$ to:

$$\begin{array}{c} \neg(A > B), i \\ \downarrow \\ ir_A j \\ A, j \\ \neg B, j \end{array}$$

(where j is new). This takes care of (1). For (2), we have to apply the following rule:

$$\begin{array}{ccc} & . & \\ \swarrow & & \searrow \\ \neg A, i & & A, i \\ & & ir_A i \\ & & Bi \end{array}$$

for every integer, i, occurring on the branch, and every A which is the antecedent of a conditional or negated conditional at a node.

5.5.4 Here is an example, to show that $A, A > B \vdash_{C^+} B$ (*modus ponens* for $>$):

$$\begin{array}{ccc} & A, 0 & \\ & A > B, 0 & \\ & \neg B, 0 & \\ \swarrow & & \searrow \\ \neg A, 0 & & A, 0 \\ \times & & 0r_A 0 \\ & & B, 0 \\ & & \times \end{array}$$

It is not difficult to check that *modus ponens* for $>$ fails in C. C^+ is therefore a proper extension of C.

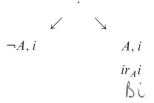

5.5.5 Here is another tableau to show that $p > r \nvdash_{C^+} p > (r \wedge q)$:

$$p > r, 0$$
$$\neg(p > (r \wedge q)), 0$$
$$0r_p1$$
$$p, 1$$
$$\neg(r \wedge q), 1$$
$$r, 1$$
$$\swarrow \quad \searrow$$
$$\neg r, 1 \qquad\qquad \neg q, 1$$
$$\times \qquad\qquad\qquad \swarrow \searrow$$
$$\neg p, 0 \qquad\qquad p, 0$$
$$0r_p0$$
$$r, 0$$
$$\swarrow \searrow$$
$$\neg p, 1 \qquad\qquad p, 1$$
$$1r_p1$$

Only the leftmost branch closes.

5.5.6 Counter-models can be read off from an open branch of a tableau as before. If A does not occur as the antecedent of a conditional or negated conditional at a node, we can no longer allow R_A to be arbitrary, however, since it must satisfy (1) and (2). The simplest trick is to let $f_A(w) = [A]$ (for every w).[2] With this definition, (1) and (2) are clearly satisfied.

5.5.7 Thus, in the counter-model for the tableau of 5.5.5, read off from the rightmost branch, $W = \{w_0, w_1\}$; $w_0 R_p w_0$, $w_0 R_p w_1$ and $w_1 R_p w_1$; for all other A, $f_A(w) = [A]$; $v_{w_0}(p) = v_{w_0}(r) = v_{w_1}(r) = v_{w_1}(p) = 1$, and $v_{w_1}(q) = 0$. In pictures:

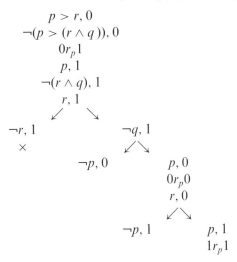

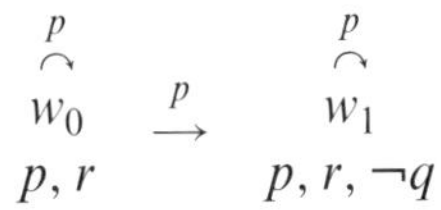

[2] This is legitimate, since f_A is not required to define the truth value of A at a world. To evaluate the truth value of A at a world, one needs to know only f_B for those B that occur as the antecedents of conditionals within A.

5.5.8 As is probably clear, the tableaux for C^+ branch very rapidly. It may often, therefore, be easier to construct counter-models directly, by trial and error. Thus, one might construct the interpretation depicted in 5.5.7 directly. (Or even a simpler one. Details are left as an exercise.)

5.5.9 Soundness and completeness proofs for the C^+ tableaux can be found in 5.9.

5.6 Similarity spheres

5.6.1 There are many other conditions that one might impose on each R_A, and so create extensions of C. Perhaps the most important constraints of this kind arise in the following way.

5.6.2 The founders of conditional logic (Stalnaker and Lewis[3]) suggested that the worlds accessible to w via R_A – that is, the worlds essentially the same as w, except that A is true there – should be thought of as the worlds *most similar* to w at which A is true. How to understand similarity in this context is a difficult question. It is clear, though, at least, that similarity is something that comes by degrees. We will return to what to make of the notion philosophically later.

5.6.3 A way of making the notion precise formally is as follows. We suppose that each world, w, comes with a system of 'spheres'. All the worlds in a sphere are more similar to w than any world outside that sphere. We may depict the idea thus. (The spheres are depicted as rectangles here for typographical reasons.)

[3] This is David Lewis, not to be confused with C. I. Lewis. All references to Lewis in this chapter are to David.

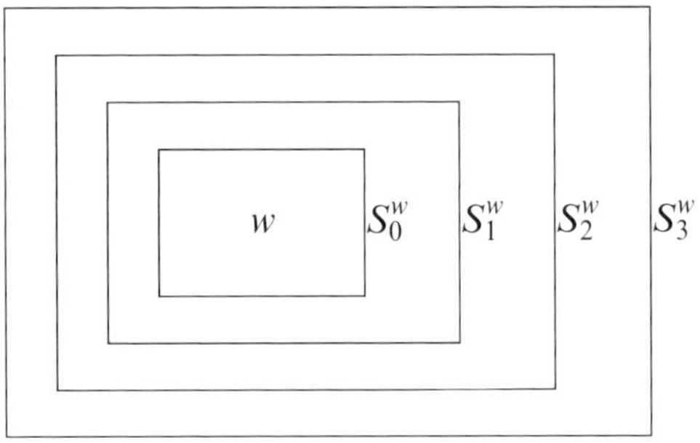

All the worlds in S_0^w are more similar to w than the worlds in S_1^w that are not in S_0^w ($S_1^w - S_0^w$). All the worlds in S_1^w are more similar than the worlds in $S_2^w - S_1^w$, etc.

5.6.4 Technically, for any world, w, there is a set of subsets of W, $\{S_0^w, S_1^w, ..., S_n^w\}$ (for some n), such that $w \in S_0^w \subseteq S_1^w \subseteq ... \subseteq S_n^w = W$. We omit the superscript when no confusion can arise as to which world's spheres it is that are at issue.

5.6.5 $f_A(w)$ may now be defined as follows. If $[A]$ is empty, then $f_A(w)$ is empty. Otherwise, there is a smallest of w's spheres whose intersection with A is not empty, S_i, and $f_A(w)$ is $S_i \cap [A]$. In terms of the motivation of 5.2.8, the sphere S_i can be thought of as containing exactly those worlds at which the *ceteris paribus* clause, C_A, is true. To help picture the situation, consider the following diagram; $f_A(w)$ is the area marked with crosses.[4]

[4] We have assumed, for simplicity, that the system of spheres is finite. This is not necessary, but infinite systems give rise to certain complications. In particular, if there is an infinite number of spheres, there may be no smallest sphere with a non-empty intersection with $[A]$. (Suppose that there is a world, w_x, at every point on the real line, x; that A holds at w_x iff $x > 0$; and that the spheres around w_0 are of the Zenonian kind $\{w_x; |x| < 1\}$, $\{w_x; |x| < 1/2\}$, $\{w_x; |x| < 1/4\}, ...$) The non-existence of a smallest sphere can be accommodated by changing the truth conditions of $>$ to: $A > B$ is true at w iff there is some sphere around w, S, such that $S \cap [A] \neq \phi$ and $S \cap [A] \subseteq [B]$, which is equivalent to the construction of the text if there is a finite number of spheres.

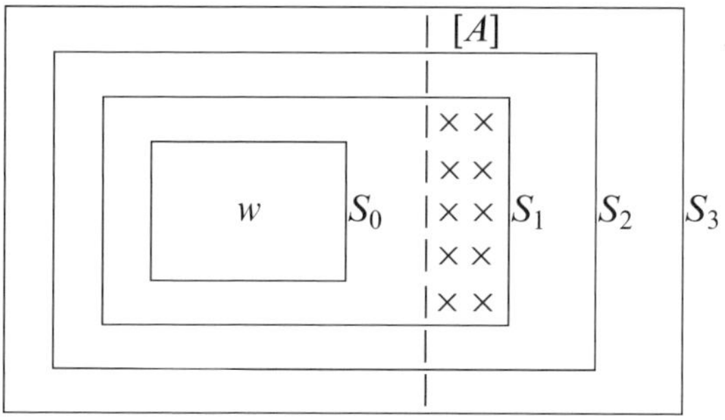

5.6.6 It is clear that this conception verifies conditions (1) and (2). For (1): if $f_A(w) = \phi$, then $f_A(w) \subseteq [A]$; and if $f_A(w) = S_i \cap [A]$, then again, $f_A(w) \subseteq [A]$. For (2): if $w \in [A]$, then $[A]$ is not empty, and since $w \in S_0$, S_0 is the smallest sphere with a non-empty intersection with $[A]$. So $w \in S_0 \cap [A] = f_A(w)$.

5.6.7 The conception also verifies further constraints on R; for example, by definition, if there are any worlds at which A is true, $f_A(w)$ is non-empty, i.e.:

(3) If $[A] \neq \phi$, then $f_A(w) \neq \phi$

5.6.8 The sphere conception also verifies the following two conditions:

(4) If $f_A(w) \subseteq [B]$ and $f_B(w) \subseteq [A]$, then $f_A(w) = f_B(w)$

(5) If $f_A(w) \cap [B] \neq \phi$, then $f_{A \wedge B}(w) \subseteq f_A(w)$

The arguments are given in 5.6.9, and can be skipped if desired.

5.6.9 For (4): suppose, for *reductio*, the antecedent and the negation of the consequent. Then either there is some $x \in f_A(w)$ such that $x \notin f_B(w)$, or vice versa. Consider the first case (the second is the same). Let $f_A(w) = S_i \cap [A]$, S_i being the smallest sphere for which this intersection is non-empty. By the first conjunct of the antecedent, $x \in [B]$. And since $x \notin f_B(w)$, and $f_B(w) \neq \phi$, by (3), there must be some $S_j \subset S_i$ such that $f_B(w) = S_j \cap [B]$. Let $y \in f_B(w)$. Then $y \in [A]$, by the second conjunct of the antecedent. But this is impossible, since $S_j \cap [A] = \phi$.

For (5): suppose that $f_A(w) \cap [B]$ is non-empty. Then $f_A(w)$ is non-empty. Let $f_A(w) = S_i \cap [A]$, S_i being the smallest sphere for which this intersection is non-empty. Hence, $S_i \cap [A] \cap [B] = S_i \cap [A \wedge B]$ is non-empty. Indeed, S_i is the smallest sphere such that the intersection is non-empty. (If $S_j \subset S_i$, then $S_j \cap [A] = \phi$.) Hence, $f_{A \wedge B}(w) = S_i \cap [A \wedge B] \subseteq S_i \cap [A] = f_A(w)$.

5.6.10 Let us call the system where validity is defined in terms of all interpretations where f satisfies conditions (1)–(5), S. S is clearly an extension of C^+.

5.6.11 It is, in fact, a proper extension. For example, the following inference is not valid in C^+, as may be checked with a tableau, or directly:

$$p > q, q > p \vdash (p > r) \equiv (q > r)$$

But it is valid in S. Suppose that the premise is true at world w, i.e., $f_p(w) \subseteq [q]$ and $f_q(w) \subseteq [p]$. Then, by condition (4), $f_p(w) = f_q(w)$. Hence, $f_p(w) \subseteq [r]$ iff $f_q(w) \subseteq [r]$, i.e., $(p > r)$ is true at w iff $(q > r)$ is true at w, i.e., $(p > r) \equiv (q > r)$ is true at w.

5.6.12 There are presently no known tableau systems of the kind used in this book for S (and its extensions that we will meet in the next section). Hence, demonstrations that an inference is valid have to be given directly, as in the previous section.

5.6.13 And demonstrations that an inference is invalid in S must be performed by constructing a counter-model directly. An easy way to do this is to construct an appropriate sphere structure. Here is an example to show that $(p \vee q) > r \nvDash_S p > r$. To invalidate this inference, we need a sphere model with a world, w_0 say, such that at the nearest worlds to w_0 where $p \vee q$ is true, so is r; but at the nearest world where p is true, r is not. Here is a simple example.

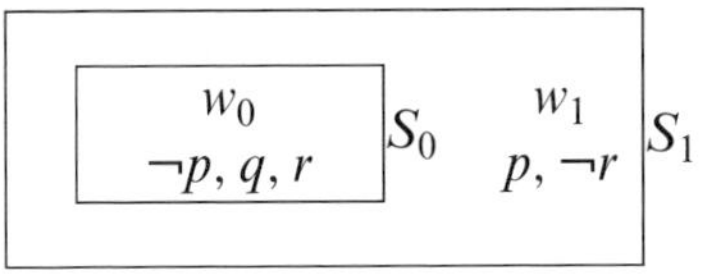

$f_{p\vee q}(w_0) = \{w_0\} \subseteq [r]$; hence, $(p \vee q) > r$ is true at w_0; but $f_p(w_0) = \{w_1\} \not\subseteq [r]$; hence, $p > r$ is false at w_0. We know that all sphere models satisfy the conditions (1)–(5) of S. Hence, the inference is invalid in S.

5.6.14 Notice that if inferences involve nested conditionals, then demonstrations of validity or invalidity may have to take into account the systems of spheres around more than one world. Here, for example, is a counter-model demonstrating that $\not\models_S \; p > (q > (p \wedge q))$:

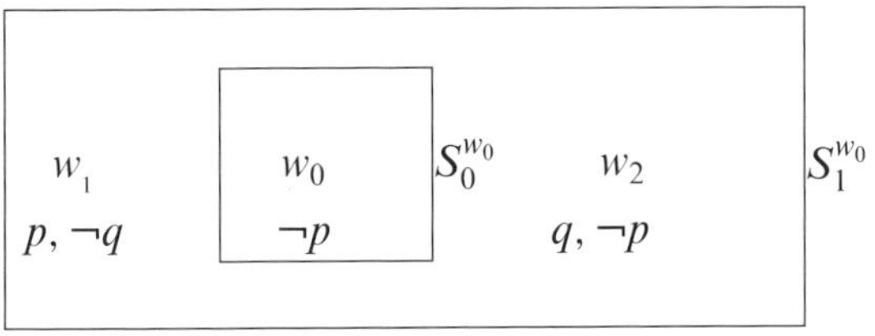

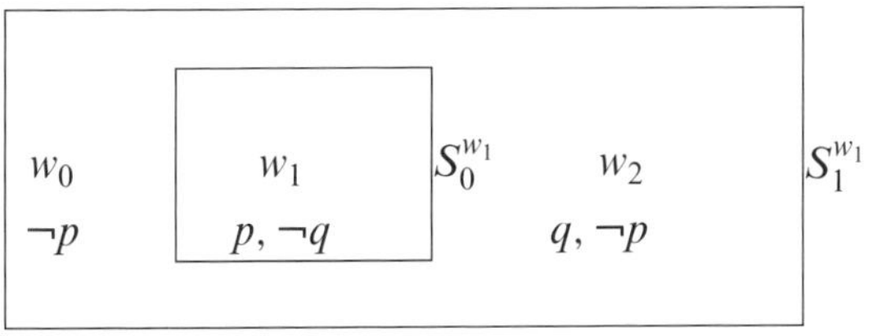

The top diagram shows the system of spheres around w_0; the bottom diagram depicts the system of spheres around w_1. $q > (p \wedge q)$ is false at w_1, since at some of the nearest worlds to w_1 where q is true (w_2), $p \wedge q$ is false. Hence, $p > (q > (p \wedge q))$ is false at w_0, since at a nearest world to w_0 where p is true (w_1), $q > (p \wedge q)$ is false. Note that the worlds in the two diagrams must be the same, as must the truth values of every formula at each world. It is only the system of spheres that may vary from picture to picture.

5.6.15 One final matter: (1) and (4) together entail that for all w:

(P) If $[A] = [B]$, then $f_A(w) = f_B(w)$

For suppose that $[A] = [B]$. Then, by (1), $f_A(w) \subseteq [A] = [B]$, and $f_B(w) \subseteq [B] = [A]$. Hence, by (4), $f_A(w) = f_B(w)$.

5.6.16 Now, the truth value of $A > B$ at a world, w, depends on $f_A(w)$. But if condition (P) holds, then $f_A(w)$ is determined completely by $[A]$. Hence, the truth value of $A > B$ depends, not on the formula A, but on the set of worlds at which A is true. (Some philosophers think of this as the *proposition* expressed by A.) If this is the case, then an interpretation can be formulated as a structure of the form $\langle W, \{R_X; X \subseteq W\}, \nu\rangle$, where truth conditions are the same as before, except that for $>$:

$\nu_w(A > B) = 1$ iff $f_{[A]}(w) \subseteq [B]$

where $f_X(w) = \{w'; wR_Xw'\}$.[5]

5.6.17 Constraints on f can then be couched in the same terms. Thus, (1) becomes $f_{[A]}(w) \subseteq [A]$, or more generally, $f_X(w) \subseteq X$, and so on.

5.7 C_1 and C_2

5.7.1 Perhaps the two best-known conditional logics are obtained from S, each by adding one further constraint. A natural thought is that, for any world, w, if there are any worlds at which A is true, then there is a *unique* world closest to w at which A is true (condition (3) guarantees that there is at least one world), i.e.:

(6) If $x \in f_A(w)$ and $y \in f_A(w)$, then $x = y$

[5] This is legitimate, since A is a subformula of $A > B$, and hence $[A]$ is determined *before* the truth value of $A > B$.

5.7.2 The system which is the same as S, except that in its interpretations f satisfies condition (6), is often called C_2.[6] What is distinctive about C_2 is that it verifies *Conditional Excluded Middle*: $(A > B) \vee (A > \neg B)$. (This is not logically valid in S; details are left as an exercise.) *Proof*: Either $[A] = \phi$ or not. In the first case, for any w, $f_A(w) = \phi$ (by (1)), and so $f_A(w) \subseteq [B]$ and $f_A(w) \subseteq [\neg B]$. Hence, the disjunction is true at w. In the second case, let $f_A(w) = \{x\}$. (It has only one member, by (6).) Either B is true at x or it is false at x. In the first case, $f_A(w) \subseteq [B]$. In the second case, $f_A(w) \subseteq [\neg B]$. In either case, the disjunction is therefore true at w.

5.7.3 One may object to condition (6) – as did Lewis – on the ground that there is no reason to believe that the nearest world to w where something holds must be unique. There may be different worlds where something holds which are symmetrical with respect to w, so that neither is nearer than the other. Consider, for example, Bizet and Verdi. These were contemporaries, but the first was French and the second was Italian. There would appear to be no unique world most similar to ours in which the two are compatriots. In some, they are both French, and in some they are both Italian. (Any world in which they are both, say, German, would be even less similar to ours.)

5.7.4 Conditional Excluded Middle is, in any case, problematic. Both of the following conditionals would appear to be false: if it will either rain tomorrow or it won't, then it will rain tomorrow; if it will either rain tomorrow or it won't, then it won't rain tomorrow.

5.7.5 In response to this, Lewis suggested dropping (6), but replacing it with:

[6] Stalnaker, whose system C_2 is, makes $f_A(w)$ a singleton for *every A*. He does this by having, in addition to all the usual worlds, one 'absurd world', where everything holds. This is the unique world in $f_A(w)$ if A is true at no ordinary worlds. Because everything holds at the absurd world, the net effect of this is the same.

(7) If $w \in [A]$ and $w' \in f_A(w)$, then $w = w'$

If A is true at w, then the most similar worlds at which A is true comprise just w itself. (Any world is more similar to itself than any other world.) (6), together with (2), obviously implies (7), but not vice versa.

5.7.6 If this replacement is made, we get a system often called C_1. What is distinctive about C_1 is that it verifies the following inference: $A \wedge B \models A > B$. (The inference is not valid in S; details are left as an exercise.) *Proof*: Suppose that $A \wedge B$ is true at w. Then A and B are true at w. Moreover, by (7), there is only one world in $f_A(w)$, and that is w. Hence $f_A(w) \subseteq [B]$.

5.7.7 This inference is itself problematic, however. Suppose that you go to a fake fortune-teller, who says that you will come in to a large sum of money. And suppose that, purely by accident, you do. The conditional 'If the fortune-teller says that you will come into a large sum of money, you will' would still appear to be false, though both antecedent and consequent are true. Or suppose that food x is normal, but food y is poisoned; and that, as a matter of fact, you will eat both and consequently become ill. According to this account, the conditional 'If you eat food x you will become ill' is true. But this seems false: it is y that will make you ill.

5.7.8 Invalidity in C_1 and C_2 may be shown in the same way as for S in 5.6.13. We just need to construct a sphere model which verifies either (6) or (7). It is easy to see that a sphere model will verify (7) if S_0 is a singleton (has just one member). For S_0 is the smallest sphere containing w, so if $w \in [A]$, $f_A(w) = \{w\}$. Similarly, a sphere model will verify (6) if S_0 is a singleton and for every other S_i, $S_i - S_{i-1}$ is also a singleton. For then if S_i is the smallest sphere such that $S_i \cap [A] \neq \phi$, $S_i \cap [A]$ must be a singleton.[7]

[7] Note that these conditions are sufficient to verify conditions (6) and (7), but they are not necessary.

5.7.9 Thus, the interpretation depicted in 5.6.13 shows that the inference in question there is also invalid in C_1 and C_2. And the following depicts a counter-model to $(p > q) \vee (p > \neg q)$ in C_1:

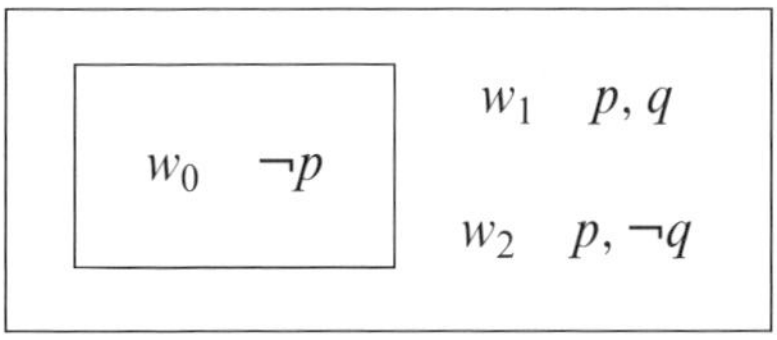

At some of the worlds nearest to w_0 where p is true, q is true; at some, it is false. Hence, neither $p > q$ nor $p > \neg q$ is true at w_0.

5.7.10 To summarise all the systems of conditional logic that we have met in this chapter: the following are systems of properly increasing strength: C, C^+, S, C_1, C_2.[8]

5.8 Further philosophical reflections

5.8.1 Let us finish by picking up a couple of philosophical loose ends. We start with the notion of similarity between worlds. The sphere models assume that there is a sensible notion of this kind, but is there? Presumably, how similar two worlds are will depend on what holds in each of these. But how can one define similarity in terms of these things?

5.8.2 One certainly cannot define it in terms of the *number* of propositions over which the worlds differ. For if there are any differences at all, there will be an infinite number. For example, if A is true at w_1 and false at w_2, then for any B false at w_1, $A \vee B$ will be true at w_1 and

[8] It should be noted that the postulates characteristic of some of the stronger systems render some of the postulates characteristic of weaker systems redundant. For example, (1), (4) and (7) together entail (5). For suppose that $f_A(w) \cap [B] \neq \phi$. By (1), $f_{A \wedge B}(w) \subseteq [A \wedge B] = [A] \cap [B] \subseteq [A]$. And since $f_A(w)$ is a singleton (by (7)), $f_A(w) \subseteq [B]$. Since $f_A(w) \subseteq [A]$ (by (1)), $f_A(w) \subseteq [A] \cap [B] = [A \wedge B]$. By (4), $f_A(w) = f_{A \wedge B}(w)$.

false at w_2. (Since there is an infinite number of sentences, and 'half' of these are false at w_1, there will be an infinite number of such B.)

5.8.3 Clearly, some changes are more important than others. The world coming to an end now, for example, would appear to be a bigger difference than my raising my arm. But how can one give an account of such importance?

5.8.4 Moreover, even if one can, is the account one that will validate the sphere models? These require of any two worlds that they have either the same degree of similarity to the actual world, or that one is more similar than the other. (All worlds are comparable in their similarity.) But why should this be the case? Consider two worlds: one is the same as ours, except that snow is green; the other is the same as ours, except that coal is green. Are these equally similar, or is one more similar than the other? I have no idea.

5.8.5 Even if there is some story to be told here, the analysis of conditionals in terms of similarity seems to be vulnerable to a more fundamental objection. Consider worlds which are like ours, except that, during the Cuban blockade, President Kennedy pushed the button. In some of these, a nuclear holocaust occurred; in others, something happened to prevent this (maybe a circuit short-circuited), and life continued much as we know it. On almost any understanding of similarity, the second scenario is more similar to the actual world than the first. Hence, according to the similarity account, the conditional 'If Kennedy had pushed the button, something would have happened to prevent a nuclear holocaust' is true; but it seems plainly false.

5.8.6 These considerations cast doubt on any theory of the behaviour of the *ceteris paribus* clause that is motivated by similarity considerations; but not C^+, which does not depend on these. This brings us to the second issue. How does the theory of C^+ fare?

5.8.7 First, consider any interpretation for $K\upsilon$. Turn this into a conditional-logic interpretation by setting $f_A(w) = [A]$. It is easy to see that this is a C^+ interpretation, since conditions (1) and (2) are satisfied. Moreover, in this interpretation $>$ is just $\prec$. Hence, if any inference is invalid in Kv, it is invalid in C^+ when $>$ is substituted for '$\prec$'. Thus, this theory does not reintroduce the problems of the material conditional, since $\prec$ is free of these (4.5).

5.8.8 But, on the other hand, it does nothing to avoid the problems of the strict conditional, on which it piggy-backs. For $\Box B \models A > B$ and $\Box\neg A \models A > B$ in C^+, as may easily be checked. In particular, $\models (A \wedge \neg A) > B$. So we still face the problems that we discussed in 4.7 and 4.8, especially the problem of explosion.

5.9 *Proofs of theorems

5.9.1 THEOREM: C is sound and complete with respect to its semantics.

Proof:

The soundness argument is essentially the same as that for K (2.9.2–2.9.4). The definition of faithfulness is modified in the obvious way. Thus, 'if irj is on b, then $f(i)Rf(j)$ in $\mathcal{I}$' is replaced by:

for every formula, A, if ir_Aj is on b, then $f(i)R_Af(j)$ in $\mathcal{I}$.[9]

In the Soundness Lemma, the cases for the truth functions, $\Box$ and $\Diamond$, are as for Kv (3.10, problem 9). For $>$: suppose that f shows that $\mathcal{I}$ is faithful to b, and that we apply the rule for $>$ to $A > B, i$ and ir_Aj to get B, j. By faithfulness, $A > B$ is true at $f(i)$ and $f(i)R_Af(j)$. Hence, B is true at $f(j)$, as required. Suppose, on the other hand, that we apply the rule for negated $>$ to $\neg(A > B), i$ to get ir_Aj, and $\neg B, j$ (j new). By faithfulness, $A > B$ is false at $f(i)$. Hence, there is some w such that w_iR_Aw and B is false at w. Let f' be the same as f, except that $f'(j) = w$. Then, as in the normal case

[9] In this proof and the next, f is always used for the function that shows a branch to be faithful to an interpretation. It is never used as the world selection function, $f_A(w)$.

for $\Diamond$, f' shows that $\mathcal{I}$ is faithful to b. The rest of the proof of the Soundness Theorem is the same.

The completeness argument is also a modification of that for K (2.9.5–2.9.7). In the induced interpretation, W and ν are defined in the same way. And, for every A:

if A occurs as the antecedent of a conditional or negated conditional at a node of b, then $w_i R_A w_j$ iff $ir_A j$ is on b;

otherwise, $w_i R_A w_j$ iff A is true at w_j.

Two comments should be made on this definition. First, the second clause is, in fact, irrelevant to the following argument. If A is not an antecedent on b, then how R_A behaves is completely irrelevant to the inference in question. We give the definition in this form, however, since the second clause is required for the completeness proof for C^+ in the next theorem. Secondly, note that the clause is well defined. The definition of A's truth at a world requires the definition of R_B only for those B that are subformulas of A.

In the Completeness Lemma, the cases for the truth functions, and for $\Box$ and $\Diamond$, are as for $K\upsilon$ (3.10, problem 9). For $>$: suppose that $A > B, i$ is on b. Then for every j such that $ir_A j$ is on b, B, j is on b. By the definition of the induced interpretation, and induction hypothesis, for every w_j such that $w_i R_A w_j$, B is true at w_j. Hence $A > B$ is true at w_i. Finally, suppose that $\neg(A > B), i$ is on b. Then there is a j such that $ir_A j$ and $\neg B, j$ is on b. By the definition of the induced interpretation, and induction hypothesis, there is a w_j such that $w_i R_A w_j$, and B is false at w_j. Hence $A > B$ is false at w_i. The Completeness Theorem then goes through as before.

5.9.2 THEOREM: C^+ is sound and complete with respect to its semantics.

Proof:

The proof is a modification of that for C. For soundness, we merely have to check the cases for the rules of 5.5.3 in the Soundness Lemma. The argument for the first of these is the same as that for the rule for negated > in C, except that we have an extra A, i to worry about. But since $f(i)R_A f(j)$, $\nu_{f(j)}(A) = 1$ by condition (1), as required. For the second, suppose that we apply the rule to obtain one branch containing $\neg A, i$, and one containing $ir_A i$ and A, i. Condition (2) tells us that either $\nu_{f(i)}(A) = 0$, or $\nu_{f(i)}(A) = 1$ and $f(i)R_A f(i)$. In the first case, f shows $\mathcal{I}$ to be faithful to the left branch; in the second case, it shows $\mathcal{I}$ to be faithful to the right branch.

For the Completeness Theorem, we have to check, in addition, only that the induced interpretation satisfies conditions (1) and (2). There are two cases, depending on whether or not A occurs as an antecedent on b. If it does not, the result holds simply by the definition of R_A (5.9.1). In the other case, let us consider the two conditions in turn. For (1), suppose that $w_i R_A w_j$; then $ir_A j$ occurs on b. The only way for this to occur is for the node to be the result of an application of one of two rules. But in each of them, when we introduce this node, we also add a node of the form A, j on the same branch. By the Completeness Lemma, $\nu_{w_j}(A) = 1$, as required. For (2), suppose that $\nu_{w_i}(A) = 1$. Then, since the second rule has been applied, either $\neg A, i$ or $ir_A i$ is on the branch. But by the Completeness Lemma, it cannot be the first. Hence, $w_i R_A w_i$, as required.

5.10 History

The first conditional logic was proposed by Stalnaker (1968), who thought it adequate for both indicative and subjunctive conditionals. His system is essentially C_2. C_1 was proposed by Lewis (1973a,b), who took it to be appropriate for subjunctive conditionals (the indicative conditional being $\supset$). C_1 is also called *VC* in the literature. Some care is required when reading the literature, since both C_1 and C_2 get formulated in slightly different ways. The versions given here are taken, essentially, from Nute (1984). The notion of sphere semantics is also due to Lewis (1973a,b). Sphere semantics not only provide a modelling for selection-function semantics for conditional logics, but, in a sense, are intertranslatable with them. In particular, the systems

S, C_1 and C_2 are sound and complete with respect to appropriate versions of the sphere semantics. Details for C_1 and C_2 can be found in Lewis (1971). The first person to realise that conditional logics could be seen as modal logics with accessibility relations indexed by formulas (or propositions) appears to have been Chellas (1975), who invented the system C. (Strictly speaking, what he calls C is what I have called C plus condition (P) of 5.6.15.) C^+ and S are not standard names. Tableaux for conditional logics of a kind very different from those used in this chapter were given by de Swart (1983) and Gent (1992). The argument of 5.8.5 is due to Fine. It is discussed in Lewis (1979).

5.11 Further reading

A good survey of conditional logics is Nute (1984). See also Nute (1980). A systematic account of many conditional logics, seen as indexed modal logics, can be found in Segerberg (1989). A debate between Stalnaker and Lewis on C_1 versus C_2 can be found in papers collected in Harper, Stalnaker and Pearce (1981), which also contains a number of other useful papers on conditionals and conditional logics. A discussion of the Lewis–Stalnaker semantics can be found in Read (1994, ch.3).

5.12 Problems

1. Complete the details left open in 5.2.1, 5.4.3, 5.5.4, 5.5.8, 5.6.11, 5.7.2, 5.7.6 and 5.8.8.
2. Show that the following are true in C:

   (*a*) $\Box(A \equiv B) \vdash (C > A) \equiv (C > B)$

   (*b*) $A > (B \wedge C) \vdash (A > B) \wedge (A > C)$

   (*c*) $(A > B) \wedge (A > C) \vdash A > (B \wedge C)$

   (*d*) $A > (B \supset C) \vdash (A > B) \supset (A > C)$

   (*e*) $\vdash A > (B \vee \neg B)$

3. Show the following are false in C, but true in C^+. Specify a C counter-model.

   (a) $\vdash p > p$

   (b) $p, p > q \vdash q$

   (c) $p \dashv q \vdash p > q$

4. Show that the following are false in C^+. Specify a counter-model, either by constructing a tableau, or directly.

   (a) $p > q \models (p \wedge r) > q$

   (b) $p > q \models \neg q > \neg p$

   (c) $p > q, q > r \models p > r$

5. Show that the following fail in C, but hold provided we add the condition on f indicated.

   (a) $(p \vee q) > r \models (p > r) \wedge (q > r)$
   $f_p(w) \cup f_q(w) \subseteq f_{p \vee q}(w)$

   (b) $(p > r) \wedge (q > r) \models (p \vee q) > r$
   $f_{p \vee q}(w) \subseteq f_p(w) \cup f_q(w)$

   (c) $p > q, q > r \models (p \wedge q) > r$
   If $f_p(w) \subseteq [q]$, then $f_{p \wedge q}(w) \subseteq f_q(w)$

6. Show that the following fail in C^+, but hold in S:

   (a) $\Diamond p \models \neg(p > (q \wedge \neg q))$

   (b) $p > q, \neg(p > \neg r) \models (p \wedge r) > q$

   (c) $\Box(p \equiv q) \models (p > r) \equiv (q > r)$

7. By constructing a suitable sphere model, show that the inferences of problem 4 also fail in C_2. Show that the following is also false in C_2: $(p \vee q) > r \models (p > r) \wedge (q > r)$.

8. Determine whether the following hold in each of C_1 and C_2:

(*a*) $p > (q \vee r) \models (p > q) \vee (p > r)$

(*b*) $p > q, \neg q \models \neg q > \neg p$

(*c*) $\Diamond p, p > q \models \neg(p > \neg q)$

(*d*) $p > (p > q) \models p > q$

(*e*) $p > (q > r) \models q > (p > r)$

9. It seems natural to suppose that the inference from $(s \vee t) > r$ to $s > r$ ought to be valid. (For example. 'If you have a broken arm or you have a broken leg, you can claim the allowance. Hence, if you have a broken arm, you can claim the allowance.') Now, suppose that $p > r$. Since $\models \Box(p \equiv ((p \wedge q) \vee (p \wedge \neg q)))$, it follows in S – and, in fact, any logic satisfying the condition (P) – that $((p \wedge q) \vee (p \wedge \neg q)) > r$. (See problem 6 (c).) If the form of inference in question were valid, then, it would follow that $(p \wedge q) > r$. But we know that the inference from $p > r$ to $(p \wedge q) > r$ is invalid. Discuss.

6 | Intuitionist logic

A modal logic

Logic of information - not so much about truth.

$A \lor \neg A$ won't be true in intuitionist logic if we may not have any info about A.

6.1 Introduction

6.1.1 In this chapter, we look at another logic that has a natural possible-world semantics: intuitionist logic, a logic that arose originally out of certain views in the philosophy of mathematics called *intuitionism*.

6.1.2 We will also look briefly at the philosophical foundations of intuitionism, and at the distinctive account of the conditional that intuitionist logic provides.

6.2 Intuitionism: the rationale

6.2.1 Let us start with a look at the original rationale for intuitionism. Consider the sentence 'Granny had led a sedate life until she decided to start pushing crack on a small tropical island just south of the Equator.' You can understand this, and indefinitely many other sentences that you have never (I presume) heard before. How is this possible?

6.2.2 We can understand a sentence of this kind because we understand its individual parts and the way they are put together; the meaning of a sentence is determined by the meanings of its parts, and of the grammatical construction which composes these. This fact is called *compositionality*.

6.2.3 An orthodox view, usually attributed to Frege, is that the meaning of a statement is given by the conditions under which it is true, its *truth conditions*. Thus, by compositionality, the truth conditions of a statement must be given in terms of the truth conditions of its parts.

Thus, for example, $\neg A$ is true iff A is not true; $A \wedge B$ is true iff A is true and B is true; and so on.

6.2.4 Now, truth, as commonly conceived, is a relationship between language and an extra-linguistic reality. Thus, 'Brisbane is in Australia' is true because of certain objective social and geographical arrangements that obtain in the southern hemisphere of our planet. But many have found the notion of an objective extra-linguistic reality problematic – for mathematics, in particular.

6.2.5 What is the extra-linguistic reality that corresponds to the truth of '$2 + 3 = 5$'? Some (mathematical *realists*) have suggested that there are objectively existing mathematical objects, like 3 and 5. To others, such a view has just seemed like mysticism. These include mathematical intuitionists, who rejected the common conception of truth, as applied to mathematics, for just this reason.

6.2.6 But in this case, how is meaning to be expressed? The intuitionist answer is that the meaning of a sentence is to be given, not by the conditions under which it is true, where truth is conceived as a relationship with some external reality, but by the conditions under which it is proved, its *proof conditions* – where a proof is a (mental) construction of a certain kind.

6.2.7 Thus, supposing that we know what counts as a proof of the simplest sentences (propositional parameters), the proof conditions for sentences constructed using the usual propositional connectives are as follows. In the following sections, it will make matters easier if we use new symbols for negation and the conditional. Hence, we will now write these as $\neg$ and $\sqsupset$, respectively.

A proof of $A \wedge B$ is a pair comprising a proof of A and a proof of B.

A proof of $A \vee B$ is a proof of A or a proof of B.

A proof of $\neg A$ is a proof that there is no proof of A.

A proof of $A \sqsupset B$ is a construction that, given any proof of A, can be applied to give a proof of B.

6.2.8 Note that these conditions fail to verify a number of standard logical principles – most notoriously, some instances of the law of excluded middle: $A \vee \to A$. For example, a famous mathematical conjecture whose status is currently undecided is the *twin prime conjecture*: there is an infinite number of pairs of primes, two apart, like 3 and 5, 11 and 13, 29 and 31. Call this claim A. Then there is presently no proof of A; nor is there a proof that there is no proof of A. Hence, there is no proof of $A \vee \to A$, which claim is not, therefore, acceptable. Thus, intuitionism generates a quite distinctive logic.

6.3 Possible-world semantics for intuitionism   K P τ

6.3.1 To obtain a better understanding of this logic, intuitionist logic, let us look at a possible-world semantics which, arguably, captures the above ideas.

6.3.2 The language of propositional intuitionist logic is a language whose only connectives are $\wedge$, $\vee$, $\to$ and $\sqsupset$.

6.3.3 An intuitionist interpretation for the language is a structure, $\langle W, R, v \rangle$, which is the same as an interpretation for the normal modal logic $K_{\rho\tau}$ (so that R is reflexive and transitive) apart from one further constraint, namely that for every propositional parameter, p:

  for all $w \in W$, if $v_w(p) = 1$ and wRw', $v_{w'}(p) = 1$

This is called the *heredity condition.* – constraint placed a v
P holds down the amous. If P is T at w
6.3.4 The assignment of values to molecular formulas is given by the   then its T in an accessible w's
following conditions:

$v_w(A \wedge B) = 1$ iff $v_w(A) = 1$ and $v_w(B) = 1$ mth conditions

$v_w(A \vee B) = 1$ iff $v_w(A) = 1$ or $v_w(B) = 1$

$v_w(\to A) = 1$ iff for all w' such that wRw', $v_{w'}(A) = 0$

⌐ A is T if A is F at all accessible words.

negation of A is T if A fails at every possible (accessible) world.

A ⊐ B is true if A fails or B holds or both.
wherever A is T B is T

$$\nu_w(A \sqsupset B) = 1 \text{ iff for all } w' \text{ such that } wRw', \text{ either } \nu_{w'}(A) = 0 \text{ or } \nu_{w'}(B) = 1$$

Note that $\rightharpoondown A$ is, in effect, $\Box\neg A$, and $A \sqsupset B$ is, in effect, $\Box(A \supset B)$.[1]

6.3.5 Given these truth conditions, the heredity condition holds, as a matter of fact, not just for propositional parameters, but for all formulas. The proof is relegated to a footnote, which can be skipped if desired.[2]

6.3.6 Before we complete the definition of validity, let us see how an intuitionist interpretation arguably captures the intuitionist ideas of the previous section. Think of a world as a state of information at a certain time; intuitively, the things that hold at it are those things which are proved at this time. uRv is thought of as meaning that v is a possible extension of u, obtained by finding some number (possibly zero) of further proofs. Given this understanding, R is clearly reflexive and transitive. (For τ: any extension of an extension is an extension.) And the heredity condition is also intuitively correct. If something is proved, it stays proved, whatever else we prove.

6.3.7 Given the provability conditions of 6.2.7, the recursive conditions of 6.3.4 are also very natural. $A \wedge B$ is proved at a time iff A is proved at that time, and so is B; $A \vee B$ is proved at a time iff A is proved at that time, or B is. If $\rightharpoondown A$ is proved at some time, then we have a proof that there is no proof of A. Hence, A will be proved at no possible later time. Conversely, if $\rightharpoondown A$ is not proved at some time,

---

[1] Sometimes, the language is taken to contain a propositional constant, $\bot$, which is true at no world. The truth conditions of $\rightharpoondown A$ then reduce to those of $A \sqsupset \bot$.

[2] The proof is by induction on the construction of formulas. Suppose that the result holds for A and B. We show that it holds for $\rightharpoondown A$, $A \wedge B$, $A \vee B$ and $A \sqsupset B$. For $\rightharpoondown A$: we prove the contrapositive. Suppose that wRw', and $\rightharpoondown A$ is false at w'. Then for some w'' such that $w'Rw''$, A is true at w''. But then wRw'', by transitivity. Hence, $\rightharpoondown A$ is false at w. For $A \wedge B$: suppose that $A \wedge B$ is true at w, and that wRw'. Then A and B are true at w. By induction hypothesis, A and B are true at w'. Hence, $A \wedge B$ is true at w'. For $A \vee B$: the argument is similar. For $A \sqsupset B$: we again prove the contrapositive. Suppose that wRw' and $A \sqsupset B$ is false at w'. Then for some w'' such that $w'Rw''$, A is true and B is false at w''. But, by transitivity, wRw''. Hence $A \sqsupset B$ is false at w.

then it is at least possible that a proof of A will turn up, so A will hold at some possible future time. Finally, if $A \sqsupset B$ is proved at a time, then we have a construction that can be applied to any proof of A to give a proof of B. Hence, at any future possible time, either there is no proof of A, or, if there is, this gives us a proof of B. Conversely, if $A \sqsupset B$ is not proved at a time, then it is at least possible that at a future time, A will be proved, and B will not be. That is, A holds and B fails at some possible future time.

6.3.8 Back to validity: this is defined as truth preservation over all worlds of all interpretations, in the usual way. We will write intuitionist logical consequence as $\models_I$, when necessary.

6.3.9 Observe that if an intuitionist interpretation has just one world, the recursive conditions for the connectives of 6.3.4 just reduce to the standard classical conditions. A one-world intuitionist interpretation is, in effect, therefore, a classical interpretation. Thus, if truth is preserved at all worlds of all intuitionist interpretations, it is preserved in all classical interpretations. If an inference is intuitionistically valid, it is therefore classically valid (when $\rightharpoondown$ and $\sqsupset$ are replaced with $\neg$ and $\supset$, respectively). The converse is not true, as we shall see. Hence, intuitionist logic is a sub-logic of classical logic.[3]

[3] This is not true of intuitionist mathematics in general. Intuitionist mathematics endorses some mathematical principles which are not endorsed in classical mathematics; in fact, they are inconsistent classically. But because intuitionist logic is weaker than classical logic, the principles are intuitionistically consistent. For the record, it is worth noting that there is a certain way of seeing classical logic as a part of intuitionist logic too. For it can be shown that if $\Sigma \vdash A$ in classical logic, then $\rightharpoondown\rightharpoondown\Sigma \vdash_I \rightharpoondown\rightharpoondown A$, when all occurrences of $\neg$ and $\supset$ are replaced by $\rightharpoondown$ and $\sqsupset$, and $\rightharpoondown\rightharpoondown\Sigma = \{\rightharpoondown\rightharpoondown A; A \in \Sigma\}$. (The converse is obviously the case, given that intuitionist logic is a sub-logic of classical logic, and the law of double negation holds for the latter.) It also follows (unobviously) that the logical truths of classical logic, expressible using only $\wedge$ and $\neg$, are identical with those of intuitionist logic (when $\neg$ is replaced by $\rightharpoondown$). Every sentence of classical propositional logic is logically equivalent to one employing only $\wedge$ and $\neg$. On these matters, see Kleene (1952, pp. 492–3).

6.4 Tableaux for intuitionist logic

6.4.1 To obtain tableaux for intuitionist logic, we modify those for normal modal logics. The first modification is that a node on the tableau is now of the form $A, +i$ or $A, -i$. The first means, intuitively, that A is true at world i; the second means that A is false at i. For previous modal logics, the fact that A was false at a world was indicated by $\neg A, i$. But now, A may be false at a world without $\to A$ being true there.

6.4.2 The initial list of a tableau for a given inference now comprises $B, +0$, for every premise, B, and $A, -0$, where A is the conclusion.

6.4.3 Closure of a branch occurs just when we have nodes of the form $A, +i$ and $A, -i$.

6.4.4 The rules of the tableau for the connectives are as follows:

$\rho \ \subset$

$\text{or} \quad \text{on} \ \text{in}$

$$A \wedge B, +i$$
$$\downarrow$$
$$A, +i$$
$$B, +i$$

$$A \wedge B, -i$$
$$\swarrow \qquad \searrow$$
$$A, -i \qquad B, -i$$

$$A \vee B, +i$$
$$\swarrow \qquad \searrow$$
$$A, +i \qquad B, +i$$

$$A \vee B, -i$$
$$\downarrow$$
$$A, -i$$
$$B, -i$$

every accessible world

$\Box \ (\text{hom}) \ A \supset B, +i$
$$irj$$
$$\swarrow \qquad \searrow$$
$$A, -j \qquad B, +j$$

$A \supset B, -i$ some accessible world
$$\downarrow$$
$$irj \qquad \text{new } j$$
$$A, +j$$
$$B, -j$$

every accessible world

$\Box \ \neg A$
$$\to A, +i$$
$$irj$$
$$\downarrow$$
$$A, -j$$

$$\to A, -i$$
$$\downarrow$$
$$irj \qquad \text{Some ...}$$
$$A, +j \qquad \text{new } j$$

$$
\begin{array}{c}
p, +i \\
irj \\
\downarrow \\
p, +j
\end{array}
$$

The rules for $\wedge$ and $\vee$ are self-explanatory. The first rule for each of $\sqsupset$ and $\neg$ is applied for every j on the branch. In the second, for each, the j is new. The rules are easier to remember if one recalls that $A \sqsupset B$ means, in effect, $\Box(A \supset B)$, and $\neg A$ means, in effect, $\Box\neg A$. Note that, in particular, we can never 'tick off' any node of the form $A \sqsupset B, +i$ or $\neg A, +i$, since we may have to come back and reapply the rule if anything of the form irj turns up. The final rule is applied only to propositional parameters, and, again, to every j (distinct from i). The rule is required by the heredity condition, and we will refer to it as the *heredity rule*. Note that there is no corresponding rule for $p, -i$.

6.4.5 We also have the rules ρ and τ (of 3.3.2), as required for the reflexivity and transitivity of R.

6.4.6 As an example, here is a tableau to show that $\vdash_I p \sqsupset \neg\neg p$:

$$
\begin{array}{cr}
p \sqsupset \neg\neg p, -0 & (1) \\
0r0 & \\
0r1 & (2) \\
p, +1 & (3) \\
\neg\neg p, -1 & (4) \\
1r1 & \\
1r2 & (5) \\
\neg p, +2 & (6) \\
2r2, 0r2 & \\
p, -2 & (7) \\
p, +2 & (8) \\
\times &
\end{array}
$$

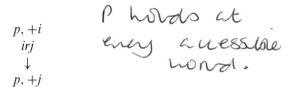

(2)–(4) are obtained from (1) by the rule for false $\sqsupset$. (5) and (6) are obtained from (4) by the rule for false $\neg$. (7) is obtained from (6) by the rule for true $\to$ (and the fact that 2r2). Finally, (8) is obtained from (3) by the heredity rule (and the fact that 1r2).[4]

6.4.7 Here is another example to demonstrate that $p \sqsupset q \nvdash_I \to p \vee q$. (Since the inference is classically valid – when $\sqsupset$ and $\to$ are replaced by $\supset$ and $\neg$ – this shows that intuitionist logic is a proper sub-logic of classical logic.)

$$
\begin{array}{c}
p \sqsupset q, +0 \\
\to p \vee q, -0 \\
0r0 \\
\to p, -0 \\
q, -0 \\
0r1 \\
p, +1 \\
1r1
\end{array}
$$

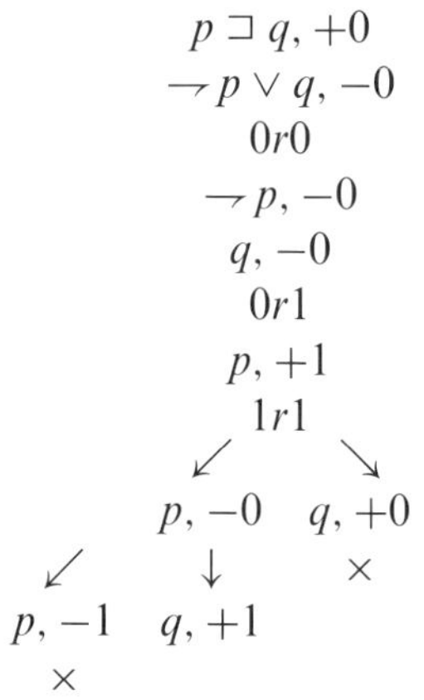

The sixth and seventh lines are given by the rule for false $\to$, applied to the fourth line. Both splits are caused by an application of the rule for true $\sqsupset$ to the first line, to worlds 0 and 1, respectively. Note that there are no possible applications of the heredity rule.

6.4.8 Counter-models are read off from an open branch of a tableau in a natural way. The worlds and accessibility relation are as the

---

[4] Note a distinctive feature of some intuitionist tableaux. Suppose that we had constructed the tableau using, not a propositional parameter, p, but an arbitrary formula, A. Then we could not apply the heredity rule to close off the tableau in the same way. But since anything of the form $A \sqsupset \to \to A$ is logically true, and the tableau system is complete, tableaux for all such formulas will close, though not in a uniform way. (That is, for each sentence that A represents, the tableau will continue to closure in a different way.) This could be changed by making the heredity rule apply to all formulas, not just propositional parameters. And since heredity does hold for arbitrary formulas (6.3.5), this rule is sound. But this complicates tableaux enormously, and, by completeness, is unnecessary anyway.

branch of the tableau specifies. If a node of the form $p, +i$ occurs on the branch, p is set to true at w_i; otherwise, p is false at w_i. (In particular, if a node of the form $p, -i$ occurs on the branch, p is set to false at w_i.) Thus, reading from the open branch of the tableau of 6.4.7, $W = \{w_0, w_1\}$; w_0Rw_0, w_0Rw_1 and w_1Rw_1; $v_{w_0}(p) = v_{w_0}(q) = 0$ and $v_{w_1}(p) = v_{w_1}(q) = 1$.

6.4.9 In pictures:

$$\begin{array}{ccc} \curvearrowright & & \curvearrowright \\ w_0 & \rightarrow & w_1 \\ -p & & +p \\ -q & & +q \end{array}$$

We indicate the fact that p is true (at a world) by $+p$, and the fact that it is false by $-p$. It is a simple matter to check directly that the interpretation is a counter-model. At every world accessible from w_0, p is false or q is true. Hence, $p \sqsupset q$ is true at w_0. p is true at w_1; hence $\neg p$ is false at w_0. But q is also false there. Hence, $\neg p \vee q$ is false there.

6.4.10 The tableaux are sound and complete with respect to the semantics. This is demonstrated in 6.7.

6.4.11 Note that, as for $K_{\rho\tau}$, open tableaux for intuitionist logic may be infinite. Here, for example, is the start of a tableau which establishes that $\nvdash_I \neg\neg p \sqsupset p$:

$$\begin{array}{c} \neg\neg p \sqsupset p, -0 \\ 0r0 \\ 0r1 \\ \neg\neg p, +1 \\ p, -1 \\ 1r1 \\ \neg p, -1 \\ 1r2 \\ p, +2 \\ 2r2, 0r2 \\ \neg p, -2 \\ 2r3 \\ \vdots \end{array}$$

Every time we open a new world, i, the fourth line (and transitivity) requires us to write $\neg p, -i$ there; but this requires us to open a new world, j, such that irj and $p, +j$, and so on.

6.4.12 Again, as with $K_{\rho\tau}$, in such cases it is usually easier to construct counter-models directly. Thus, for $\neg\neg p \sqsupset p$, the following will work:

$$\begin{array}{ccc} \curvearrowright & & \curvearrowright \\ w_0 & \rightarrow & w_1 \\ -p & & +p \end{array}$$

Since p is true at w_1, $\neg p$ is false at w_0 and w_1. Hence, $\neg\neg p$ is true at w_0. Since p is false there, $\neg\neg p \sqsupset p$ is false at w_0.

6.5 The foundations of intuitionism

6.5.1 So much for formal details: in this section we look a little further into the foundations of intuitionism.

6.5.2 The intuitionist critique of classical logic described in 6.2, is not, as a matter of fact, very persuasive. For even if one rejects a realm of independently existing mathematical objects, one might simply say that, for atomic sentences, truth is to be considered as provability. Yet once truth is defined in this way for atomic sentences, truth conditions for connectives are given as in classical logic. Thus, if we are dealing with arithmetic, something like '$2 + 3$' $= 5$ is true if the numerical algorithm for addition verifies it. Then, for any sentence, A, $\neg A$ is true iff A is not true, and so on. Thus, classical logic is not impugned.

6.5.3 A much more subtle but radical argument for intuitionism has been elaborated in recent years by a number of people, but most notably by Dummett, based on quite different considerations. *In nuce*, it goes as follows. Someone who understands the meaning of a sentence must be able to demonstrate that they grasp its meaning, or we would not be able to recognise that they understood it (nor, the argument sometimes continues, would we ever be able to learn the meaning of the sentence from others). In particular, we demonstrate our understanding of the meaning of a sentence by being prepared to assert it in those conditions under which it obtains (and just those). But if classical truth conditions were employed, this would be impossible. For such conditions allow for the possibility that a sentence could be true, even though we could never recognise this. For example, the sentence 'It is not the case that there are unicorn-like creatures somewhere in space and time' might be true, even though we could never establish this. Hence, meanings must be specified in terms of something which we can recognise as obtaining, namely the conditions under which a sentence is shown to be true, that is, *verified.*

6.5.4 Clearly, Dummett's argument applies to all language, not just to mathematical language. Intuitionist claims about mathematics are just a special case, proof being mathematical verification. If this critique is right, then, intuitionist logic would be correct quite generally.

6.5.5 But one may have doubts about Dummett's argument for several reasons. For a start, why must it always be necessary to be able to manifest a grasp of meaning? Some aspects of meaning might simply be innate, or hard-wired into us. We do not need to learn them; nor do we need an *a posteriori* guarantee that a speaker possesses them. (Chomsky has argued that our grammar is innate in just this way.)

6.5.6 But even granting that the grasp of meaning must be manifestable, why does it have to be manifestable in a way as strong as the argument requires? Why is it not sufficient simply to assent to a sentence when the state of affairs it describes *is* manifest, and not when it isn't?

6.5.7 It might be suggested that such a manifestation would not be adequate. There will be cases where people assent to the same sentence, but do not mean the same thing by it, as would be demonstrated by some situation that will never, as a matter of fact, come to light, but in which they would differ. Thus, for example, you and I might agree that standard objects are red, but yet mean different things by the word, as would be exposed by a disagreement about the redness of some totally novel object that will, as a matter of fact, never come to light.

6.5.8 This may be so. But if people not only agree on given cases, but also manifest a disposition to agree on novel cases when they do arise, this is sufficient to show (if not, perhaps, conclusively, then at least beyond reasonable doubt) that they are operating with the notion in question in the same way. (This is essentially what following an appropriate rule comes to, in Wittgensteinian terms.)

6.6 The intuitionist conditional

6.6.1 Setting aside the intuitionist critique in general, let us finish by considering the intuitionist conditional in its own right. All the claims about $\models_I$ in the following subsections can be checked by suitable tableaux, and are left as exercises.

6.6.2 The intuitionist conditional has an unusual mixture of properties. It validates the paradoxes of the material conditional, $q \models p \sqsupset q$, $\neg p \models p \sqsupset q$, and so is liable to the objections of 1.7 (which, as we saw there, are not conclusive). However, the following are false:

$$(p \wedge q) \sqsupset s \models (p \sqsupset s) \vee (q \sqsupset s)$$

$$(p \sqsupset q) \wedge (s \sqsupset t) \models (p \sqsupset t) \vee (s \sqsupset q)$$

$$\neg (p \sqsupset q) \models p$$

So the conditional does not fall to the more damaging objections of 1.9.

6.6.3 The following hold in intuitionist logic:

$$p \sqsupset q \models \neg q \sqsupset \neg p$$

$$p \sqsupset q, q \sqsupset s \models p \sqsupset s$$

$$p \sqsupset s \models (p \wedge q) \sqsupset s$$

Hence, the intuitionist conditional is not suitable as an account of a conditional with an enthymematic *ceteris paribus* clause, for reasons that we saw in 5.2.

6.6.4 Most importantly, the intuitionist conditional also validates the strict paradox: $\models (p\wedge \neg p) \sqsupset q$, and so is not suitable as an account of the ordinary conditional, for reasons that we saw in 4.8.

6.6.5 Intuitionist logic also validates the strict paradox $\Box q \models p \sqsupset q$ – or, at least, obviously would do so if the language were augmented with the modal operator. But it does not validate the classical instance: $\models p \sqsupset (q\vee \neg q)$. The reason for this is that $q\vee \neg q$ is not a logical truth: there are situations in which something of the form $q\vee \neg q$ may fail. This thought takes us into the next chapter.

6.7 *Proofs of theorems

6.7.1 The soundness and completeness proofs for intuitionist tableaux are modifications of those for normal modal logics. We start by re-defining faithfulness.

6.7.2 DEFINITION: Let $\mathcal{I} = \langle W, R, \nu\rangle$ be any intuitionist interpretation, and b be any branch of a tableau. Then $\mathcal{I}$ is *faithful* to b iff there is a map, f, from the natural numbers to W such that:

for every node $A, +i$ on b, A is true at $f(i)$ in $\mathcal{I}$.

for every node $A, -i$ on b, A is false at $f(i)$ in $\mathcal{I}$.

if irj is on b, $f(i)Rf(j)$ in $\mathcal{I}$.

6.7.3 SOUNDNESS LEMMA: Let b be any branch of a tableau, and $\mathcal{I} = \langle W, R, \nu\rangle$ be any intuitionist interpretation. If $\mathcal{I}$ is faithful to b, and a tableau rule is applied to b, then this produces at least one extension, b', such that $\mathcal{I}$ is faithful to b'.

Proof:

Let f be a function which shows $\mathcal{I}$ to be faithful to b. The proof proceeds by a case-by-case consideration of the tableau rules. The cases for the rules ρ and τ are as 3.7.1. The propositional rules for $\wedge$ and $\vee$ are straightforward. For $\sqsupset$: suppose that $A \sqsupset B, +i$ and irj are on b, and that we apply the rule, splitting the branch, to get $A, -j$ on one branch and $B, +j$, on the other. Then $A \sqsupset B$ is true at $f(i)$, and $f(i)Rf(j)$; hence, either A is false at $f(j)$ and $\mathcal{I}$ is faithful to the first branch, or B is true at $f(j)$ and it is faithful to the second. Suppose that $A \sqsupset B, -i$ is on b, and that we apply the rule to get irj, $A, +j$ and $B, -j$, where j is new. Then $A \sqsupset B$ is false at $f(i)$. Hence, there is a w such that $f(i)Rw$, A is true at w, and B is false at w. Let f' be the same as f, except that $f'(j) = w$. Then f' shows that $\mathcal{I}$ is faithful to the extended branch, as usual. For $\neg$: suppose that $\neg A, +i$ and irj are on b, and that we apply the rule to get $A, -j$. Then $\neg A$ is true at $f(i)$, and $f(i)Rf(j)$; hence, A is false at $f(j)$, as required. Suppose that $\neg A, -i$ is on b, and that we apply the rule to get irj, $A, +j$, where j is new. Then $\neg A$ is false at $f(i)$. Hence, there is a w such that $f(i)Rw$, and A is true at w. Let f' be the same as f, except that $f'(j) = w$. Then f' shows that $\mathcal{I}$ is faithful to the extended branch, as usual. This leaves the heredity rule. Suppose that $p, +i$ and irj are on b, and that we apply the rule to get $p, +j$. Since p is true at $f(i)$ and $f(i)Rf(j)$, p is true at $f(j)$, by the heredity condition.

6.7.4 SOUNDNESS THEOREM: For finite Σ, if $\Sigma \vdash_I A$ then $\Sigma \models_I A$.

Proof:

This follows from the Soundness Lemma in the usual way.

6.7.5 DEFINITION: Let b be an open branch of a tableau. The interpretation, $\mathcal{I} = \langle W, R, v\rangle$, induced by b, is defined as in 6.4.8. $W = \{w_i;\ i \text{ occurs on } b\}$. $w_i R w_j$ iff irj occurs on b. $v_{w_i}(p) = 1$ iff $p, +i$ occurs on b.

6.7.6 LEMMA: If b is an open branch of a tableau, and $\mathcal{I}$ is the interpretation it induces, $\mathcal{I}$ is an intuitionist interpretation.

Proof:

First, R satisfies the conditions ρ and τ, as in 3.7.3. For the heredity condition, suppose that p is true at w_i and $w_i R w_j$. Then $p, +i$ and irj occur on b. Since the heredity rule has been applied, $p, +j$ is on b, and hence p is true at w_j in $\mathcal{I}$, as required.

6.7.7 COMPLETENESS LEMMA: Let b be any open completed branch of a tableau. Let $\mathcal{I} = \langle W, R, \nu \rangle$ be the interpretation induced by b. Then:

if $A, +i$ is on b, then A is true at w_i
if $A, -i$ is on b, then A is false at w_i

Proof:

The proof is by recursion on the complexity of A. If A is atomic, the result is true by definition, and the fact that b is open. If $B \vee C, +i$ is on b, then either $B, +i$ or $C, +i$ is on b. By induction hypothesis, either B or C is true at w_i. So $B \vee C$ is true at w_i. If $B \vee C, -i$ is on b, then $B, -i$ and $C, -i$ are on b. By induction hypothesis, B and C are false at w_i. Hence, $B \vee C$ is false at w_i. The argument for $B \wedge C$ is similar. If $B \sqsupset C, +i$ is on b, then for every j such that irj is on b, either $B, -j$ or $C, +j$ is on b. Hence, by construction and induction hypothesis, for every w_j such that $w_i R w_j$, either B is false at w_j or C is true at w_j. Thus, $B \sqsupset C$ is true at w_i. If $B \sqsupset C, -i$ is on b, then for some j, irj, $B, +j$ and $C, -j$ are on b. By construction and induction hypothesis, there is a w_j such that $w_i R w_j$, B is true at w_j, and C is false at w_j. Hence, $B \sqsupset C$ is false at w_i. Finally, if $\neg B, +i$ is on b, then for every j such that irj is on b, $B, -j$ is on b. By construction and induction hypothesis, for every w_j such that $w_i R w_j$, B is false at w_j. Thus, $\neg B$ is true at w_i. If $\neg B, -i$ is on b, then for some j, irj and $B, +j$ are on b. By construction and induction hypothesis, there is a w_j such that $w_i R w_j$ and B is true at w_j. Hence, $\neg B$ is false at w_i.

6.7.8 COMPLETENESS THEOREM: For finite Σ, if $\Sigma \models_I A$ then $\Sigma \vdash_I A$.

Proof:

The result follows from the previous two lemmas in the usual fashion.

6.8 History

Intuitionism was first advocated by the Dutch mathematician Brouwer in a number of papers from just before the First World War until the early 1950s. (The name 'intuitionism' comes from the fact that Brouwer took himself to be endorsing the Kantian claim that arithmetic is the pure form of temporal intuition.) Intuitionist logic was formulated first (as an axiom system) by the Dutch logician Heyting in 1930. For a history of the intuitionist movement, see Fraenkel, Bar-Hillel and Levy (1973, ch. 4). The close connection between intuitionist logic and $K\rho\tau$ was observed (before the advent of possible-world semantics) by Gödel (1933a). (See 6.10, problem 8.) The possible-world semantics for intuitionist logic were first given by Kripke (1965b). Frege expressed the view that meaning is determined by truth conditions in section 32 of volume 1 of his *Grundgesetze der Arithmetik*. Dummett advocated intuitionist logic in a number of places starting in the mid-1970s (see the next section). The innateness of grammar was advocated by Chomsky (1971). Innateness was advocated in semantics by Fodor (1975). Cryptic remarks on rule-following can be found in Wittgenstein (1953, esp. sects. 201–40).

6.9 Further reading

A gentle introduction to intuitionism can be found in Haack (1974, ch. 5). A more technical introduction can be found in Fraenkel, Bar-Hillel and Levy (1973, ch. 4). A systematic account of intuitionist logic, mathematics and philosophy can be found in Dummett (1977). His argument for intuitionism is spelled out there in 7.1, and also in Dummett (1978). It is generalised to all language in Dummett (1976). A critique of Dummett's position can be found in Wright (1987). For a readable introduction to constructivism in general, see Read (1994, ch. 8).

6.10 Problems

1. Verify the claims made about intuitionist validity, left as exercises in 6.6.

2. Show that in an intuitionist interpretation, $\neg\neg A$ is true at a world, w, iff for all w' such that wRw', there is a w'' such that $w'Rw''$ and A is true at w''.

3. Show the following in intuitionist logic:

   (*a*) $\vdash (p \wedge (\neg p \vee q)) \sqsupset q$

   (*b*) $\vdash \neg(p \wedge \neg p)$

   (*c*) $\neg p \vee q \vdash p \sqsupset q$

   (*d*) $\neg(p \vee q) \vdash \neg p \wedge \neg q$

   (*e*) $\neg p \wedge \neg q \vdash \neg(p \vee q)$

   (*f*) $\neg p \vee \neg q \vdash \neg(p \wedge q)$

   (*g*) $p \sqsupset (p \sqsupset q) \vdash p \sqsupset q$

   (*h*) $\vdash \neg\neg(p \vee \neg p)$

4. Either using tableaux, or by constructing counter-models directly, show each of the following. In each case, define the interpretation and draw a picture of it. (For simplicity, omit the extra arrows required by transitivity. Take them as read.) Check that the interpretation works.

   (*a*) $\nvDash p \vee \neg p$

   (*b*) $\neg p \sqsupset p \nvDash p$

   (*c*) $\neg(p \wedge q) \nvDash \neg p \vee \neg q$

   (*d*) $\neg p \sqsupset \neg q \nvDash q \sqsupset p$

   (*e*) $p \sqsupset (q \vee r) \nvDash (p \sqsupset q) \vee (p \sqsupset r)$

5. How else might one manifest an understanding of the meaning of a sentence, other than by asserting it when it becomes manifest that the situation described obtains?

6. * Consider the following tableau rule:

$$\begin{array}{c} p, -j \\ irj \\ \downarrow \\ p, -i \end{array}$$

   Show that if this rule is added to tableaux for intuitionist logic, they are still sound. Use the completeness of intuitionist tableaux to infer that the rule is redundant.

7. *Call a *strong intuitionist interpretation* one where R satisfies the additional condition: for all $x, y \in W$, if xRy and yRx, then $x = y$. (This makes R a partial order.) If an inference is intuitionistically valid, it is obviously truth-preserving in all worlds of strong intuitionist interpretations. Show the converse. (*Hint*: Consider the interpretation induced by an open branch of a tableau for an invalid inference.)

8. *The *Gödel translation* is a map, G, from the sentences of intuitionist propositional logic into the language of $K\rho\tau$, defined, by recursion, thus:

$$\begin{array}{rcl} p^G & = & \Box p \\ (A \wedge B)^G & = & A^G \wedge B^G \\ (A \vee B)^G & = & A^G \vee B^G \\ (A \sqsupset B)^G & = & \Box(A^G \supset B^G) \\ (\neg A)^G & = & \Box\neg A^G \end{array}$$

   Given an intuitionist interpretation (which is also, of course, a $K\rho\tau$ interpretation), show by recursion on the construction of sentences that A is true at a world, w, iff A^G is true at w. Let $\Sigma^G = \{A^G; A \in \Sigma\}$. Infer that if $\Sigma^G \models_{K\rho\tau} A^G$, then $\Sigma \models_I A$. Suppose that $\Sigma^G \not\models_{K\rho\tau} A^G$ (and hence that $\Sigma^G \nvdash_{K\rho\tau} A^G$), and consider the interpretation induced by an open branch of the tableau. Show that this satisfies the heredity condition, and hence infer the converse.

7 Many-valued logics

7.1 Introduction

7.1.1 In this chapter, we leave possible-world semantics for a time, and turn to the subject of propositional many-valued logics. These are logics in which there are more than two truth values.

7.1.2 We have a look at the general structure of a many-valued logic, and some simple but important examples of many-valued logics. The treatment will be purely semantic: we do not look at tableaux for the logics, nor at any other form of proof procedure. Tableaux for some many-valued logics will emerge in the next chapter.

7.1.3 We also look at some of the philosophical issues that have motivated many-valued logics, how many-valuedness affects the issue of the conditional, and the relationship between modal and many-valued logics.

7.2 Many-valued logic: the general structure

7.2.1 Let us start with the general structure of a many-valued logic. To simplify things, we take, henceforth, $A \equiv B$ to be defined as $(A \supset B) \wedge (B \supset A)$.

7.2.2 Let $\mathcal{C}$ be the class of connectives of classical propositional logic $\{\wedge, \vee, \neg, \supset\}$. The classical propositional calculus can be thought of as defined by the structure $\langle \mathcal{V}, \mathcal{D}, \{f_c; c \in \mathcal{C}\} \rangle$. $\mathcal{V}$ is the set of truth values $\{1, 0\}$. $\mathcal{D}$ is the set of *designated* values $\{1\}$; these are the values that are preserved in valid inferences. For every connective, c, f_c is the truth function it denotes. Thus, $f_\neg$ is a one-place function such that $f_\neg(0) =$

1 and $f_\neg(1) = 0$; $f_\wedge$ is a two-place function such that $f_\wedge(x, y) = 1$ if $x = y = 1$, and $f_\wedge(x, y) = 0$ otherwise; and so on. These functions can be (and often are) depicted in the following 'truth tables'.

$f_\neg$	
1	0
0	1

$f_\wedge$	1	0
1	1	0
0	0	0

7.2.3 An interpretation, ν, is a map from the propositional parameters to $\mathcal{V}$. An interpretation is extended to a map from all formulas into $\mathcal{V}$ by applying the appropriate truth functions recursively. Thus, for example, $\nu(\neg(p \wedge q)) = f_\neg(\nu(p \wedge q)) = f_\neg(f_\wedge(\nu(p), \nu(q)))$. (So if $\nu(p) = 1$ and $\nu(q) = 0$, $\nu(\neg(p \wedge q)) = f_\neg(f_\wedge(1, 0)) = f_\neg(0) = 1$.) Finally, an inference is semantically valid just if there is no interpretation that assigns all the premises a value in $\mathcal{D}$, but assigns the conclusion a value not in $\mathcal{D}$.

7.2.4 A many-valued logic is a natural generalisation of this structure. Given some propositional language with connectives $\mathcal{C}$ (maybe the same as those of the classical propositional calculus, maybe different), a logic is defined by a structure $\langle \mathcal{V}, \mathcal{D}, \{f_c; c \in \mathcal{C}\} \rangle$. $\mathcal{V}$ is the set of truth values: it may have any number of members (≥ 1). $\mathcal{D}$ is a subset of $\mathcal{V}$, and is the set of designated values. For every connective, c, f_c is the corresponding truth function. Thus, if c is an n-place connective, f_c is an n-place function with inputs and outputs in $\mathcal{V}$.

7.2.5 An interpretation for the language is a map, ν, from propositional parameters into $\mathcal{V}$. This is extended to a map from all formulas of the language to $\mathcal{V}$ by applying the appropriate truth functions recursively. Thus, if c is an n-place connective, $\nu(c(A_1, \ldots, A_n)) = f_c(\nu(A_1), \ldots, \nu(A_n))$. Finally, $\Sigma \models A$ iff there is no interpretation, ν, such that for all $B \in \Sigma$, $\nu(B) \in \mathcal{D}$, but $\nu(A) \notin \mathcal{D}$. A is a logical truth iff $\phi \models A$, i.e., iff for every interpretation $\nu(A) \in \mathcal{D}$.

7.2.6 If $\mathcal{V}$ is finite, the logic is said to be *finitely many-valued*. If $\mathcal{V}$ has n members, it is said to be an n-valued logic.

7.2.7 For any finitely many-valued logic, the validity of an inference with finitely many premises can be determined, as in the classical propositional calculus, simply by considering all the possible cases. We list all the possible combinations of truth values for the propositional parameters employed. Then, for each combination, we compute the value of each premise and the conclusion. If, in any of these, the premises are all designated and the conclusion is not, the inference is invalid. Otherwise, it is valid. We will have an example of this procedure in the next section.

7.2.8 This method, though theoretically adequate, is often impractical because of exponential explosion. For if there are m propositional parameters employed in an inference, and n truth values, there are m^n possible cases to consider. This grows very rapidly. Thus, if the logic is 4-valued and we have an inference involving just four propositional parameters, there are already 256 cases to consider!

K3 – (3 valued).

7.3 The 3-valued logics of Kleene and Łukasiewicz

7.3.1 In what follows, we consider some simple examples of the above general structure. All the examples that we consider are 3-valued logics. The language, in every case, is that of the classical propositional calculus.

7.3.2 A simple example of a 3-valued logic is as follows. $\mathcal{V} = \{1, i, 0\}$. 1 and 0 are to be thought of as *true* and *false*, as usual. i is to be thought of as *neither true nor false*. $\mathcal{D}$ is just $\{1\}$. The truth functions for the connectives are depicted as follows:

$f_\neg$	
1	0
i	i
0	1

$f_\wedge$	1	i	0
1	1	i	0
i	i	i	0
0	0	0	0

$f_\vee$	1	i	0
1	1	1	1
i	1	i	i
0	1	i	0

$f_\supset$	1	i	0
1	1	i	0
i	1	i	i
0	1	1	1

Thus, if $\nu(p) = 1$ and $\nu(q) = i$, $\nu(\neg p) = 0$ (top row of $f_\neg$), $\nu(\neg p \vee q) = i$ (bottom row, middle column of $f_\vee$), etc.

7.3.3 Note that if the inputs of any of these functions are classical (1 or 0), the output is exactly the same as in the classical case. We compute the other entries as follows. Take $A \wedge B$ as an example. If A is false, then, whatever B is, this is (classically) sufficient to make $A \wedge B$ false. In particular, if B is neither true nor false, $A \wedge B$ is false. If A is true, on the other hand, and B is neither true nor false, there is insufficient information to compute the (classical) value of $A \wedge B$; hence, $A \wedge B$ is neither true nor false. Similar reasoning justifies all the other entries.

7.3.4 The logic specified above is usually called the (strong) Kleene 3-valued logic, often written K_3.[1]

7.3.5 The following table verifies that $p \supset q \models_{K_3} \neg q \supset \neg p$:

p	q	$p \supset q$	$\neg q$	$\supset$	$\neg p$
1	1	**1**	0	**1**	0
1	i	**i**	i	**i**	0
1	0	**0**	1	**0**	0
i	1	**1**	0	**1**	i
i	i	**i**	i	**i**	i
i	0	**i**	1	**i**	i
0	1	**1**	0	**1**	1
0	i	**1**	i	**1**	1
0	0	**1**	1	**1**	1

In the last three columns, the first number is the value of $\neg q$; the last number is that of $\neg p$, and the central number (printed in bold) is the value of the whole formula. As can be seen, there is no interpretation where the premise is designated, that is, has the value 1, and the conclusion is not.

7.3.6 In checking for validity, it may well be easier to work backwards. Consider the formula $p \supset (q \supset p)$. Suppose that this is un-

[1] Weak Kleene logic is the same as K_3, except that, for every truth function, if any input is i, so is the output.

designated. Then it has either the value 0 or the value i. If it has the value 0, then p has the value 1 and $q \supset p$ has the value 0. But if p has the value 1, so does $q \supset p$. This situation is therefore impossible. If it has the value i, there are three possibilities:

p	$q \supset p$
1	i
i	i
i	0

The first case is not possible, since if p has the value 1, so does $q \supset p$. Nor is the last case, since if p has the value i, $q \supset p$ has value either i or 1. But the second case is possible, namely when both p and q have the value i. Thus, $v(p) = v(q) = i$ is a counter-model to $p \supset (q \supset p)$, as a truth-table check confirms. So $\not\models_{K_3} p \supset (q \supset p)$.

7.3.7 A distinctive thing about K_3 is that the law of excluded middle is not valid: $\not\models_{K_3} p \vee \neg p$. (Counter-model: $v(p) = i$.) However, K_3 is distinct from intuitionist logic. As we shall see in 7.10.8, intuitionist logic is not the same as any finitely many-valued logic.

7.3.8 In fact, K_3 has no logical truths at all (7.14, problem 3)! In particular, the law of identity is not valid: $\not\models_{K_3} p \supset p$. (Simply give p the value i.) This may be changed by modifying the middle entry of the truth function for $\supset$, so that $f_\supset$ becomes:

$f_\supset$	1	i	0
1	1	i	0
i	1	1	i
0	1	1	1

(The old meaning of $A \supset B$ can still be expressed by $\neg A \vee B$, since this has the same truth table, as may be checked.) Now, $A \supset A$ always takes the value 1.

7.3.9 The logic resulting from this change is one originally given by Łukasiewicz, and is often called $Ł_3$.

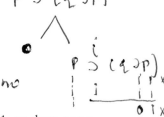

7.4 *LP* and RM_3

7.4.1 Another 3-valued logic is the one often called *LP*. This is exactly the same as K_3, except that $\mathcal{D} = \{1, i\}$.

7.4.2 In the context of *LP*, the value i is thought of as *both true and false*. Consequently, 1 and 0 have to be thought of as *true and true only*, and *false and false only*, respectively. This change does not affect the truth tables, which still make perfectly good sense under the new interpretation. For example, if A takes the value 1 and B takes the value i, then A and B are both true; hence, $A \wedge B$ is true; but since B is false, $A \wedge B$ is false. Hence, the value of $A \wedge B$ is i. Similarly, if A takes the value 0, and B takes the value i, then A and B are both false, so $A \wedge B$ is false; but only B is true, so $A \wedge B$ is not true. Hence, $A \wedge B$ takes the value 0.

7.4.3 However, the change of designated values makes a crucial difference. For example, $\models_{LP} p \vee \neg p$. (Whatever value p has, $p \vee \neg p$ takes either the value 1 or i. Thus it is always designated.) This fails in K_3, as we saw in 7.3.7.

7.4.4 On the other hand, $p \wedge \neg p \not\models_{LP} q$. Counter-model: $\nu(p) = i$ (making $\nu(p \wedge \neg p) = i$), $\nu(q) = 0$. But $p \wedge \neg p$ can never take the value 1 and so be designated in K_3. Thus, the inference is valid in K_3.

7.4.5 A notable feature of *LP* is that *modus ponens* is invalid: $p, p \supset q \not\models_{LP} q$. (Assign p the value i, and q the value 0.)

7.4.6 One way to rectify this is to change the truth function for $\supset$ to the following:

$f_\supset$	1	i	0
1	1	0	0
i	1	i	0
0	1	1	1

(As with K_3, the old meaning of $A \supset B$ can still be expressed by $\neg A \vee B$.) Now, if A and $A \supset B$ have designated values (1 or i), so does B, as a moment checking the truth table verifies.

7.4.7 This change gives the logic often called RM_3.

7.5 Many-valued logics and conditionals

7.5.1 Further details of the properties of $\wedge$, $\vee$ and $\neg$ in the logics we have just met will emerge in the next chapter. For the present, let us concentrate on the conditional.

7.5.2 In past chapters, we have met a number of problematic inferences concerning conditionals. The following table summarises whether or not they hold in the various logics we have looked at. (A tick means *yes*; a cross means *no*.)

		K_3	$Ł_3$	LP	RM_3
(1)	$q \models p \supset q$	✓	✓	✓	×
(2)	$\neg p \models p \supset q$	✓	✓	✓	×
(3)	$(p \wedge q) \supset r \models (p \supset r) \vee (q \supset r)$	✓	✓	✓	✓
(4)	$(p \supset q) \wedge (r \supset s) \models (p \supset s) \vee (r \supset q)$	✓	✓	✓	✓
(5)	$\neg(p \supset q) \models p$	✓	✓	✓	✓
(6)	$p \supset r \models (p \wedge q) \supset r$	✓	✓	✓	✓
(7)	$p \supset q, q \supset r \models p \supset r$	✓	✓	×	✓
(8)	$p \supset q \models \neg q \supset \neg p$	✓	✓	✓	✓
(9)	$\models p \supset (q \vee \neg q)$	×	×	✓	×
(10)	$\models (p \wedge \neg p) \supset q$	×	×	✓	×

(1) and (2) we met in 1.7, and (3)–(5) we met in 1.9, all in connection with the material conditional. (6)–(8) we met in 5.2, in connection with conditional logics. (9) and (10) we met in 4.6, in connection with the strict conditional. The checking of the details is left as a (quite lengthy) exercise. For K_3, a generally good strategy is to start by assuming that the premises take the value 1 (the only designated value), and recall that, in K_3, if a conditional takes the value 1, then

either its antecedent takes the value 0 or the consequent takes the value 1. For $Ł_3$, it is similar, except that a conditional with value 1 may also have antecedent and consequent with value *i*. For *LP*, a generally good strategy is to start by assuming that the conclusion takes the value 0 (the only undesignated value), and recall that, in *LP*, if a conditional takes the value 0, then the antecedent takes the value 1 and the consequent takes the value 0. For RM_3, it is similar, except that if a conditional has value 0, the antecedent and consequent may also take the values 1 and *i*, or *i* and 0, respectively. And recall that classical inputs (1 or 0) always give the classical outputs.

7.5.3 As can be seen from the number of ticks, the conditionals do not fare very well. If one's concern is with the ordinary conditional, and not with conditionals with an enthymematic *ceteris paribus* clause, then one may ignore lines (6)–(8). But all the logics suffer from some of the same problems as the material conditional. K_3 and $Ł_3$ also suffer from some of the problems that the strict conditional does. In particular, even though (10) tells us that $(p \wedge \neg p) \supset q$ is not valid in these logics, contradictions still entail everything, since $p \wedge \neg p$ can never assume a designated value. By contrast, this is not true of *LP* (as we saw in 7.4.4), but this is so only because *modus ponens* is invalid, since $(p \wedge \neg p) \supset q$ is valid, as (10) shows. (*Modus ponens* is valid for the other logics, as may easily be checked.) About the best of the bunch is RM_3.

7.5.4 But there are quite general reasons as to why the conditional of any finitely many-valued logic is bound to be problematic. For a start, if disjunction is to behave in a natural way, the inference from A (or B) to $A \vee B$ must be valid. Hence, we must have:

(i) if A (or B) is designated, so is $A \vee B$

Also, $A \equiv A$ ought to be a logical truth. (Even if A is neither true nor false, for example, it would still seem to be the case that *if* A then A, and so, that A iff A.) Hence:

(ii) if A and B have the same value, $A \equiv B$ must be designated (since $A \equiv A$ is). Note that both of these conditions hold for all the logics that we have looked at, with the exception of K_3, for which (ii) fails.

7.5.5 Now, take any n-valued logic that satisfies (i) and (ii), and consider $n+1$ propositional parameters, $p_1, p_2, ..., p_{n+1}$. Since there are only n truth values, in any interpretation, two of these must receive the same value. Hence, by (ii), for some j and k, $p_j \equiv p_k$ must be designated. But then the disjunction of all biconditionals of this form must also be designated, by (i). Hence, this disjunction is logically valid.

7.5.6 But this seems entirely wrong. Consider $n+1$ propositions such as 'John has 1 hair on his head', 'John has 2 hairs on his head', ... , 'John has $n+1$ hairs on his head'. Any biconditional relating a pair of these would appear to be false. Hence, the disjunction of all such pairs would also appear to be false – certainly not logically true.

7.6 Truth-value gluts: inconsistent laws

7.6.1 Let us now turn to the issue of the philosophical motivations for many-valued logics and, in particular, the 3-valued logics we have met. Typically, the motivations for those logics that treat i as both true and false (a *truth-value glut*), like LP and RM_3, are different from those that treat i as neither true nor false (a *truth-value gap*), like K_3 and $Ł_3$. Let us start with the former. We will look at two reasons for supposing that there are truth-value gluts.[2]

[2] Other examples of truth-value gluts that have been suggested include the state of affairs realised at an instant of change; statements about some object in the border-area of a vague predicate; contradictory statements in the dialectical tradition of Hegel and Marx; statements with predicates whose criteria of application are over-determined; and certain statements about micro-objects in quantum mechanics.

7.6.2 The first concerns inconsistent laws, and the rights and obligations that agents have in virtue of these. We have already had an example of this in 4.8.3 concerning inconsistent traffic regulations.

7.6.3 Here is another example. Suppose that in a certain (entirely hypothetical) country the constitution contains the following clauses:

(1) No aborigine shall have the right to vote.

(2) All property-holders shall have the right to vote.

We may suppose that when the law was made, the possibility of an aboriginal property-holder was so inconceivable as not to be taken seriously. Despite this, as social circumstances change, aborigines do come to hold property. Let one such be John. John, it would appear, both does and does not have the right to vote.

7.6.4 Of course, if a situation of this kind comes to light, the law is likely to be changed to resolve the contradiction. The fact remains, though, that until the law is changed the contradiction is true.

7.6.5 One way that one might object to this conclusion is as follows. The law contains a number of principles for resolving apparent contradictions, for example *lex posterior* (that a later law takes precedence over an earlier law), or that constitutional law takes precedence over statute law, which takes precedence over case law. One might insist that all contradictions are only apparent, and can be defused by applying one or other of these principles.

7.6.6 It is clear, however, that there could well be cases where none of these principles are applicable. Both laws are made at the same time; they are both laws of the same rank, and so on. Hence, though some legal contradictions may be only apparent, this need not always be the case.

7.7 Truth-value gluts: paradoxes of self-reference

7.7.1 A second argument for the existence of truth-value gluts concerns the paradoxes of self-reference. There are many of these; some very old; some very modern. Here are a couple of well-known ones.

7.7.2 THE LIAR PARADOX: Consider the sentence 'this sentence is false'. Suppose that it is true. Then what it says is the case. Hence it is false. Suppose, on the other hand, that it is false. That is just what it says, so it is true. In either case – one of which must obtain by the law of excluded middle – it is both true and false.

7.7.3 RUSSELL'S PARADOX: Consider the set of all those sets which are not members of themselves, $\{x; x \notin x\}$. Call this r. If r is a member of itself, then it is one of the sets that is not a member of itself, so r is not a member of itself. On the other hand, if r is not a member of itself, then it is one of the sets in r, and hence it is a member of itself. In either case – one of which must obtain by the law of excluded middle – it is both true and false.

7.7.4 These (and many others like them) are both *prima facie* sound arguments, and have conclusions of the form $A \wedge \neg A$. If the arguments are sound, the conclusions are true, and hence there are truth-value gluts.

7.7.5 Many people have claimed that the arguments are not, despite appearances, sound. The reasons given are many and complex; let us consider, briefly, just a couple.

7.7.6 Some have argued that any sentence which is self-referential, like the liar sentence, is meaningless. (Hence, such sentences can play no role in logical arguments at all.) This, however, is clearly false. Consider: 'this sentence has five words', 'this sentence is written on page 127 of *An Introduction to Non-Classical Logic*', 'this sentence refers to itself'.

hierarchies of metalanguages.

7.7.7 The most popular objection to the argument is that the liar sentence is neither true nor false. In this case, we can no longer appeal to the law of excluded middle, and so the arguments to contradiction are broken. (Thus, the paradoxes of self-reference are sometimes used as an argument for the existence of truth-value gaps, too.)

7.7.8 This suggestion does not avoid contradiction, however, because of 'extended paradoxes'.[3] Consider the sentence 'This sentence is either false or neither true nor false.' If it is true, it is either false or neither. In both cases it is not true. If, on the other hand, it is either false or neither (and so not true), then that is exactly what it claims, and so it is true. In either case, therefore, it is both true and not true.

7.8 Truth-value gaps: denotation failure

7.8.1 Let us now turn to the question of why one might suppose there to be truth-value gaps. One reason for this, we saw in the last chapter. If one identifies truth with verification then, since there may well be sentences, A, such that neither A nor $\neg A$ can be verified, there may well be truth-value gaps. Intuitionism can be thought of as a particular case of this.[4] Since we discussed intuitionism in the last chapter, we will say no more about this argument here. Instead, we will look at two different arguments.[5]

7.8.2 The first concerns sentences that contain noun phrases that do not appear to refer to anything, like names such as 'Sherlock Holmes', and descriptions such as 'the largest integer' (there is no largest).

[3] Moreover, and in any case, not all of the paradoxical arguments invoke the law of excluded middle. Berry's paradox, for example, does not.

[4] Though, note, in the Kripke semantics for intuitionist logic, every formula takes the value of either 1 or 0 at every world.

[5] Other examples of truth-value gaps that are sometimes given include category mistakes, such as 'The number 3 is thinking about Sydney', and other 'nonsense' statements; statements in the border-area of some vague predicate; and cases of presupposition failure.

7.8.3 It was suggested by Frege that all sentences containing such terms are neither true nor false.[6] This seems unduly strong. Think, for example, of 'Sherlock Holmes does not really exist', or 'either 2 is even or the greatest prime number is'.

7.8.4 Still, there are some sentences containing non-denoting terms that can plausibly be taken as neither true nor false. One sort of example concerns 'truths of fiction'. It is natural to suppose that 'Holmes lived in Baker Street' is true, because Conan Doyle says so; 'Holmes' friend, Watson, was a lawyer' is false, since Doyle tells us that Watson was a doctor; and 'Holmes had three maiden aunts' is neither true nor false, since Doyle tells us nothing about Holmes' aunts or uncles.

7.8.5 This reason is not conclusive, though. An alternative view is that *all* such sentences are simply false. A fictional truth is really a shorthand for the truth of a sentence prefixed by 'In the play/novel/film (etc.), it is the case that'. Thus, in Doyle's stories (it is the case that) Holmes lived in Baker Street. Fictional falsities are similar. Thus, in Doyle's stories it is not the case that Watson was a lawyer. And a fictional truth-value gap, A, is just something where neither A nor $\neg A$ holds in the fiction. Thus, it is not the case in Doyle's stories that Holmes had three maiden aunts; and it is not the case that he did not.

7.8.6 Another sort of example of a sentence that can plausibly be seen as neither true nor false is a subject/predicate sentence containing a non-denoting description, like 'the greatest integer is even'. (Maybe not every predicate, though: 'The greatest integer exists' would seem to be false. But existence is a contentious notion anyway.)[7]

---

[6] Though he also thought that denotation failure ought not to arise in a properly constructed language. Non-denoting terms should be assigned an arbitrary reference.

[7] A related suggestion concerns names that may denote objects, but not objects that exist in the world or situation at which truth is being evaluated. Thus, Aristotle exists in this world, but consider some world at which he does not exist. It may be suggested that 'Aristotle is a philosopher' is neither true nor false at that world.

7.8.7 But again, this view is not mandatory. One may simply take such sentences to be false (so that their negations are true, etc.). This was, essentially, Russell's view.

7.8.8 And Russell's view would seem to work better than a truth-value gap view in many cases. Thus, let 'Father Christmas' be short for the description 'the old man with a white beard who comes down the chimney at Christmas bringing presents'. Then the following would certainly appear to be false: 'The Greeks worshipped Father Christmas' and 'Julius Caesar thought about Father Christmas.'

7.8.9 Note, though, that even Russell's view appears to be in trouble with some similar examples. For example, it appears to be true that the Greeks worshipped the gods who lived on Mount Olympus, and that little Johnny does think about Father Christmas on 24 December.

7.8.10 Thus, though non-denotation does give some reason for supposing there to be truth-value gaps, the view has its problems, as do most views concerning non-denotation.

7.9 Truth-value gaps: future contingents

7.9.1 The second argument for the existence of truth-value gaps concerns certain statements about the future – future contingents. The suggestion is that statements such as 'The first pope in the twenty-second century will be Chinese' and 'It will rain in Brisbane some time on 6/6/2066' are now neither true nor false. The future does not yet exist; there are therefore, presently, no facts that makes such sentences true or false.

7.9.2 It might be replied that such sentences *are* either true or false; it's just that we do not know which yet. But there is a very famous argument, due to Aristotle, to the effect that this cannot be the case. It can be put in different ways; here is a standard version of it.

7.9.3 Let S be the sentence 'The first pope in the twenty-second century will be Chinese.' If S were true now, then it would necessarily be the case that the first pope in the twenty-second century will be Chinese. If S were false now, then it would necessarily be the case that the first pope in the twenty-second century will not be Chinese. Hence, if S were either true or false now, then whatever the state of affairs concerning the first pope in the twenty-second century, it will arise of necessity. But this is impossible, since what happens then is still a contingent matter. Hence, it is neither true nor false now.

7.9.4 One might say much about this argument, but a standard, and very plausible, response to it is that it hinges on a fallacy of ambiguity. Statements of the form 'if A then necessarily B' are ambiguous between 'if A, then, it necessarily follows that B' – $\Box(A \supset B)$ – and 'if A, then B is true of necessity' – $A \supset \Box B$. Moreover, neither of these entails the other (even in $K\upsilon$).

7.9.5 Now, consider the sentence 'If S were true now, then it would necessarily be the case that the first pope in the twenty-second century will be Chinese', which is employed in the argument. If this is interpreted in the first way ($\Box(A \supset B)$), it is true, but the argument is invalid. (Since $A, \Box(A \supset B) \not\models \Box B$.) If we interpret it in the second way ($A \supset \Box B$), the argument is certainly valid, but now there is no reason to believe the conditional to be true (or, if there is, this argument does not provide it). Similar considerations apply to the second part of the argument. Aristotle's argument does not, therefore, appear to work.

7.10 Supervaluations, modality and many-valued logic

7.10.1 Let us finish with a couple of comments on some other matters of note. These arise in connection with Aristotle's argument of the previous section.

7.10.2 First, those who have taken future contingents to be neither true nor false, like Aristotle, have not normally taken all statements about the future to be truth-valueless. Only those statements whose truth value is as yet undetermined have that status. In particular, instances of the law of excluded middle, $S \vee \neg S$, are usually endorsed, even if S is a future contingent. Since this is not valid in K_3 or $Ł_3$, these logics do not appear to be the appropriate ones for future statements.

7.10.3 A better logic can be obtained by a technique called *supervaluation*. Even if neither S nor $\neg S$ is presently true, one or other will be true eventually, presumably. Given a K_3 interpretation, ν, let us write $\nu \leq \nu'$ to mean that ν' is a classical interpretation which is the same as ν, except where $\nu(p) = i$, in which case $\nu'(p)$ is either 1 or 0. ν' represents one of the ways that things could turn out to be eventually. It is called a *supervaluation* of ν.

7.10.4 Now, we want our logic to work however things turn out to be. Hence, it is natural to define a notion of consequence thus:

$\Sigma \models_S A$ iff for every interpretation, ν, every supervaluation of ν that makes every $B \in \Sigma$ true makes A true.

7.10.5 Since every supervaluation is a classical interpretation, and every classical interpretation is a supervaluation of some K_3 interpretation (namely itself), this definition just reduces to truth preservation under all classical interpretations. Hence, $\models_S$ is just classical logic – even though it allows for truth-value gaps! In particular, $\models_S A \vee \neg A$.[8]

7.10.6 The second main issue concerns the connection between modality and many-valued logic. Notwithstanding the issue concerning the law of excluded middle that we have just discussed, Łukasiewicz was motived to construct his logic $Ł_3$ by the problem about future contingents. According to him, statements about the past and present

[8] A similar construction will work with $Ł_3$, but is less appropriate. For, on an Aristotelian view, it is natural to suppose that, as time passes, more becomes true; things already true should not cease to be so. In K_3 anything true under an evaluation is true under any of its supervaluations. This is not the case with $Ł_3$. See 7.14, problem 4, below.

are now unalterable in truth value. If they are true, they are necessarily true; if they are false, they are necessarily false. But future contingents, those things taking the value i, are merely possible. Things that are true are also possible, of course. He therefore augmented the language with a modal possibility operator, $\diamond$, and gave it the following truth table:

$f_\diamond$	
1	1
i	1
0	0

Defining $\Box A$ in the standard way, as $\neg\diamond\neg A$, gives it the truth table:

$f_\Box$	
1	1
i	0
0	0

7.10.7 These definitions give a modal logic that, in the light of modern modal logic, has some rather strange properties. For example, it is easy to check that $p \models_{L_3} \Box p$. (This is *not* the Rule of Necessitation.) Given the Aristotelian motivation, this may be acceptable. But there are other consequences that are certainly not. For example, it is easy to check that $\diamond A, \diamond B \models_{L_3} \diamond(A \wedge B)$. This is not acceptable – even to an Aristotelian. It is possible that the first pope in the twenty-second century will be Chinese and possible that she will not. But it is not possible that she both will and will not be.

7.10.8 In fact, none of the modal logics that we have looked at (nor conditional logics, nor intuitionist logic) is a finitely many-valued logic. The proof of this is essentially a version of the argument of 7.5.4, 7.5.5. The proof is given in 7.11.1–7.11.3.

7.10.9 There is a certain sense in which every logic can be thought of as an infinitely many-valued logic, however. A *uniform substitution* of a set of formulas is the result of replacing each propositional parameter uniformly with some formula or other (maybe itself). Thus, for example, a uniform substitution of the set $\{p,\ p \supset (p \vee q)\}$ is $\{r \wedge s, (r \wedge s) \supset ((r \wedge s) \vee q)\}$. A logic is *closed under uniform substitution* when any inference that is valid is also valid for every uniform substitution of the premises and conclusion. All standard logics are closed under uniform substitution.[9]

7.10.10 Now, it can be shown that every logical consequence relation, $\vdash$, closed under uniform substitution, is weakly complete with respect to a many-valued semantics. That is, $\vdash A$ iff A is logically valid in the semantics. This is proved in 7.11.5. The semantics is somewhat fraudulent, though, since it involves taking every formula as a truth value. Moreover, it appears that the result does not extend to strong completeness, that is, to inferences with arbitrary (as opposed to empty) premise sets.

7.11 *Proofs of theorems

7.11.1 DEFINITION: Let $A ⥼⥽ B$ be $(A ⥽ B) \wedge (B ⥽ A)$, and let $A \sqsubset\!\sqsupset B$ be $(A \sqsupset B) \wedge (B \sqsupset A)$. Let D_{n+1} be the disjunction of all sentences of the form $p_j ⥼⥽ p_k$ (if we are dealing with a modal logic), or $p_j \sqsubset\!\sqsupset p_k$ (if we are dealing with intuitionist logic), for $1 \leq j < k \leq n+1$.

7.11.2 LEMMA: For no n is D_{n+1} a logical truth of any modal logic weaker than $K\upsilon$ or of intuitionist logic.

[9] The general reason is as follows. Suppose that some substitution instance of an inference is invalid. Then there is some interpretation, $\mathcal{I}$ (appropriate for the logic in question), which makes the premises true and the conclusion untrue (at some world). Now consider the interpretation that is exactly the same as $\mathcal{I}$, except that it assigns to every parameter (at a world) the value of whatever formula was substituted for it (at that world) in $\mathcal{I}$. It is not difficult to check that the truth value of every formula (at every world) is the same in this interpretation as its substitution instance was in $\mathcal{I}$. Hence, the inference is invalid also.

Proof:

The proof is by constructing counter-models in $K\upsilon$ and I, either directly or with the aid of tableaux. Details are left as an exercise.

7.11.3 THEOREM: No modal logic between N and $K\upsilon$ is a finitely many-valued logic.

Proof:

Suppose that it were, and that it had n truth values. Since $A \models_N A \vee B$:

(i) whenever $A \in \mathcal{D}$, $A \vee B \in \mathcal{D}$

Since $A \wedge B \models_N A$:

(ii) whenever $A \wedge B \in \mathcal{D}$, $A \in \mathcal{D}$

(and the same for B in both cases). Moreover, since $\models_N p \strictif p$:

(iii) for any $x \in \mathcal{V}$, $f_{\strictif}(x, x) \in \mathcal{D}$

Now, consider any interpretation, ν. Since there are only n truth values, for some $1 \leq j < k \leq n+1$, $\nu(p_j) = \nu(p_k)$. Hence, $\nu(p_j \strictif p_k) \in \mathcal{D}$ and $\nu(p_k \strictif p_j) \in \mathcal{D}$, by (iii), $\nu(p_j \strictiff p_k) \in \mathcal{D}$, by (ii), and $\nu(D_{n+1}) \in \mathcal{D}$, by (i). Thus, D_{n+1} is logically valid, which it is not, by the preceding lemma.

7.11.4 THEOREM: Intuitionist logic is not a finitely many-valued logic. Nor is any logic that extends intuitionist logic or any of the modal logics above with extra connectives. In particular, no conditional logic is a finitely many-valued logic.

Proof:

The proof for intuitionist logic is exactly the same, replacing $\strictiff$ with $\sqsubset\sqsupset$. The argument for any linguistic extension of the logics in question is also exactly the same.

7.11.5 THEOREM: Any logical consequence relation, $\vdash$, closed under uniform substitution, is weakly complete with respect to a many-valued semantics.

Proof:

We define the components of a many-valued logic as follows. Let $\mathcal{V}$ be the set of formulas of the language. Let $\mathcal{D} = \{A; \vdash A\}$. For every n-place connective, c, let $f_c(A_1, ..., A_n) = c(A_1, ..., A_n)$. Now, suppose that $\vdash A$. Consider any interpretation, ν. Then it is easy to check that $\nu(A)$ is simply the formula A with every propositional parameter, p, replaced by $\nu(p)$. Call this A_ν. Since $\vdash$ is closed under uniform substitution, $\vdash A_\nu$. That is, $\nu(A) \in \mathcal{D}$. Conversely, suppose that $\nvdash A$. Consider the interpretation, ν, which maps every propositional parameter to itself. It is easy to check that $\nu(A) = A$. Hence, $\nu(A) \notin \mathcal{D}$.

7.12 History

The first many-valued logic was $Ł_3$. This, and its generalisation to n-valued logics, $Ł_n$, were invented by the Polish logician Łukasiewicz (pronounced Woo/ka/syey/vitz) around 1920. See Łukasiewicz (1967). (This paper also discusses future contingents and Łukasiewicz' modal logic.) At about the same time, the US mathematician Post (1921) was also constructing a many-valued logic. (Post's system has no simple philosophical motivation, though.) The logic K_3 was invented by Kleene (1952, sect. 64). He was brought to it by considering partial functions, that is, functions that may have no value for certain inputs (such as division when this is by 0). An expression such as 3/0 can be thought of as an instance of denotation failure. Some, such as Kripke (1975), have argued that i should be thought of as a lack of truth value, rather than as a third truth value; but this is a subtle distinction to which it is hard to give substance. *LP* (which stands for 'Logic of Paradox') was given by Priest (1979). RM_3 is one of a family of n-valued logics, RM_n, related to the logic R-Mingle. (We will meet the relevant logic R in a later chapter.) See Anderson and Belnap (1975, pp. 470f.).

The view that there are true contradictions, *dialetheism*, had a number of historical adherents; but, in its modern form, is relatively recent. For its history, see Priest (1998). Frege's views on non-denotation can be found in Frege (1970). A more nuanced defence of the same idea is in Strawson (1950). Russell's account of descriptions appeared in Russell (1905). Aristotle's argument for truth-value gaps is to be found in *De Interpretatione*, chapter 9.

Supervaluations were invented by van Fraassen (1969). The proof that intuitionist logic is not many-valued was first given by Gödel (1933b). The idea was applied to modal logic by Dugunji (1940). The proof that every logic is weakly characterised by a many-valued logic is duc to Lindenbaum (see Rescher 1969, p. 157).

7.13 Further reading

For an excellent overview of many-valued logics, including their history, see Rescher (1969). Urquhart (1986) is shorter and also very good. The literature on the paradoxes of self-reference is enormous, but reasonable places to start are Haack (1979, ch. 8), Sainsbury (1995, ch. 5) and Priest (1987, chs. 1 and 2). Chapter 13 of the last of these also contains a discussion of inconsistent laws. The literature on non-denotation is also enormous. A suitable place to start is Haack (1979, ch. 5). A good discussion of Aristotle's argument for truth-value gaps, and its employment by Łukasiewicz, is Haack (1974, ch. 4). Many of the possible examples of truth-value gluts are discussed in Priest and Routley (1989a,b). Many of the possible examples of truth-value gaps are discussed in Blamey (1986, sect. 2).

7.14 Problems

1. Check all the details omitted in 7.5.2.
2. Call a many-valued logic in the language of the propositional calculus *normal* if, amongst its truth values are two, 1 and 0, such that 1 is designated, 0 is not, and for every truth function corresponding to a connective, the output for those inputs is the same as the classical output. (K_3, $Ł_3$, *LP* and

RM_3 are all normal.) Show that every normal many-valued logic is a sub-logic of classical logic.

3. Observe that in K_3 if an interpretation assigns the value i to every propositional parameter that occurs in a formula, then it assigns the value i to the formula itself. Infer that there are no logical truths in K_3. Are there any logical truths in $Ł_3$?

4. Let ν_1 and ν_2 be any interpretations of K_3 or LP. Write $\nu_1 \preceq \nu_2$ to mean that for every propositional parameter, p:

$$\text{if } \nu_1(p) = 1, \text{ then } \nu_2(p) = 1; \text{and if } \nu_1(p) = 0, \text{ then } \nu_2(p) = 0$$

Show by induction on the way that formulas are constructed, that if $\nu_1 \preceq \nu_2$, then the displayed condition is true for all formulas. Does the result hold for $Ł_3$ and RM_3?

5. By problem 2, if $\models_{LP} A$, then A is a classical logic truth. Use problem 4 to show the converse. (*Hint*: Suppose that ν is an LP interpretation such that $\nu(A) = 0$. Consider the interpretation, ν', which is the same as ν, except that if $\nu(p) = i$, $\nu'(p) = 0$.)

6. What is the truth value of ‘this sentence is true’?

7. Tolkien tells us in *The Hobbit* that Bilbo Baggins is a hobbit, and all hobbits are short. Graham Priest is 6′4″. What is the truth value of ‘Graham Priest is taller than Bilbo Baggins’, and why?

8. * Fill in the details omitted in 7.11.2.

8 First degree entailment

8.1 Introduction

8.1.1 In this chapter we look at a logic called *first degree entailment* (*FDE*). This is formulated, first, as a logic where interpretations are *relations* between formulas and standard truth values, rather than as the more usual *functions*. Connections between *FDE* and the many-valued logics of the last chapter will emerge.

8.1.2 We also look at an alternative possible-world semantics for *FDE*, which will introduce us to a new kind of semantics for negation.

8.1.3 Finally, we look at the relation of all this to the explosion of contradictions, and to the disjunctive syllogism.

8.2 The semantics of *FDE*

8.2.1 The language of *FDE* contains just the connectives $\wedge$, $\vee$ and $\neg$. $A \supset B$ is defined, as usual, as $\neg A \vee B$.

8.2.2 In the classical propositional calculus, an interpretation is a function from formulas to the truth values 0 and 1, written thus: $\nu(A) = 1$ (or 0). Packed into this formalism is the assumption (usually made without comment in elementary logic texts) that every formula is either true or false; never neither, and never both.

8.2.3 As we saw in the last chapter, there are reasons to doubt this assumption. If one does, it is natural to formulate an interpretation, not as a function, but as a relation between formulas and truth values. Thus, a formula may relate to 1; it may relate to 0; it may relate to both; or it may relate to neither. This is the main idea behind the following semantics for *FDE*.

8.2.4 Note that it is now very important to distinguish between being false in an interpretation and not being true in it. (There is, of course, no difference in the classical case.) The fact that a formula is false (relates to 0) does not mean that it is untrue (it may also relate to 1). And the fact that it is untrue (does not relate to 1) does not mean that it is false (it may not relate to 0 either).

8.2.5 An *FDE* interpretation is a relation, ρ,[1] between propositional parameters and the values 1 and 0. (In mathematical notation, $\rho \subseteq \mathcal{P} \times \{1, 0\}$, where $\mathcal{P}$ is the set of propositional parameters.) Thus, $p\rho 1$ means that p relates to 1, and $p\rho 0$ means that p relates to 0.

8.2.6 Given an interpretation, ρ, this is extended to a relation between all formulas and truth values by the recursive clauses:

$A \wedge B\rho 1$ iff $A\rho 1$ and $B\rho 1$
$A \wedge B\rho 0$ iff $A\rho 0$ or $B\rho 0$

$A \vee B\rho 1$ iff $A\rho 1$ or $B\rho 1$
$A \vee B\rho 0$ iff $A\rho 0$ and $B\rho 0$

$\neg A\rho 1$ iff $A\rho 0$
$\neg A\rho 0$ iff $A\rho 1$

Note that these are exactly the same as the classical truth conditions, stripped of the assumption that truth and falsity are exclusive and exhaustive. Thus, a conjunction is true (under an interpretation) if both conjuncts are true (under that interpretation); it is false if at least one conjunct is false, etc.

8.2.7 As an example of how these conditions work, consider the formula $\neg p \wedge (q \vee r)$. Suppose that $p\rho 1$, $p\rho 0$, $q\rho 1$ and $r\rho 0$, and that ρ

[1] Not to be confused with the reflexive ρ of normal modal logics.

relates no parameter to anything else. Since p is true, $\neg p$ is false; and since p is false, $\neg p$ is true. Thus $\neg p$ is both true and false. Since q is true, $q \vee r$ is true; and since q is not false, $q \vee r$ is not false. Thus, $q \vee r$ is simply true. But then, $\neg p \wedge (q \vee r)$ is true, since both conjuncts are true; and false, since the first conjunct is false. That is, $\neg p \wedge (q \vee r)\rho 1$ and $\neg p \wedge (q \vee r)\rho 0$.

8.2.8 Semantic consequence is defined, in the usual way, in terms of truth preservation, thus:

$\Sigma \models A$ iff for every interpretation, ρ, if $B\rho 1$ for all $B \in \Sigma$ then $A\rho 1$

and:

$\models A$ iff $\phi \models A$, i.e., for all ρ, $A\rho 1$

8.3 Tableaux for *FDE*

8.3.1 Tableaux for *FDE* can be obtained by modifying those for the classical propositional calculus as follows.

8.3.2 Each entry of the tableau is now of the form $A, +$ or $A, -$. Intuitively, $A, +$ means that A is true, $A, -$ means that it isn't. As we noted in 8.2.4, and as with intuitionist logic (6.4.1), $\neg A, +$ no longer means the same, intuitively, as $A, -$.

8.3.3 To test the claim that $A_1, \ldots, A_n \vdash B$, we start with an initial list of the form:

$$\begin{array}{c} A_1, + \\ \vdots \\ A_n, + \\ B, - \end{array}$$

8.3.4 The tableaux rules are as follows:

$$\begin{array}{c} A \wedge B, + \\ \downarrow \\ A, + \\ B, + \end{array} \qquad \begin{array}{ccc} & A \wedge B, - & \\ \swarrow & & \searrow \\ A, - & & B, - \end{array}$$

$$\begin{array}{ccc} & A \vee B, + & \\ \swarrow & & \searrow \\ A, + & & B, + \end{array} \qquad \begin{array}{c} A \vee B, - \\ \downarrow \\ A, - \\ B, - \end{array}$$

$$\begin{array}{c} \neg(A \wedge B), + \\ \downarrow \\ \neg A \vee \neg B, + \end{array} \qquad \begin{array}{c} \neg(A \wedge B), - \\ \downarrow \\ \neg A \vee \neg B, - \end{array}$$

$$\begin{array}{c} \neg(A \vee B), + \\ \downarrow \\ \neg A \wedge \neg B, + \end{array} \qquad \begin{array}{c} \neg(A \vee B), - \\ \downarrow \\ \neg A \wedge \neg B, - \end{array}$$

$$\begin{array}{c} \neg\neg A, + \\ \downarrow \\ A, + \end{array} \qquad \begin{array}{c} \neg\neg A, - \\ \downarrow \\ A, - \end{array}$$

The first two rules speak for themselves: if $A \wedge B$ is true, A and B are true; if $A \wedge B$ is not true, then one or other of A and B is not true. Similarly for the rules for disjunction. The other rules are also easy to remember, since $\neg(A \wedge B)$ and $\neg A \vee \neg B$ have the same truth values in *FDE*, as do $\neg(A \vee B)$ and $\neg A \wedge \neg B$, and $\neg\neg A$ and A. (De Morgan's laws and the law of double negation, respectively.)

8.3.5 Finally, a branch of a tableau closes if it contains nodes of the form $A, +$ and $A, -$.

8.3.6 For example, the following tableau demonstrates that $\neg(B \wedge \neg C) \wedge A \vdash (\neg B \vee C) \vee D$:

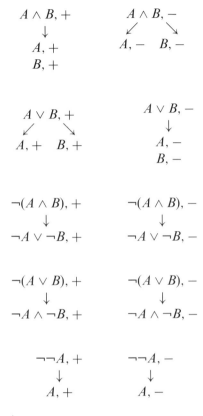

$$
\begin{array}{ccc}
 & \neg(B \wedge \neg C) \wedge A, + & \\
 & (\neg B \vee C) \vee D, - & \\
 & \neg(B \wedge \neg C), + & \\
 & A, + & \\
 & \neg B \vee \neg\neg C, + & \\
 & \neg B \vee C, - & \\
 & D, - & \\
 & \neg B, - & \\
 & C, - & \\
\swarrow & & \searrow \\
\neg B, + & & \neg\neg C, + \\
\times & & C, + \\
 & & \times
\end{array}
$$

The third and fourth lines come from the first, by the rule for true conjunctions. The next line comes from the third by De Morgan's laws. The next two lines come from the second by the rule for untrue disjunctions, which is then applied again, to get the next two lines. The branching arises because of the rule for true disjunctions, applied to line five. The left branch is now closed because of $\neg B, -$ and $\neg B, +$; an application of double negation then closes the righthand branch.

8.3.7 Here is another example, to show that $p \wedge (q \vee \neg q) \nvdash r$:

$$
\begin{array}{ccc}
 & p \wedge (q \vee \neg q), + & \\
 & r, - & \\
 & p, + & \\
 & q \vee \neg q, + & \\
\swarrow & & \searrow \\
q, + & & \neg q, +
\end{array}
$$

8.3.8 Counter-models can be read off from open branches in a simple way. For every parameter, p, if there is a node of the form $p, +$, set $p\rho 1$; if there is a node of the form $\neg p, +$, set $p\rho 0$. No other facts about ρ obtain.

8.3.9 Thus, the counter-model defined by the righthand branch of the tableau in 8.3.7 is the interpretation ρ, where $p\rho 1$ and $q\rho 0$ (and no other relations hold). It is easy to check directly that this interpretation makes the premises true and the conclusion untrue.

8.3.10 The tableaux are sound and complete with respect to the semantics. This is proved in 8.7.1–8.7.7.

8.4 *FDE* and many-valued logics

8.4.1 Given any formula, A, and any interpretation, ρ, there are four possibilities: A is true and not also false, A is false and not also true, A is true and false, A is neither true nor false. If we write these possibilities as 1, 0, b and n, respectively, this makes it possible to think of *FDE* as a 4-valued logic.

8.4.2 The truth conditions of 8.2.6 give the following truth tables:

$f_\neg$	
1	0
b	b
n	n
0	1

$f_\wedge$	1	b	n	0
1	1	b	n	0
b	b	b	0	0
n	n	0	n	0
0	0	0	0	0

$f_\vee$	1	b	n	0
1	1	1	1	1
b	1	b	1	b
n	1	1	n	n
0	1	b	n	0

The details are laborious, but easy enough to check. Thus, suppose that A is n and B is b. Then it is not the case that A and B are both true; hence, $A \wedge B$ is not true. But B is false; hence, $A \wedge B$ is false. Thus, $A \wedge B$ is false but not true, 0. Since B is true, $A \vee B$ is true; and since A and B are not both false, $A \vee B$ is not false. Hence, $A \vee B$ is true and not false, 1. The other cases are left as an exercise.

8.4.3 An easy way to remember these values is with the following diagram, the 'diamond lattice':

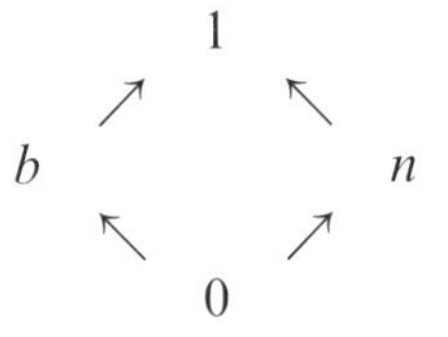

The conjunction of any two elements, x and y, is their greatest lower bound, that is, the greatest thing from which one can get to both x and y going up the arrows. Thus, for example, $b \wedge n = 0$ and

$b \wedge 1 = b$. The disjunction of two elements, x and y, is the least upper bound, that is, the least thing from which one can get to both x and y going down the arrows. Thus, for example, $b \vee n = 1$, $b \vee 1 = 1$. Negation toggles 0 and 1, and maps each of n and b to itself.[2]

8.4.4 Since validity in *FDE* is defined in terms of truth preservation, the set of designated values is $\{1, b\}$ (true only, and both true and false).

8.4.5 This is not one of the many-valued logics that we met in the last chapter, but two of the ones that we did meet there are closely related to *FDE*.

8.4.6 Suppose that we consider an *FDE* interpretation that satisfies the constraint:

Exclusion: for no p, $p\rho 1$ and $p\rho 0$

i.e., no propositional parameter is both true and false. Then it is not difficult to check that the same holds for every sentence, A.[3] That is, nothing takes the value b.

8.4.7 The logic defined in terms of truth preservation over all interpretations satisfying this constraint is, in fact, K_3. For if we take the above matrices, and ignore the rows and columns for b, we get exactly the matrices for K_3 (identifying n with i). (In K_3, $A \supset B$ can be defined as $\neg A \vee B$, as we observed in 7.3.8.)

[2] In fact, this structure is more than a mnemonic. The lattice is one of the most fundamental of a group of structures called 'De Morgan lattices', which can be used to give a different semantics for *FDE*.

[3] *Proof*: The proof is by an induction over the complexity of sentences. Suppose that it is true for A and B; we show that it is true for $\neg A$, $A \wedge B$ and $A \vee B$. Suppose that $\neg A\rho 1$ and $\neg A\rho 0$; then $A\rho 0$ and $A\rho 1$, contrary to supposition. Suppose that $A \wedge B\rho 1$ and $A \wedge B\rho 0$; then $A\rho 1$ and $B\rho 1$, and either $A\rho 0$ or $B\rho 0$; hence, either $A\rho 1$ and $A\rho 0$, or the same for B. Both cases are false, by assumption. The argument for $A \vee B$ is similar.

8.4.8 K_3 is sound and complete with respect to the tableaux of the previous section, augmented by one extra closure rule: a branch closes if it contains nodes of the form $A, +$ and $\neg A, +$. (This is proved in 8.7.8.) Here, for example, is a tableau showing that $p \wedge \neg p \vdash_{K_3} q$. (The tableau is open in *FDE*.)

$$\begin{array}{c} p \wedge \neg p, + \\ q, - \\ p, + \\ \neg p, + \\ \times \end{array}$$

Counter-models are read off from open branches of tableaux in exactly the same way as in *FDE*.

8.4.9 Suppose, on the other hand, that we consider an *FDE* interpretation that satisfies the constraint:

Exhaustion: for all p, either $p\rho 1$ or $p\rho 0$

i.e., every propositional parameter is either true and false – and maybe both. Then it is not difficult to check that, again, the same holds for every sentence, A.[4] That is, nothing takes the value n.

8.4.10 The logic defined by truth preservation over all interpretations satisfying this constraint is, in fact, *LP*. For if we take the matrices of 8.4.2 and ignore the rows and columns for n, we get exactly the matrices for *LP* (identifying b with i). (Again, in *LP*, $A \supset B$ can be defined as $\neg A \vee B$, as we observed in 7.4.6.)

8.4.11 *LP* is sound and complete with respect to the tableaux of the previous section, augmented by one extra closure rule: a branch closes if it contains nodes of the form $A, -$ and $\neg A, -$. (This is proved in

[4] *Proof*: The proof is by an induction over the complexity of sentences. Suppose that it is true for A and B; we show that it is true for $\neg A$, $A \wedge B$ and $A \vee B$. Suppose that either $A\rho 1$ or $A\rho 0$; then either $\neg A\rho 0$ or $\neg A\rho 1$. Since $A\rho 1$ or $A\rho 0$, and $B\rho 1$ or $B\rho 0$, then either $A\rho 1$ and $B\rho 1$, and so $A \wedge B\rho 1$; or $A\rho 0$ or $B\rho 0$, and so $A \wedge B\rho 0$. The argument for $A \vee B$ is similar.

8.7.9.) Here, for example, is a tableau showing that $p \vdash_{LP} q \vee \neg q$. (The tableau is open in *FDE*.)

$$p, +$$
$$q \vee \neg q, -$$
$$q, -$$
$$\neg q, -$$
$$\times$$

Counter-models are read off from open branches of tableaux by employing the following rule: if $p, -$ is not on the branch (and so, in particular, if $p, +$ is), set $p \rho 1$; and if $\neg p, -$ is not on the branch (and so, in particular, if $\neg p, +$ is), set $p \rho 0$.

8.4.12 Finally, and of course, if an interpretation satisfies both *Exclusion* and *Exhaustion*, then for every p, $p \rho 0$ or $p \rho 1$, but not both, and the same follows for arbitrary A. In this case, we have what is, in effect, an interpretation for classical logic. Adding the closure rules for K_3 and *LP* to those of *FDE*, therefore gives us a new tableau procedure for classical logic. In counter eg –

In q – set $q \rho 0$ ($\neg q, -$ it would have to be.
eg k ($\ 8 \cdot 2$)

8.4.13 Since all K_3 interpretations are *FDE* interpretations, and all *LP* interpretations are *FDE* interpretations, *FDE* is a sub-logic of K_3 and *LP*. It is a proper sub-logic of each, as the tableaux of 8.4.8 and 8.4.11 show.

8.5 The Routley star

8.5.1 We now have two equivalent semantics for *FDE*, a relational semantics and a many-valued semantics.[5] For reasons to do with later chapters, we should have a third. This is a two-valued possible-world semantics, which treats negation as an intensional operator; that is, as

---

[5] At least, they are equivalent given the standard set-theoretic reasoning employed in the reformulation. Such reasoning employs classical logic, however, and in a set theory based on a paraconsistent logic it may fail. See Priest (1993).

an operator whose truth conditions require reference to worlds other than the world at which truth is being evaluated.

8.5.2 Specifically, we assume that each world, w, comes with a mate, w^*, its *star world*, such that $\neg A$ is true at w if A is false, not at w, but at w^*. If $w = w^*$ (which may happen), then these conditions just collapse into the classical conditions for negation; but if not, they do not. The star operator is often described with a variety of metaphors; for example, it is sometimes described as a reversal operator; but it is hard to give it and its role in the truth conditions for negation a satisfying intuitive interpretation.

8.5.3 Formally, a *Routley interpretation* is a structure $\langle W, *, \nu\rangle$, where W is a set of worlds, $*$ is a function from worlds to worlds such that $w^{**} = w$, and ν assigns each propositional parameter either the value 1 or the value 0 at each world. ν is extended to an assignment of truth values for all formulas by the conditions:

$$\nu_w(A \wedge B) = 1 \text{ if } \nu_w(A) = 1 \text{ and } \nu_w(B) = 1\text{; otherwise it is } 0.$$

$$\nu_w(A \vee B) = 1 \text{ if } \nu_w(A) = 1 \text{ or } \nu_w(B) = 1\text{; otherwise it is } 0.$$

$$\nu_w(\neg A) = 1 \text{ if } \nu_{w^*}(A) = 0\text{; otherwise it is } 0.$$

Note that $\nu_{w^*}(\neg A) = 1$ iff $\nu_{w^{**}}(A) = 0$ iff $\nu_w(A) = 0$. In other words, exactly one of A and $\neg A$ is true in each of w or w^*; and, whichever it is, the other is true in the other. Validity is defined in terms of truth preservation over all worlds of all interpretations.

8.5.4 Appropriate tableaux for these semantics are easy to construct. Nodes are now of the form $A, +x$ or $A, -x$, where x is either i or $i^{\#}$, i being a natural number. (In fact, i will always be 0, but we set things up in a slightly more general way for reasons to do with later chapters.) Intuitively, $i^{\#}$ represents the star world of i. Closure occurs if we have a pair of the form $A, +x$ and $A, -x$. The initial list comprises a node $B, +0$ for every premise, B, and $A, -0$, where A is the conclusion. The tableau rules are as follows, where x is either i or $i^{\#}$, and whichever of these it is, $\overline{x}$ is the other.

$$\begin{array}{c} A \wedge B, +x \\ \downarrow \\ A, +x \\ B, +x \end{array} \qquad \begin{array}{c} A \wedge B, -x \\ \swarrow \quad \searrow \\ A, -x \quad B, -x \end{array}$$

$$\begin{array}{c} A \vee B, +x \\ \swarrow \quad \searrow \\ A, +x \quad B, +x \end{array} \qquad \begin{array}{c} A \vee B, -x \\ \downarrow \\ A, -x \\ B, -x \end{array}$$

$$\begin{array}{c} \neg A, +x \\ \downarrow \\ A, -\overline{x} \end{array} \qquad \begin{array}{c} \neg A, -x \\ \downarrow \\ A, +\overline{x} \end{array}$$

8.5.5 Here are tableaux demonstrating that $\neg(B \wedge \neg C) \wedge A \vdash (\neg B \vee C) \vee D$ and $p \wedge (q \vee \neg q) \nvdash r$:

$$\begin{array}{c} \neg(B \wedge \neg C) \wedge A, +0 \\ (\neg B \vee C) \vee D, -0 \\ (\neg B \vee C), -0 \\ D, -0 \\ \neg B, -0 \\ C, -0 \\ B, +0^{\#} \\ \neg(B \wedge \neg C), +0 \\ A, +0 \\ B \wedge \neg C, -0^{\#} \\ \swarrow \qquad \searrow \\ B, -0^{\#} \qquad \neg C, -0^{\#} \\ \times \qquad\qquad C, +0 \\ \qquad\qquad\quad \times \end{array}$$

Line two is pursued as far as possible. Then line one is pursued to produce closure.

$$
\begin{array}{c}
p \wedge (q \vee \neg q), +0 \\
r, -0 \\
p, +0 \\
q \vee \neg q, +0 \\
\swarrow \qquad \searrow \\
q, +0 \qquad \neg q, +0 \\
\qquad\qquad q, -0^{\#}
\end{array}
$$

8.5.6 To read off a counter-model from an open branch: $W = \{w_0, w_{0^\#}\}$ (there are only ever two worlds); $w_0^* = w_{0^\#}$ and $(w_{0^\#})^* = w_0$. (W and $*$ are always the same, no matter what the tableau.) v is such that if $p, +x$ occurs on the branch, $v_{w_x}(p) = 1$, and if $p, -x$ occurs on the branch, $v_{w_x}(p) = 0$. Thus, the counter-model defined by the right-hand open branch of the second tableau of 8.5.5 has $v_{w_0}(p) = 1$, $v_{w_0}(r) = 0$ and $v_{w_{0^\#}}(q) = 0$. It is easy to check directly that this interpretation does the job. Since q is false at $w_{0^\#}$, $\neg q$ is true at w_0, as, therefore, is $q \vee \neg q$; but p is true at w_0, hence $p \wedge (q \vee \neg q)$ is true at w_0. But q is false at w_0, as required.

8.5.7 The soundness and completeness of this tableau procedure is proved in 8.7.10–8.7.16.

8.5.8 It is not at all obvious that the $*$ semantics are equivalent to the relational semantics, but it is not too difficult to establish this. Essentially, it is because a relational interpretation, ρ, is equivalent to a pair of worlds, w and w^*. Specifically, the relation and the worlds do exactly the same job when they are related by the condition:

$$v_w(p) = 1 \text{ iff } p\rho 1$$

$$v_{w^*}(p) = 0 \text{ iff } p\rho 0$$

for all parameters, p. The proof of the equivalence is given in 8.7.17 and 8.7.18.

Explosion - once you have a contradiction everything explodes.

8.6 Paraconsistency and the disjunctive syllogism

8.6.1 As we have seen (8.4.8 and 8.4.11), both of the following are false in *FDE*: $p \models q \vee \neg q$, $p \wedge \neg p \models q$. This is essentially because there are truth-value gaps (for the former) and truth-value gluts (for the latter). In particular, then, *FDE* does not suffer from the problem of explosion (4.8).

8.6.2 A logic in which the inference from p and $\neg p$ to an arbitrary conclusion is not valid is called *paraconsistent*. *FDE* is therefore paraconsistent, as is *LP* (7.4.4).

8.6.3 It is not only explosion that fails in *FDE* (and *LP*). The disjunctive syllogism (*DS*) is also invalid: $p, \neg p \vee q \not\models_{FDE} q$. (Relational counter-model: $p\rho 1$ and $p\rho 0$, but just $q\rho 0$.)

8.6.4 This is a significant plus. We have seen the *DS* involved in two problematic arguments: the argument for the material conditional of 1.10, and the Lewis argument for explosion of 4.9.2. We can now see that these arguments do not work, and (at least one reason) why.[6]

8.6.5 Note, also, that the *DS* is just *modus ponens* for the material conditional. Since this fails, we have another argument against the adequacy of the material conditional to represent the real conditional.

8.6.6 The failure of the *DS* has also been thought by some to be a significant minus. First, it is claimed that the *DS* is intuitively valid. For if $\neg p \vee q$ is true, either $\neg p$ or q is true. But, the argument continues, if p is true, this rules out the truth of $\neg p$. Hence, it must be q that is true. But once one countenances the possibility of truth-value gluts, this argument is patently wrong. The truth of p does not rule out the truth of $\neg p$: both may hold. From this perspective, the inference is intuitively invalid.

[6] For good measure, the argument of 4.9.3 for the validity of the inference from A to $B \vee \neg B$ is also invalid in *FDE*, since $p \not\models (p \wedge q) \vee (p \wedge \neg q)$, as may be checked.

8.6.7 A more persuasive objection is that we frequently use, and seem to need to use, the *DS* to reason, and we get the right results. Thus, we know that you are either at home or at work. We ascertain that you are not at home, and infer that you are at work – which you are. If the *DS* is invalid, this form of reasoning would seem to be incorrect.

8.6.8 If the *DS* fails, then the inference about being at home or work is not deductively valid. It may be perfectly legitimate to use it, none the less. There are a number of ways of spelling this idea out in detail, but at the root of all of them is the observation that when the *DS* fails, it does so because the premise p involved is a truth-value glut. If the situation about which we are reasoning is consistent – as it is, presumably, in this case – the *DS* cannot lead us from truth to untruth. So it is legitimate to use it. This fact will underwrite its use in most situations we come across, since consistency is, arguably, the norm.

8.6.9 In the same way, if we have some collection, X, one cannot infer from the fact that some other collection, Y, is a proper subset of X that it is smaller.[7] But provided that we are working with collections that are finite, this inference is perfectly legitimate: violations can occur only when infinite sets are involved.

8.6.10 Thus, this objection can also be set aside.

D.S is OK as a default inference eg Tweetie is a bird, birds fly so tweetie can fly.

8.7 *Proofs of theorems

Penguins don't fly but OK ∵ things

8.7.1 The soundness and completeness proofs for the relational semantics for *FDE* modify those for classical logic (1.11).

seem consistent normally

---

[7] For example, the set of all natural numbers is the same size as the set of all even numbers, as can be seen by making the following correlation:

$$\begin{array}{cccccc} 0 & 1 & 2 & 3 & 4 & \cdots \\ \updownarrow & \updownarrow & \updownarrow & \updownarrow & \updownarrow & \\ 0 & 2 & 4 & 6 & 8 & \cdots \end{array}$$

Addition | $\frac{A}{A \vee B}$ $\neg A$ } DS B = explosion C. I. Lewis

8.7.2 DEFINITION: Let ρ be any relational interpretation. Let b be any branch of a tableau. ρ is *faithful* to b iff for every node, $A, +$, on the branch, $A\rho 1$, and for every node, $A, -$, on the branch, it is not the case that $A\rho 1$.

8.7.3 SOUNDNESS LEMMA: If ρ is faithful to a branch of a tableau, b, and a tableau rule is applied to b, then ρ is faithful to at least one of the branches generated.

Proof:

The proof is by a case-by-case examination of the tableau rules. First, the rules for $\wedge$. Suppose that we apply the rule for $A \wedge B, +$; then since ρ is faithful to the branch, $A \wedge B\rho 1$. Hence, $A\rho 1$ and $B\rho 1$. Hence, ρ is faithful to the extended branch. Next, suppose that we apply the rule for $A \wedge B, -$; then since ρ is faithful to the branch, it is not the case that $A \wedge B\rho 1$. Hence, either it is not the case that $A\rho 1$ or it is not the case that $B\rho 1$. Hence, ρ is faithful to either the left branch or the right branch. The argument for $\vee$ is similar. For the other rules, it is easy to check that in *FDE*, $\neg(A \wedge B)$ is true under an evaluation iff $\neg A \vee \neg B$ is true; the same goes for $\neg(A \vee B)$ and $\neg A \wedge \neg B$, and $\neg\neg A$ and A. (Details are left as an exercise.) The cases for the other rules follow simply from these facts.

8.7.4 SOUNDNESS THEOREM FOR *FDE*: For finite Σ, if $\Sigma \vdash A$ then $\Sigma \models A$.

Proof:

The proof follows from the Soundness Lemma in the usual way.

8.7.5 DEFINITION: Let b be an open branch of a tableau. The interpretation *induced* by b is the interpretation, ρ, such that for every propositional parameter, p:

$p\rho 1$ iff $p, +$ occurs on b

$p\rho 0$ iff $\neg p, +$ occurs on b

8.7.6 COMPLETENESS LEMMA: Let b be an open completed branch of a tableau. Let ρ be the interpretation induced by b. Then:

if $A, +$, occurs on b, then $A\rho 1$

if $A, -$ occurs on b, then it is not the case that $A\rho 1$

if $\neg A, +$, occurs on b, then $A\rho 0$

if $\neg A, -$ occurs on b, then it is not the case that $A\rho 0$

Proof:

The proof is by an induction on the complexity of A. If A is a propositional parameter, p: if $p, +$ occurs on b, then $p\rho 1$ by definition. If $p, -$ occurs on b, then $p, +$ does not occur on b, since it is open. Hence, by definition, it is not the case that $p\rho 1$. The cases for 0 are similar. For $B \wedge C$: if $B \wedge C, +$ occurs on b, then $B, +$ and $C, +$ occur on b. By induction hypothesis, $B\rho 1$ and $C\rho 1$. Hence, $B \wedge C\rho 1$ as required. The argument for $B \wedge C, -$ is similar. If $\neg(B \wedge C), +$ occurs on b, then by applications of a De Morgan rule and a disjunction rule, either $\neg B, +$ or $\neg C, +$ are on b. By induction hypothesis, either $B\rho 0$ or $C\rho 0$. In either case, $B \wedge C\rho 0$. The case for $\neg(B \wedge C), -$ is similar. The argument for $\vee$ is symmetric. This leaves negation. Suppose that $\neg B, +$ occurs on b. Since the result holds for B, $B\rho 0$. Hence, $\neg B\rho 1$, as required. Similarly for $\neg B, -$. If $\neg\neg B, +$ is on b, $B, +$ is on b. Hence, by induction hypothesis, $B\rho 1$, and so $\neg\neg B\rho 1$ as required. The case for $\neg\neg B, -$ is similar.

8.7.7 COMPLETENESS THEOREM FOR *FDE*: For finite Σ, if $\Sigma \models A$ then $\Sigma \vdash A$.

Proof:

The proof follows from the Completeness Lemma in the usual way.

8.7.8 THEOREM: The tableau rules of 8.4.8 are sound and complete for K_3.

Proof:

The soundness proof is exactly the same as that for *FDE*. (If the rules are sound with respect to *FDE* interpretations, they are sound with respect to K_3 interpretations, which are a special case.) The completeness proof is also essentially the same. All we have to check, in addition, is that the induced interpretation is a K_3 interpretation. It cannot be the case that $p\rho 1$ and $p\rho 0$, for then we would have both $p, +$ and $\neg p, +$ on b. But this is impossible, or b would be closed by the new closure rule.

8.7.9 THEOREM: The tableau rules of 8.4.11 are sound and complete for *LP*.

Proof:

The soundness proof is exactly the same as that for *FDE*. (If the rules are sound with respect to *FDE* interpretations, they are sound with respect to *LP* interpretations, which are a special case.) In the completeness proof, the induced interpretation is defined slightly differently, thus:

$p\rho 1$ iff $p, -$ is not on b

$p\rho 0$ iff $\neg p, -$ is not on b

Note that this makes ρ an *LP* interpretation. By the new closure rule, either $p, -$ or $\neg p, -$ is not on b. Hence, either $p\rho 1$ or $p\rho 0$. In the Completeness Lemma, the new definition makes the argument for the basis case different. If $p, +$ occurs on b, then $p, -$ does not occur on b, by the *FDE* closure rule, so $p\rho 1$. If $p, -$ occurs on b, then it is not the case that $p\rho 1$, by definition. The argument for $\neg p$ is the same. The rest of the the Completeness Lemma, and the proof of the Completeness Theorem itself, are as usual.

8.7.10 The soundness and completeness proofs for the $*$ semantics are variations on those for intuitionist tableaux (6.7). We start off, as usual, with a redefinition of faithfulness.

8.7.11 DEFINITION: Let $\mathcal{I} = \langle W, *, \nu \rangle$ be any Routley interpretation, and b be any branch of a tableau. Then $\mathcal{I}$ is faithful to b iff there is a map, f, from the natural numbers to W such that:

for every node $A, +x$ on b, A is true at $f(x)$ in $\mathcal{I}$,

for every node $A, -x$ on b, A is false at $f(x)$ in $\mathcal{I}$,

where $f(i^{\#})$ is, by definition, $f(i)^*$.

8.7.12 SOUNDNESS LEMMA: Let b be any branch of a tableau, and $\mathcal{I} = \langle W, *, \nu \rangle$ be any Routley interpretation. If $\mathcal{I}$ is faithful to b, and a tableau rule is applied, then it produces at least one extension, b', such that $\mathcal{I}$ is faithful to b'.

Proof:

Let f be a function which shows $\mathcal{I}$ to be faithful to b. The proof proceeds by a case-by-case consideration of the tableau rules. Suppose we apply the rule to $A \wedge B, +x$, then, by assumption $A \wedge B$ is true at $f(x)$. Thus, A and B are both true at $f(x)$, and so f shows that $\mathcal{I}$ is faithful to b'. If we apply the rule to $A \wedge B, -x$, then, by assumption, $A \wedge B$ is false at $f(x)$. Consequently, A is false at $f(x)$ or B is false at $f(x)$, i.e., f shows that $\mathcal{I}$ is faithful to either the left branch or the right branch. The arguments for the rules for disjunction are also similar. This leaves the rules for negation. Suppose that we apply the rule to $\neg A, +i$. Then, by assumption, $\neg A$ is true at $f(i)$. Hence, A is false at $f(i)^*$, as required. If we apply the rule to $\neg A, +i^{\#}$, then we know that $\neg A$ is true at $f(i)^*$. Hence, A is false at $f(i)$, as required. The argument for the other negation rule is similar.

8.7.13 SOUNDNESS THEOREM: For finite Σ, if $\Sigma \vdash A$ then $\Sigma \models A$.

Proof:

This follows from the Soundness Lemma in the usual way.

8.7.14 DEFINITION: Let b be an open branch of a tableau. The interpretation, $\mathcal{I} = \langle W, *, \nu \rangle$, induced by b, is defined as in 8.5.6. $W = \{w_0, w_{0^\#}\}$. $w_0^* = w_{0^\#}$, $(w_{0^\#})^* = w_0$. ν is such that:

$$\nu_{w_x}(p) = 1 \text{ if } p, +x \text{ is on } b$$

$$\nu_{w_x}(p) = 0 \text{ if } p, -x \text{ is on } b$$

(where x is either 0 or $0^\#$). Since the branch is open, this is well defined. Note also that, by the definition of $*$, $w_x^{**} = w_x$, i.e., the induced interpretation is a Routley interpretation.

8.7.15 COMPLETENESS LEMMA: Let b be any open completed branch of a tableau. Let $\mathcal{I} = \langle W, *, \nu \rangle$ be the interpretation induced by b. Then:

if $A, +x$ is on b, A is true at w_x

if $A, -x$ is on b, A is false at w_x

Proof:

This is proved by induction on the complexity of A. If A is atomic, the result is true by definition. If $B \wedge C, x$ occurs on b, then B, x and C, x occur on b. By induction hypothesis, B and C are true at w_x. Hence, $B \wedge C$ is true at w_x. If $B \wedge C, -x$ occurs on b, then either $B, -x$, or $C, -x$ occurs on b. By induction hypothesis, B is false at w_x or C is false at w_x. Hence, $B \wedge C$ is false at w_x as required. The cases for disjunction are similar. For negation: if $\neg B, +x$ occurs on b, then $B, -\overline{x}$ occurs on b. By induction hypothesis, B is false at $w_{\overline{x}}$; hence, by the definition of $*$, B is false at w_x^*, that is, $\neg B$ is true at w_x, as required. The other negation rule is the same.

8.7.16 COMPLETENESS THEOREM: For finite Σ, if $\Sigma \models A$ then $\Sigma \vdash A$.

Proof:

The result follows from the Completeness Lemma in the usual fashion.

8.7.17 THEOREM: If $\Sigma \models A$ under the relational semantics, $\Sigma \models A$ under the Routley semantics.

Proof:

We prove the contrapositive. Suppose that there is a Routley interpretation, $\langle W, *, \nu \rangle$, and a world $w \in W$, which makes all the members of Σ true and A false (i.e., untrue). Define a relational interpretation, ρ, by the following conditions:

$$p\rho 1 \text{ iff } \nu_w(p) = 1$$

$$p\rho 0 \text{ iff } \nu_{w^*}(p) = 0$$

If it can be shown that the displayed conditions hold for all formulas, then the result follows. This is proved by induction on the construction of A. If A is a propositional parameter, the result holds by definition. Suppose that the result holds for B and C. $B \wedge C\rho 1$ iff $B\rho 1$ and $C\rho 1$; iff $\nu_w(B) = 1$ and $\nu_w(C) = 1$, by induction hypothesis; iff $\nu_w(B \wedge C) = 1$. $B \wedge C\rho 0$ iff $B\rho 0$ or $C\rho 0$; iff $\nu_{w^*}(B) = 0$ or $\nu_{w^*}(C) = 0$, by induction hypothesis; iff $\nu_{w^*}(B \wedge C) = 0$, as required. The cases for disjunction are similar. $\neg A\rho 1$ iff $A\rho 0$; iff $\nu_{w^*}(A) = 0$, by induction hypothesis; iff $\nu_w(\neg A) = 1$. $\neg A\rho 0$ iff $A\rho 1$; iff $\nu_w(A) = 1$, by induction hypothesis; iff $\nu_{w^*}(\neg A) = 0$, as required.

8.7.18 THEOREM: If $\Sigma \models A$ under the Routley semantics, $\Sigma \models A$ under the relational semantics.

Proof:

We prove the contrapositive. Suppose that there is a relational interpretation, ρ, which makes all the members of Σ true and A untrue. Define a Routley interpretation, $\langle W, *, \nu \rangle$, where $W = \{a, b\}$, $a^* = b$ and $b^* = a$, and ν is defined by the conditions:

$$\nu_a(p) = 1 \text{ iff } p\rho 1$$

$$\nu_b(p) = 1 \text{ iff it is not the case that } p\rho 0$$

If it can be shown that the displayed condition holds for all formulas, then the result follows. This is proved by induction on the construction of A. If A is a propositional parameter, the result holds by definition. Suppose that the result holds for B and C. $\nu_a(B \wedge C) = 1$ iff $\nu_a(B) = 1$ and $\nu_a(C) = 1$; iff $B\rho 1$ and $C\rho 1$, by induction hypothesis; iff $B \wedge C\rho 1$. $\nu_b(B \wedge C) = 1$ iff $\nu_b(B) = 1$ and $\nu_b(C) = 1$; iff it is not the case that $B\rho 0$ and it is not the case that $C\rho 0$, by induction hypothesis; iff it is not the case that $B \wedge C\rho 0$. The cases for disjunction are similar. $\nu_a(\neg B) = 1$ iff $\nu_{a^*}(B) = 0$; iff $\nu_b(B) = 0$; iff $B\rho 0$, by induction hypothesis; iff $\neg B\rho 1$. $\nu_b(\neg B) = 1$ iff $\nu_{b^*}(B) = 0$; iff $\nu_a(B) = 0$; iff it is not the case that $B\rho 1$, by induction hypothesis; iff it is not the case that $\neg B\rho 0$.

8.8 History

The logic *FDE* is the core of a family of relevant logics (which we will meet in later chapters), developed by the US logicians Anderson and Belnap, starting at the end of the 1950s. (Strictly speaking, $A \models_{FDE} B$ iff $A \to B$ is valid in their system of first degree entailment.) See Anderson and Belnap (1975, esp. ch. 3). The relational semantics were discovered by Dunn in the 1960s as a spin-off from his algebraic semantics for *FDE* (on which, see Anderson and Belnap 1975, sect. 18). He published them only later, however, by which time they had been discovered by others too. The Routley semantics for *FDE* were first given by Richard Routley (later Sylvan) and Val Routley (later Plumwood) in Routley and Routley (1972). There are many paraconsistent logics. *FDE*, *LP* and the relevant logics that we will meet in later chapters constitute one kind. Paraconsistent logics of different kinds were developed by the Polish logician Jaśkowski in 1948 (see Jaśkowski 1969) and the Brazilian logician da Costa in the 1960s (see da Costa 1974). A general history and survey of paraconsistent logics can be found in Priest (2000a).

8.9 Further reading

On the various semantics for *FDE* covered in this chapter, see Priest (2000a, sects. 4.6 and 4.7); and for a much more detailed account, see

Routley, Plumwood, Meyer and Brady (1982, sects. 3.1 and 3.2). For the Routleys' own discussion of the meaning of the star operator, see Routley and Routley (1985). For a defence of the Routley star, see Restall (1999). Discussions of the disjunctive syllogism can be found in Burgess (1983), Mortensen (1983) and Priest (1987, ch. 8).

8.10 Problems

1. Using the tableau procedure of 8.3, determine whether or not the following are true in *FDE*. If the inference is invalid, specify a relational counter-model.

   (*a*) $p \wedge q \vdash p$

   (*b*) $p \vdash p \vee q$

   (*c*) $p \wedge (q \vee r) \vdash (p \wedge q) \vee (p \wedge r)$

   (*d*) $p \vee (q \wedge r) \vdash (p \vee q) \wedge (p \vee r)$

   (*e*) $p \vdash \neg\neg p$

   (*f*) $\neg\neg p \vdash p$

   (*g*) $(p \wedge q) \supset r \vdash (p \wedge \neg r) \supset \neg q$

   (*h*) $p \wedge \neg p \vdash p \vee \neg p$

   (*i*) $p \wedge \neg p \vdash q \vee \neg q$

   (*j*) $p \vee q \vdash p \wedge q$

   (*k*) $p, \neg(p \wedge \neg q) \vdash q$

   (*l*) $(p \wedge q) \supset r \vdash p \supset (\neg q \vee r)$

2. For the inferences of problem 1 that are invalid, determine which ones are valid in K_3 and *LP*, using the appropriate tableaux.

3. Check all the details omitted in 8.4.2.

4. By checking the truth tables of 8.4.2, note that if A and B have truth value n, then so do $A \vee B$, $A \wedge B$ and $\neg A$. Infer that if A is any formula all of whose propositional parameters take the value n, it, too, takes the value n. Hence infer that there is no formula, A, such that $\models_{FDE} A$.

5. Similarly, show that if A is a formula all of whose propositional parameters take the value b, then A takes the value b. Hence, show that if A and B have no propositional parameters in common, $A \not\models_{FDE} B$. (*Hint*: Assign all the parameters in A the value b, and all the parameters in B the value n.)

6. Repeat problem 1 with the $*$ semantics and tableaux of 8.5.

7. Using the $*$ semantics, show that if $A \models_{FDE} B$, then $\neg B \models_{FDE} \neg A$. (*Hint*: Assume that there is a counter-model for the consequent.) Why is this not obvious with the many-valued or the relational semantics? (Note that contraposition of this kind does not extend to multiple-premise inferences: $p, q \models_{FDE} p$, but $p, \neg p \not\models_{FDE} \neg q$.)

8. Under what conditions is it legitimate to employ a deductively invalid inference?

9. *Check the details omitted in 8.7.3.

9 Basic relevant logic

9.1 Introduction

9.1.1 In this chapter, we consider the addition of a conditional operator to *FDE*, and semantics for a basic relevant logic. The semantics has both a relational version and a $*$ version.

9.1.2 To obtain a relevant logic it is necessary to bring back the non-normal worlds of chapter 4. We also discuss further exactly what non-normal worlds are.

9.2 Adding →

9.2.1 *FDE* has no conditional operator. The material conditional, $A \supset B$, does not even satisfy *modus ponens*, as we saw in 8.6.5. In any case, as we have seen, using possible-world semantics provides a much more promising approach to the logic of conditional operators. Thus, an obvious thing to do is to build a possible-world semantics on top of the relational semantics of *FDE*.

9.2.2 To effect this, let us add a new binary connective, $\rightarrow$, to the language of *FDE* to represent the conditional. By analogy with $K\upsilon$, a relational interpretation for such a language is a pair $\langle W, \rho \rangle$, where W is a set of worlds, and for every $w \in W$, ρ_w is a relation between propositional parameters and the values 1 and 0.

9.2.3 The truth and falsity conditions for the extensional connectives ($\wedge$, $\vee$ and $\neg$) are exactly those of 8.2.6, except that they are relativised to each world, w. Thus, for example, the truth and falsity conditions for conjunction are:

$A \wedge B\rho_w 1$ iff $A\rho_w 1$ and $B\rho_w 1$

$A \wedge B\rho_w 0$ iff $A\rho_w 0$ or $B\rho_w 0$

9.2.4 For the truth and falsity conditions for $\rightarrow$, recall that the truth and falsity conditions for $\dashv$ in $K\upsilon$ come to this: $v_w(A \dashv B) = 1$ if for all w' such that $v_{w'}(A) = 1$, $v_{w'}(B) = 1$; and $v_w(A \dashv B) = 0$ if for some w', $v_{w'}(A) = 1$ and $v_{w'}(B) = 0$. Making the obvious generalisation:

$A \rightarrow B\rho_w 1$ iff for all $w' \in W$ such that $A\rho_{w'} 1$, $B\rho_{w'} 1$

$A \rightarrow B\rho_w 0$ iff for some $w' \in W$, $A\rho_{w'} 1$ and $B\rho_{w'} 0$

9.2.5 Semantic consequence is defined in terms of truth preservation at all worlds of all interpretations: *says which propos-*

$K\upsilon$ no accessibility relation *itional variables*

$\Sigma \vDash A$ iff for every interpretation, $\langle W, \rho \rangle$, and all $w \in W$: if *relate to*
$B\rho_w 1$ for all $B \in \Sigma$, $A\rho_w 1$ *what at each world.*

9.2.6 A natural name for this logic would be $K\upsilon_4$. We will call it, more *john* simply, K_4. *→ Satisfies modus ponens* *while behaving like a conditional — much like $\dashv$*

9.3 Tableaux for K_4 *4 valued logic in $K\upsilon$.*

9.3.1 A tableau system for K_4 can be obtained by modifying the system for *FDE* of 8.3, in the same way that the tableau system for classical propositional logic is modified in order to obtain one for $K\upsilon$ (3.5.3).

9.3.2 A node now has the form $A, +i$ or $A, -i$, where i is a natural number. The initial list comprises a node of the form $B, +0$ for every premise, B, and $A, -0$, where A is the conclusion. A branch closes if it contains pairs of the form $A, +i$ and $A, -i$.

Pluses + minuses say about holding or failing.

9.3.3 The rules for the extensional connectives are exactly the same as those of 8.3.4 for *FDE*, except that i is carried through each rule.

Can have a world where contradictions hold + excluded middle doesn't

Thus, for example, the rules for $\wedge$ are:

$$
\begin{array}{c}
A \wedge B, +i \\
\downarrow \\
A, +i \\
B, +i
\end{array}
\qquad
\begin{array}{ccc}
 & A \wedge B, -i & \\
\swarrow & & \searrow \\
A, -i & & B, -i
\end{array}
$$

9.3.4 The rules for the conditional are as follows:

every no. splits

$$
\begin{array}{ccc}
 & A \rightarrow B, +i & \\
\swarrow & & \searrow \\
A, -j & & B, +j
\end{array}
\qquad
\begin{array}{c}
A \rightarrow B, -i \\
\downarrow \\
A, +j \\
B, -j
\end{array}
$$

new no.

new no

$$
\begin{array}{c}
\neg(A \rightarrow B), +i \\
\downarrow \\
A, +j \\
\neg B, +j
\end{array}
\qquad
\begin{array}{ccc}
 & \neg(A \rightarrow B), -i & \\
\swarrow & & \searrow \\
A, -j & & \neg B, -j
\end{array}
$$

every no. splits

In the rules that split the branch, j is every number that occurs on the branch. In the other two rules, j is a new number.

Thus

9.3.5 Example: $A \rightarrow B, B \rightarrow C \vdash A \rightarrow C$:

$$
\begin{array}{ccccc}
 & & A \rightarrow B, +0 & & \\
 & & B \rightarrow C, +0 & & \\
 & & A \rightarrow C, -0 & & \\
 & & A, +1 & & \\
 & & C, -1 & & \\
 & \swarrow & & \searrow & \\
A, -1 & & & & B, +1 \\
\times & & & & \swarrow \searrow \\
 & & & B, -1 & C, +1 \\
 & & & \times & \times
\end{array}
$$

The fourth and fifth lines are obtained by applying the rule for untrue $\rightarrow$ to the third line. The two splits are then obtained by applying the rule for true $\rightarrow$ to the first and second lines respectively.

⊨B (suppose B is a logical truth i.e. true at any world. This leads to ⊨ A→B is a logical truth and ⊨ p→p ⇒ q → (p→B) *contraposition*

9.3.6 Example: $p \to q \nvdash \neg q \to \neg p$:

$$p \to q, +0$$
$$\neg q \to \neg p, -0$$
$$\neg q, +1$$
$$\neg p, -1$$

$$p, -0 \qquad\qquad q, +0$$

$$p, -1 \quad q, +1 \qquad p, -1 \quad q, +1$$

9.3.7 Counter-models are read off from open branches of tableaux in the natural way. There is a world w_i for each i on the branch; for propositional parameters, p, if p, $+i$ occurs on the tableau, set $p\rho_{w_i}1$; if $\neg p$, $+i$ occurs on the branch, set $p\rho w_i 0$. ρ relates no parameter to anything else. Thus, the counter-model defined by the leftmost branch of the tableau of 9.3.6 may be depicted thus:

$$
\begin{array}{ll}
w_0 & w_1 \\
-p & -p \\
 & -\neg p \\
 & +\neg q \\
\end{array}
$$

w0 +q⊘ w1 +q { ¬p.1 +¬q } pρo1

(+A indicates that A is true; $-A$ indicates that it is untrue.) At every world, p is untrue. Hence, $p \to q$ is true at w_0. But $\neg q$ is true at w_1, and $\neg p$ is not true there. Hence, $\neg q \to \neg p$ is not true at w_0.
1   4

9.3.8 The tableaux are sound and complete with respect to the semantics. This is proved in 9.8.1–9.8.7. *Can td. but P→P is a law of logic - need to say similar laws of logic may fail (logically impossible worlds where laws of logic fail. Conditionals must behave differently in these worlds.*

9.4 Non-normal worlds again

9.4.1 As is to be expected, and is not difficult to check, the following do not hold in K_4: $\models p \to (q \vee \neg q)$, $\models (p \wedge \neg p) \to q$. The conditional of K_4 does not, therefore, suffer from these paradoxes of the strict conditional.

9.4.2 But, as is also easy to see, it is still the case that if $\models A$ then $\models B \rightarrow A$. (If A is true at all worlds of all interpretations, it is true at all worlds of all interpretations where B is true).[1] In particular, for example, since $\models q \rightarrow q$, $\models p \rightarrow (q \rightarrow q)$.

9.4.3 This may well be felt to be unsatisfactory. $q \rightarrow q$ is an instance of the law of identity. Yet the following conditional would hardly seem to be true: if every instance of the law of identity failed, then, if cows were black, cows would be black. If every instance of the law failed, then it would precisely *not* be the case that if cows were black, they would be black.

9.4.4 Clearly, if we are thinking in terms of worlds, to do justice to this conditional, we need to countenance worlds where the laws of logic are different, and so where laws of logic, like the law of identity, may fail. This is exactly what non-normal worlds are, as we saw in 4.4.8. Hence, it is natural to augment the semantic machinery with appropriate non-normal worlds.

9.4.5 Now, it is exactly conditionals – which guarantee truth preservation from antecedent to consequent at all worlds – that express laws of logic. (A conditional such as 'If it does not rain, we will go to the cricket' does not express a law of logic, of course. But, as we noted in 5.2.4, such a conditional is not, strictly speaking, true.) Hence, we need to consider worlds where formulas of the form $A \rightarrow B$ may take values different from the values they may take in K_4.

9.4.6 How different? If logical laws may change, then there would seem to be no *a priori* bound on how this may happen. Hence, at a non-normal world $A \rightarrow B$ might be able to take on any sort of value.

9.4.7 A way of making these ideas precise is to take an interpretation to be a structure $\langle W, N, \rho\rangle$, where W is a set of worlds, $N \subseteq W$ is the

[1] The dual (if $\models \neg A$ then $\models A \rightarrow B$) does not hold. For example, even though $\models \neg\neg(p \rightarrow p)$, $\not\models \neg(p \rightarrow p) \rightarrow q$, as may be checked.

set of normal worlds (so that $W - N$ is the set of non-normal worlds), and ρ does two things. For every w, ρ_w is a relation between propositional parameters and the truth values 1 and 0, in the usual way. But also, for every *non-normal* world, w, ρ_w is a relation between formulas of the form $A \rightarrow B$ and truth values.

9.4.8 The truth conditions for all the connectives are exactly as in K_4 (9.2.4), except that at non-normal worlds, the truth values of $\rightarrow$ formulas are not determined recursively: they are already determined by ρ.

9.4.9 Validity is defined in terms of truth preservation at all normal worlds of all interpretations, as in 4.2.5. (After all, we are interested in what follows from what in the worlds where logic is *not* different.) Call this logic N_4.

9.5 Tableaux for N_4

9.5.1 Tableaux for N_4 can be obtained by modifying those for K_4. Specifically, the rules are exactly the same as those for K_4, except that the rules for $\rightarrow$ apply at world 0 only. (It turns out that we never need to assume that there is more than one normal world in a counter-model.)

9.5.2 For example: $\nvdash \neg(p \rightarrow p) \rightarrow (q \rightarrow q)$:

$$\neg(p \rightarrow p) \rightarrow (q \rightarrow q), -0$$
$$\neg(p \rightarrow p), +1$$
$$(q \rightarrow q), -1$$

The tableau finishes there! (In K_4 an application of the rule for untrue $\rightarrow$ to the last line would immediately close it.)

9.5.3 We read off a counter-model from an open branch exactly as for K_4 (9.3.7), except that the only normal world is w_0 – all others are non-normal – and the recipe for determining ρ is applied to propositional parameters at all worlds, and to any formula of the form e tells of truth values of every conditionals at non-normal worlds (not at normal worlds

∴ they're taken care of) and truth values of propositional parameters.

$A \to B$ at *non-normal* worlds. Thus, in the tableau of the previous paragraph, $W = \{w_0, w_1\}$; $N = \{w_0\}$ and $p \to p\rho_{w_1}0$, there being no other facts about ρ. Since $\neg(p \to p)$ is true at w_1, and $q \to q$ is not true at w_1, $\neg(p \to p) \to (q \to q)$ is not true at w_0.

Validity truth preservation just in normal worlds.

9.5.4 Since interpretations for K_4 are special cases of interpretations for N_4 (namely, when $W - N = \phi$), N_4 is a sub-logic of K_4, but not the other way around, as this example shows.

Like non-normal modal logic but 4 valued.

9.5.5 The tableaux for N_4 are sound and complete with respect to the semantics. This is proved in 9.8.8–9.8.9.

Truth value of A→B in non-normal worlds can be anything you like: don't look at their parts, but their whole.

9.6 Star again

9.6.1 Before we move on to consider some of the implications of the preceding, let us pause to note that exactly the same sorts of construction can be performed with respect to the $*$ semantics.

9.6.2 Let $\langle W, *, \nu\rangle$ be any Routley interpretation (8.5.3). This becomes an interpretation for the augmented language when we add the following truth condition for $\to$:

$$\nu_w(A \to B) = 1 \text{ iff for all } w' \in W \text{ such that } \nu_{w'}(A) = 1,\ \nu_{w'}(B) = 1$$

Call the logic that this generates, K_*.

9.6.3 Tableaux for K_* can be obtained by adding to the rules of 8.5.4, these rules for $\to$:

$$\begin{array}{ccc} & A \to B, +x & \\ \swarrow & & \searrow \\ A, -y & & B, +y \end{array} \qquad \begin{array}{c} A \to B, -x \\ \downarrow \\ A, +j \\ B, -j \end{array}$$

where x is either i or $i^{\#}$; y is anything of the form j or $j^{\#}$, where one or other (or both) of these is on the branch; and in the second rule, j must be new. (Note that we do not need rules for negated $\to$. The $*$ rules take care of that.)

9.6.4 Here is a tableau to show that $p \wedge \neg q \nvdash \neg(p \rightarrow q)$:

$$
\begin{array}{c}
p \wedge \neg q, +0 \\
\neg(p \rightarrow q), -0 \\
p, +0 \\
\neg q, +0 \\
q, -0^{\#} \\
p \rightarrow q, +0^{\#} \\
\swarrow \qquad \searrow \\
\begin{array}{cc}
p, -0 & q, +0 \\
\times & \swarrow \searrow \\
 & \begin{array}{cc} p, -0^{\#} & q, +0^{\#} \\ & \times \end{array}
\end{array}
\end{array}
$$

The splits are caused by applying the rule for true $\rightarrow$ to the line immediately before the first split. There are two worlds, 0 and $0^{\#}$, so the rule has to be applied to both of them.

9.6.5 Counter-models are read off as is done without $\rightarrow$ (8.5.6), except that there may be more than two worlds now. Thus, W is the set of worlds which contains w_i and $w_{i^{\#}}$ for every i that occurs on the branch. For all i, $w_i^* = w_{i^{\#}}$ and $w_{i^{\#}}^* = w_i$. v is such that if $p, +x$ occurs on the branch, $v_x(p) = 1$, and if $p, -x$ occurs on the branch, $v_x(p) = 0$. Thus, the counter-model from the open branch of the tableau of 9.6.4 may be depicted thus:

$$
\begin{array}{cc}
+p & -p \\
+q & -q \\
w_0 & w_0^*
\end{array}
$$

Since q is not true at w_0^*, $\neg q$ is true at w_0, as, then, is $p \wedge \neg q$. But at every world where p is true, q is true. Hence, $p \rightarrow q$ is true at w_0^*, and so $\neg(p \rightarrow q)$ is false (untrue) at w_0.

9.6.6 As in K_4, in K_*, $\models p \rightarrow (q \rightarrow q)$, as may easily be checked. To change this, we may add non-normal worlds in the same way. An interpretation is a structure $\langle W, N, *, v\rangle$, where $N \subseteq W$; for all

$w \in W$, $w^{**} = w$; v assigns a truth value to every parameter at every world, and to every formula of the form $A \rightarrow B$ at every non-normal world. The truth conditions are exactly the same as for K_*, except that the truth conditions for $\rightarrow$ apply only at normal worlds; at non-normal worlds, they are already given by v. Validity is defined in terms of truth preservation at normal worlds. Call this logic N_*.

9.6.7 The tableaux for N_* are the same as those for K_*, except that the rules for $\rightarrow$ (9.6.3) are applied only at 0. Counter-models are also read off in the same way. Again, only w_0 is normal.

9.6.8 Soundness and completeness for the tableaux for K_* and N_* are proved in 9.8.10–9.8.13.

9.6.9 It should be noted that although the relational semantics and the $*$ semantics are equivalent for *FDE*, as we saw in 8.5.8, this equivalence no longer obtains once we add $\rightarrow$. For a start, the $*$ systems (K and N) validate contraposition: $p \rightarrow q \models \neg q \rightarrow \neg p$. (Details are left as an exercise.) The relational systems do not. (We saw that this is not valid in K_4, and *a fortiori* N_4, in 9.3.6.)[2]

9.6.10 More fundamentally, because of the falsity conditions for $\rightarrow$, the relation semantics (normal and non-normal) verify $p \wedge \neg q \models \neg(p \rightarrow q)$. (Details are left as an exercise.) But this inference fails in K_* (and *a fortiori* N_*), as we saw in 9.6.4.

[2] This may be changed by redefining the truth conditions of $\rightarrow$ (at normal worlds) in the relational semantics, as:

$$A \rightarrow B\rho_w 1 \text{ iff for all } w' \in W \text{ (if } A\rho_{w'} 1 \text{ then } B\rho_{w'} 1, \text{and if } B\rho_{w'} 0 \text{ then } A\rho_{w'} 0).$$

Or, more simply, and equivalently, defining a new conditional $A \Rightarrow B$ as $(A \rightarrow B) \wedge (\neg B \rightarrow \neg A)$, and working with this.

9.7 Impossible worlds and relevant logic

9.7.1 Let us finish with some comments on the import of the previous constructions.

9.7.2 As we saw (9.4.4–9.4.6), non-normal worlds of the kind we have employed in this chapter are worlds where the laws of logic are different. Let us call these 'logically impossible worlds'.

9.7.3 There seems to be no reason why there should not be logically impossible worlds, in whatever sense there are possible worlds. Physically impossible worlds, where the laws of physics are different, are entirely routine (see 3.6.5). And just as there are worlds where the laws of physics are different, there must be worlds where the laws of logic are different.

9.7.4 After all, we seem to envisage just such worlds when we evaluate conditionals such as 'if intuitionist logic were correct, the law of double negation would fail' (true), 'if intuitionist logic were correct, the law of identity would fail' (false). Even if one is a modal realist (2.6), why should there not be such worlds?

9.7.5 One might suggest that there can be no worlds at which logical laws fail: by definition, logical laws hold at *all* possible worlds. Maybe so. But it is precisely *impossible* worlds that we are dealing with here. Or one might say: take a world in which it is a logical law that $A \rightarrow (B \wedge \neg B)$ and in which A is also true. It would follow that $B \wedge \neg B$ is true at that world, which cannot be the case. This argument is hardly likely to persuade someone who accepts the possibility of truth-value gluts. But in any case, it is fallacious. For who says that *modus ponens* holds at that world? In the semantics we have looked at, it is entirely possible to have both A and $A \rightarrow C$ holding at a non-normal world, without C holding there.

9.7.6 Note that one might take 'logically impossible world' to mean something other than 'world where the laws of logic are different'. One might equally take it to mean 'world where the logically impossible happens'. This need not be the same thing. If this is not clear, just consider physically impossible worlds. The fact that the laws of physics are different does not necessarily mean that physically impossible things happen there (though the converse is true). For example, even if the laws of physics were to permit things to accelerate past the speed of light, it does not follow that anything actually would. Things at that world might be accelerating very slowly, and the world might not last long enough for any of them to reach super-luminal speeds.

9.7.7 But logically impossible worlds, in the sense that these occur in the semantics we have been looking at, may be logically impossible in the second sense as well. For example, there are, as has just been noted, worlds where A and $A \to C$ are true, but C is not.[3]

9.7.8 A propositional logic is *relevant* iff whenever $A \to B$ is logically valid, A and B have a propositional parameter in common. Obviously, any conditional that suffers from paradoxes of implication (material implication, strict implication, the intuitionist conditional) is not relevant. Neither are K_4 and K_* relevant, as we have seen (9.4.2 and 9.6.6).

9.7.9 But N_4 is a relevant logic. This can be seen by modifying the argument of 8.10, problem 5. Suppose that A and B share no propositional parameters, and consider an interpretation $\langle W, N, \rho \rangle$, where $W = \{w_0, w_1\}$; $N = \{w_0\}$; if D is a propositional parameter or a conditional in A, $D\rho_{w_1}1$ and $D\rho_{w_1}0$; if D is a propositional parameter or a conditional in B, neither $D\rho_{w_1}1$ nor $D\rho_{w_1}0$. (D cannot occur in both, since A and B have no parameters in common.) It is easy to check that $A\rho_{w_1}1$ and $A\rho_{w_1}0$, but neither $B\rho_{w_1}1$ nor $B\rho_{w_1}0$.[4] In particular, A is true at w_1 and B is not. Hence $A \to B$ is not true at w_0.

---

[3] There are no worlds at which $A \wedge B$ is true, but A is not, or at which $\neg\neg A$ is true, but A is not. But it is conditionals that express the laws of logic, not conjunctions or negations. That is why it is their behaviour (and only theirs) that changes at non-normal worlds.

[4] *Proof*: For the first, what we show is that every formula made up from the propositional parameters occurring in A – and so, in particular, A – the result holds. Similarly for B. This is proved by induction on the construction of sentences, but an induction slightly different from the normal kind. Note that every formula can be built up from

9.7.10 A similar argument shows that N_* is a relevant logic. Take a $*$ interpretation $\langle W, N, *, \nu\rangle$, where $W = \{w_0, w_1, w_2\}$; $N = \{w_0\}$, $w_0^* = w_0$, $w_1^* = w_2$, $w_2^* = w_1$; for every propositional parameter or conditional, D, in A, $\nu_{w_1}(D) = 1$ and $\nu_{w_2}(D) = 0$; for every propositional parameter or conditional, D, in B, $\nu_{w_1}(D) = 0$ and $\nu_{w_2}(D) = 1$. One can check that $\nu_{w_1}(A) = 1$, and $\nu_{w_1}(B) = 0$. Hence $\nu_{w_0}(A \to B) = 0$. Details are left as an exercise.

9.7.11 It is a natural thought that for a conditional to be true there must be some connection between its antecedent and consequent. It was precisely this idea that led to the development of relevant logic. A sensible notion of connection is not so easy to spell out, however (as we saw, in effect, in 4.9.2). The parameter-sharing condition of 9.7.8 gives some content to the idea.

9.7.12 There are some approaches to relevant logic where a conditional is taken to be valid iff it is classically valid *and* satisfies some extra constraint, for example that antecedent and consequent share a parameter. (These are sometimes called *filter logics*, since the extra constraint filters out 'undesirables'.) Characteristically, such approaches give rise to relevant logics of a kind different from those considered in this book. For example, if the parameter-sharing filter is used, $(p \wedge (\neg p \vee q)) \to q$ is valid, which it is not in the relevant logics of this, and subsequent, chapters. Typically (though not invariably), a feature of filter logics is the failure of the principle of transitivity: if $A \models B$ and $B \models C$ then $A \models C$ (thus breaking the argument of 4.9.2).

9.7.13 In the present approach, relevance is not some extra condition imposed *on top* of classical validity. Rather, relevance, in the form of

Footnote 4 (continued)
conditionals and parameters using the extensional connectives. Hence, the result may be proved by induction, with parameters and conditionals as the basis case, and induction cases for the extensional connectives. The basis case is true by definition. The induction cases are as in the notes to 8.4.6 and 8.4.9.

parameter sharing, falls out of something more fundamental, namely the taking into account of a suitably wide range of situations.

9.7.14 One final comment: one might hold that truth – real truth, not just truth in some world – has some special properties; that unlike truth in an arbitrary world, truth itself can have no gaps or gluts. To accommodate this view, one could take an interpretation to include a distinguished normal world, @ (for actuality), such that truth (*simpliciter*) is truth at @. Validity would then be defined as truth preservation at @ in all interpretations.[5] The special properties of truth would be reflected in semantic constraints on @. Thus, if it be held that there are no truth-value gluts in @, one would impose the constraint that $\rho_@$ satisfy the condition *Exclusion* of 8.4.6. If it be held that there are no truth-value gaps in @, then one would impose the constraint that $\rho_@$ satisfy the condition *Exhaustion* of 8.4.9.[6] Or in a $*$ interpretation, one might require that $w_@ = w^*_@$, which rules out gaps and gluts. But from the present perspectives, these conditions would require justification by some novel considerations.

9.8 *Proofs of theorems

9.8.1 Soundness and completeness proofs for K_4 and N_4 can be obtained by modifying the proofs for *FDE*, as the proofs for classical

[5] One could, in fact, set up all the possible-world semantics that we have had till now in this way. But since these semantics contain nothing to distinguish @ from any other normal world, this would have had no effect on validity.

[6] Strictly speaking, these conditions are not sufficient. To rule out truth-value gluts and gaps with formulas containing $\rightarrow$s, we need to make another change as well. Specifically, to rule out truth-value gaps, the falsity conditions for $A \rightarrow B$ at @ have to read:

$A \rightarrow B\rho_@ 0$ iff (for some w', $A\rho_{w'}1$ and $B\rho_{w'}0$) or (it is not the case that $A \rightarrow B\rho_w 1$)

and to rule out truth-value gluts, they have to read:

$A \rightarrow B\rho_@ 0$ iff (for some w', $A\rho_{w'}1$ and $B\rho_{w'}0$) and (it is not the case that $A \rightarrow B\rho_w 1$).

logic were modified for normal and non-normal logics, respectively. Let us start with K_4.

9.8.2 DEFINITION: Let $\mathcal{I} = \langle \mathcal{W}, \rho \rangle$ be any relational interpretation, and b be any branch of a tableau. Then $\mathcal{I}$ is *faithful* to b iff there is a map, f, from the natural numbers to W such that:

for every node $A, +i$ on b, $A\rho_{f(i)}1$ in $\mathcal{I}$.

for every node $A, -i$ on b, it is not the case that $A\rho_{f(i)}1$ in $\mathcal{I}$.

9.8.3 SOUNDNESS LEMMA: Let b be any branch of a tableau, and $\mathcal{I} = \langle W, \rho \rangle$ be any K_4 interpretation. If $\mathcal{I}$ is faithful to b, and a tableau rule is applied to it, then it produces at least one extension, b', such that $\mathcal{I}$ is faithful to b'.

Proof:

Let f be a function which shows $\mathcal{I}$ to be faithful to b. The proof proceeds by a case-by-case consideration of the tableau rules. The cases for the extensional rules are essentially as for *FDE* (8.7.3). We simply rewrite ρ as $\rho_{f(i)}$. For the rules for $\rightarrow$: suppose that we apply the rule to $A \rightarrow B, +i$. Then by assumption, $A \rightarrow B$ is true at $f(i)$. Hence, for any j on the branch, either A is not true at $f(j)$ or B is true at $f(j)$. In the first case, f shows $\mathcal{I}$ to be faithful to the lefthand branch; in the second, it shows $\mathcal{I}$ to be faithful to the righthand branch. Next, suppose that we apply the rule to $A \rightarrow B, -i$. Then $A \rightarrow B$ is not true at $f(i)$. Hence, there is some w such that A is true at w and B is not. Let f' be the same as f, except that $f'(j) = w$. Then f' shows $\mathcal{I}$ to be faithful to the extended branch, as usual. The cases for $\neg(A \rightarrow B), +$ and $\neg(A \rightarrow B), -$ are similar.

9.8.4 SOUNDNESS THEOREM FOR K_4: For finite Σ, if $\Sigma \vdash A$ then $\Sigma \models A$.

Proof:

This follows from the Soundness Lemma in the usual way.

9.8.5 DEFINITION: Let b be an open branch of a tableau. The interpretation, $\mathcal{I} = \langle W, \rho \rangle$, induced by b, is defined as in 9.3.7. $W = \{w_i;\ i$ occurs on $b\}$. For every parameter, p:

$p\rho_{w_i}1$ iff $p, +i$ occurs on b

$p\rho_{w_i}0$ iff $\neg p, +i$ occurs on b

9.8.6 COMPLETENESS LEMMA: Let b be any open completed branch of a tableau. Let $\mathcal{I} = \langle W, \rho \rangle$ be the interpretation induced by b. Then:

if $A, +i$ is on b, then A is true at w_i

if $A, -i$ is on b, then it is not the case that A is true at w_i

if $\neg A, +i$ is on b, then A is false at w_i

if $\neg A, -i$ is on b, then it is not the case that A is false at w_i

Proof:

The proof is by recursion on the complexity of A. If A is atomic, the result is true by definition, and the fact that b is open. The cases for the extensional connectives are essentially the same as for *FDE* (8.7.6). We merely rewrite ρ as ρ_{w_i}. This leaves the cases for $\rightarrow$. Suppose that $B \rightarrow C, +i$ is on b. Then for all j, either $B, -j$ or $C, +j$ is on b. By induction hypothesis, either B is not true at w_j or C is true at w_j. Thus, $B \rightarrow C$ is true at w_i. Suppose that $B \rightarrow C, -i$ is on b. Then there is a j, such that $B, +j$ and $C, -j$ are on b. By induction hypothesis, B is true at w_j and C is not true at w_j. Thus, $B \rightarrow C$ is not true at w_i. The cases for negated $\rightarrow$ are similar.

9.8.7 COMPLETENESS THEOREM FOR K_4: For finite Σ, if $\Sigma \models A$ then $\Sigma \vdash A$.

Proof:

The result follows from the Completeness Lemma in the usual fashion.

9.8.8 SOUNDNESS THEOREM FOR N_4: The tableau system for N_4 is sound with respect to its semantics.

Proof:

The proof is exactly the same as for K_4, except that in the definition of faithfulness, we add the clause: $f(0) \in N$. In the Soundness Lemma, the rules for $\rightarrow$ are applied only at $f(0)$; and this is normal.

9.8.9 COMPLETENESS THEOREM FOR N_4: The tableau system for N_4 is complete with respect to its semantics.

Proof:

The induced interpretation is now defined as follows (as in 9.5.3). $W = \{w_i; i \text{ occurs on } b\}$. $N = \{w_0\}$. For every parameter, p:

$p\rho_{w_i}1$ iff $p, +i$ occurs on b

$p\rho_{w_i}0$ iff $\neg p, +i$ occurs on b

and for every formula $A \rightarrow B$, and $i > 0$:

$A \rightarrow B\rho_{w_i}1$ iff $A \rightarrow B, +i$ occurs on b

$A \rightarrow B\rho_{w_i}0$ iff $\neg(A \rightarrow B), +i$ occurs on b

The proof of the Completeness Theorem is then as for K_4. Only the induction cases for $\rightarrow$ in the Completeness Lemma are different. In these, if w_i is normal, the arguments are exactly the same as before. If w_i is non-normal, the result holds simply by definition.

9.8.10 Soundness and completeness proofs for K_* and N_* can be obtained by modifying those for the $*$ semantics for *FDE* (8.7.10–8.7.16).

9.8.11 SOUNDNESS THEOREM: K_* is sound with respect to its semantics.

Proof:

The proof is exactly the same as that for *FDE*. All we need to check, in addition, are the new rules for $\rightarrow$ in the Soundness

Lemma. So suppose that we apply the rule to $A \rightarrow B, +x$, then, by assumption, $A \rightarrow B$ is true at some world. Hence, for any y, either A is not true at $f(y)$, in which case f shows $\mathcal{I}$ to be faithful to the left branch, or B is true at $f(y)$, in which case f shows $\mathcal{I}$ to be faithful to the right branch. If we apply the rule to $A \rightarrow B, -x$, then $A \rightarrow B$ is false at some world. Hence, there is a world, w, at which A is true and B is false. Consider an f' which is the same as f, except that $f'(j) = w$. Then the result follows as usual.

9.8.12 COMPLETENESS THEOREM: K_* is complete with respect to its semantics.

Proof:

The interpretation induced by an open branch is defined in exactly the same way as in *FDE* (8.7.14), except that there may be more than two worlds. Thus, $W = \{w_i; i \text{ occurs on } b\} \cup \{w_i^*; i \text{ occurs on } b\}$, and for all i, $w_i^* = w_{i\#}$ and $w_{i\#}^* = w_i$. The only things that need additional checking are the cases for $\rightarrow$ in the Completeness Lemma. So suppose that $A \rightarrow B, +x$ occurs on b; then for all y either $A, -y$ or $B, +y$ occurs on b. By induction hypothesis and the definition of W, for all $w \in W$, either A is false at w or B is true at w. Hence $A \rightarrow B$ is true at w_x. Suppose, on the other hand, that $A \rightarrow B, -x$ occurs on b. Then for some j, $A, +j$ and $B, -j$ occur on b. By induction hypothesis, A is true at w_j and B is false at w_j. Hence, $A \rightarrow B$ is false at w_x, as required. The rest of the proof is the same.

9.8.13 SOUNDNESS AND COMPLETENESS FOR N_*: N_* is sound and complete with respect to its tableaux.

Proof:

The proof modifies the proof for K_*, as that for N_4 modifies that for K_4. Details are left as an exercise.

9.9 History

The terminology of degrees (as in 'first degree entailment') comes from Anderson and Belnap (1975, p. 150). The degree of a formula is the largest number of nestings of $\rightarrow$ within it. So the logics of this chapter have formulas of arbitrarily high degree. These logics are not to be found in the literature, though a version of K_4 occurs in Priest (1987, ch. 5). The idea of giving conditionals arbitrary truth values at some worlds was first used in Routley and Loparić (1978) in connection with a certain family of paraconsistent logics. The analysis of these worlds as worlds where logic is different comes from Priest (1992). The notion of an impossible world, as such, started to appear in the literature in the late 1980s. On filter logics, see Priest (2000a, sects. 4.1 and 5.1).

9.10 Further reading

Discussions of impossible worlds can be found in Yagisawa (1988), Stalnaker (1996) and all the papers in Priest (1997b). The editor's introduction to the third of these is a useful orientation. An argument that truth proper has no gaps is mounted in Priest (1987, ch. 4).

9.11 Problems

1. Complete the details left as exercises in 9.4.1, 9.4.2, 9.6.6, 9.6.9, 9.6.10 and 9.7.10.

2. Show the following in K_4 (where $A \leftrightarrow B$ is $(A \rightarrow B) \wedge (B \rightarrow A)$): try ∧ + not ∧ splitting.

   (*a*) $\vdash A \rightarrow A$

   (*b*) $\vdash A \leftrightarrow \neg\neg A$

   (*c*) $\vdash (A \wedge B) \rightarrow A$

   (*d*) $\vdash A \rightarrow (A \vee B)$

(*e*) $\vdash (A \wedge (B \vee C)) \leftrightarrow ((A \wedge B) \vee (A \wedge C))$

(*f*) $A \rightarrow B, A \rightarrow C \vdash A \rightarrow (B \wedge C)$

(*g*) $A \rightarrow C, B \rightarrow C \vdash (A \vee B) \rightarrow C$

(*h*) $A \rightarrow C \vdash (A \wedge B) \rightarrow C$

(*i*) $\vdash ((A \rightarrow B) \wedge (A \rightarrow C)) \rightarrow (A \rightarrow (B \wedge C))$

(*j*) $\vdash ((A \rightarrow C) \wedge (B \rightarrow C)) \rightarrow ((A \vee B) \rightarrow C)$

(*k*) $A \rightarrow B \vdash (B \rightarrow C) \rightarrow (A \rightarrow C)$

(*l*) $A \rightarrow B \vdash (C \rightarrow A) \rightarrow (C \rightarrow B)$

(*m*) $A \rightarrow B, B \rightarrow C \vdash A \rightarrow C$

3. Show that the following are not true in K_4, and specify a counter-model.

   (*a*) $\vdash (p \wedge (\neg p \vee q)) \rightarrow q$

   (*b*) $(p \wedge q) \rightarrow r \vdash p \rightarrow (\neg q \vee r)$

   (*c*) $\vdash p \rightarrow (q \vee \neg q)$

   (*d*) $\vdash (p \wedge \neg p) \rightarrow q$

   (*e*) $\vdash (p \rightarrow q) \rightarrow (\neg q \rightarrow \neg p)$

4. Determine which of the inferences in problem 2 are valid in N_4. Where invalid, specify a counter-model.

5. Repeat problems 2–4 with K_* and N_*.

6. In the semantics for N_4 and N_*, there may be many normal worlds, but the tableaux show us that it suffices to suppose that there is only one normal world. Why is this?

7. What reasons might there be against supposing that there are logically impossible worlds?

8. Suppose that we add the modal operators $\Box$ and $\Diamond$ to the language. What are the most appropriate truth/falsity conditions for them in the non-normal semantics, and why? (Should the truth of $\Box A$ at a normal world depend on the truth of A at all worlds, or just at normal worlds? What truth conditions are appropriate at non-normal worlds? How does this bear on the question of relevance?)

9. * Fill in the details of 9.8.13.

10. * Design tableaux for the systems of 9.7.14, and prove them sound and complete.

10 Mainstream relevant logics

10.1 Introduction

10.1.1 In this chapter we look at logics in the family of mainstream relevant logics. These are obtained by employing a ternary relation to formulate the truth conditions of $\rightarrow$. In the most basic logic, there are no constraints on the relation. Stronger logics are obtained by adding constraints.

10.1.2 We also see how these semantics can be combined with the semantics of conditional logics of chapter 5 to give an account of *ceteris paribus* enthymemes.

10.2 The logic *B*

10.2.1 N_4 and N_* are relevant logics, but, as relevant logics go, they are relatively weak. Many proponents of relevant logic have thought that the relevant logics of the last chapter are too weak, on the ground that there are intuitively correct principles concerning the conditional that they do not validate. A way to accommodate such principles within a possible-world semantics is to use a relation on worlds to give the truth conditions of conditionals at non-normal worlds. Unlike the binary relation of modal logic, xRy, though, this relation is a ternary, that is, three-place, relation, $Rxyz$.[1]

[1] Using a binary relation would produce irrelevance, since $p \rightarrow p$ would be true at all worlds, and hence, $q \rightarrow (p \rightarrow p)$ would be logically valid.

10.2.2 Intuitively, the ternary relation $Rxyz$ means something like: for all A and B, if $A \to B$ is true at x, and A is true at y, then B is true at z. What philosophical sense to make of this, we will come back to later.

10.2.3 The technique can be applied to both the relational semantics and the $*$ semantics. As we noted in 9.6.9 and 9.6.10, these semantics diverge once we add $\to$ to the language. Though the ternary relation *relational* semantics are perfectly good, it is, as a matter of historical fact, the logics with the ternary relation $*$ semantics that occur in the literature. Hence, we look only at those.

10.2.4 A ternary ($*$) interpretation is a structure $\langle W, N, R, *, \nu \rangle$, where W, N, $*$ and ν are as in the semantics for N_* (9.6.6), and R is any ternary relation on worlds. (So, technically, $R \subseteq W \times W \times W$.)

10.2.5 With one exception, the truth conditions for all connectives are as for N_*. In particular, at normal worlds, the truth conditions for $\to$ are:

$$\nu_w(A \to B) = 1 \text{ iff for all } x \in W \text{ such that } \nu_x(A) = 1, \nu_x(B) = 1$$

The exception is that if w is a non-normal world:

$$\nu_w(A \to B) = 1 \text{ iff for all } x, y \in W \text{ such that } Rwxy, \text{ if } \nu_x(A) = 1, \text{ then } \nu_y(B) = 1$$

10.2.6 Validity is defined as truth preservation over all normal worlds, as in N_*.

10.2.7 The logic generated in this way is usually called B (for basic).[2] Clearly, B is a sub-logic of K_* (since any K_* interpretation is a B interpretation, with $W - N = \phi$). Moreover, any B interpretation, $\mathcal{I}$, is equivalent to an N_* interpretation. We just take that N_* interpretation which is the same as $\mathcal{I}$, except that it assigns to each conditional at each non-normal world, w, whatever value it has at w in $\mathcal{I}$. Hence, N_* is a sub-logic of B.

[2] We continue to use B as a letter for formulas, too. Context will disambiguate.

10.2.8 The bipartite truth conditions of $\rightarrow$ can be simplified if one thinks of R as *defined* at normal worlds. Specifically, if w is normal, we specify R by the following condition:

$Rwxy$ iff $x = y$

Call this the *normality condition*. If we define R at normal worlds in this way, we may take the ternary truth conditions to govern conditionals at *all* worlds. For, given this condition, the ternary truth conditions:

for all $x, y \in W$ such that $Rwxy$, if $\nu_x(A) = 1$, then $\nu_y(B) = 1$

become:

for all $x, y \in W$ such that $x = y$, if $\nu_x(A) = 1$, then $\nu_y(B) = 1$

And given the standard properties of $=$, this is logically equivalent to:

for all $x \in W$ such that $\nu_x(A) = 1$, $\nu_x(B) = 1$

which gives the standard truth conditions of $\rightarrow$ at normal worlds. We adopt this simplification in what follows.

10.2.9 Notice that the normality condition falls apart into two halves. From left to right:

if $Rwxy$ then $x = y$

and from right to left, since $x = x$:

$Rwxx$.

10.3 Tableaux for *B*

10.3.1 Tableaux for B are the same as those for N_* (9.6.7), except that nodes may now be of the form $A, +x$, or $A, -x$ (where x is i or $i^{\#}$), or of the form $rxyz$; the tableaux rules for the conditional are:

$$
\begin{array}{ccc}
\begin{array}{c}
A \to B, +x \\
rxyz \\
\swarrow \quad \searrow \\
A, -y \quad B, +z
\end{array}
& \qquad &
\begin{array}{c}
A \to B, -x \\
\downarrow \\
rxjk \\
A, +j \\
B, -k
\end{array}
\end{array}
$$

In the first rule, y and z are anything of the form j or $j^{\#}$, where either of these occurs on the branch. In the second rule, j and k are new. Moreover, in this, if x is 0, j and k must be the same, as required by one half of the normality condition. For the other half, we need one further rule:

$$
\begin{array}{c}
. \\
\downarrow \\
r0xx
\end{array}
$$

where x is either j or $j^{\#}$, where either of these occurs on the branch – and, as usual, $r0xx$ is not already on the branch. We will call this the *normality rule*. It is simplest to apply it as soon as conveniently possible on a branch.

10.3.2 Example: $(A \to B) \models_B (B \to C) \to (A \to C)$:

$$
\begin{array}{cr}
(A \to B), +0 & \\
(B \to C) \to (A \to C), -0 & (1) \\
r000,\ r00^{\#}0^{\#} & \\
r011,\ r01^{\#}1^{\#} & (2) \\
(B \to C), +1 & (3) \\
(A \to C), -1 & (4) \\
r123 & (5) \\
A, +2 & (6) \\
C, -3 & (7) \\
r022,\ r02^{\#}2^{\#},\ r033,\ r03^{\#}3^{\#} & \\
\swarrow \qquad\qquad \searrow & \\
A, -2 \qquad\qquad B, +2 \qquad & \\
\times \qquad\qquad\quad \swarrow\searrow \qquad & \\
\qquad\qquad\qquad B, -2 \quad C, +3 & \\
\qquad\qquad\qquad \times \qquad \times &
\end{array}
$$

Line (1) and the normality rule give lines (2)–(4). Line (4) gives lines (5)–(7). The first line of the tableau, and the fact that $r022$, give the first split; and line (3), plus the fact that $r123$, give the second.

10.3.3 In practice, it is simplest to omit the lines of the form $r0xx$ in a tableau for B, since they cause much clutter – as long as one remembers that they are there for the purpose of applying a rule to something of the form $A \to B, +0$. Another example: $\nvDash_B p \to ((p \to q) \to q)$.

$$p \to ((p \to q) \to q), -0$$
$$p, +1$$
$$(p \to q) \to q, -1$$
$$r123$$
$$(p \to q), +2$$
$$q, -3$$

The rule for true conditionals never gets applied in this tableau, since the only true conditional holds at world 2, and we have nothing of the form $r2xy$.

10.3.4 Counter-models are read off open branches as in N_* (9.6.7), except that the information about R is now included. Thus, in the counter-model given by the tableau of 10.3.3, $W = \{w_0, w_1, w_2, w_3, w_{0^\#}, w_{1^\#}, w_{2^\#}, w_{3^\#}\}$; $N = \{w_0\}$; $w_i^* = w_{i^\#}$ and $w_{i^\#}^* = w_i$; $Rw_1w_2w_3$, and for all $w \in W$, Rw_0ww; v is such that $v_{w_1}(p) = 1$, and $v_{w_3}(q) = 0$. The interpretation may be depicted thus:

$$
\begin{array}{cccc}
w_0 & & & w_0^* \\
& & & \\
w_1 & +p & & w_1^* \\
\diagdown & & & \\
w_2 \quad w_3 & -q & & w_2^* \quad w_3^*
\end{array}
$$

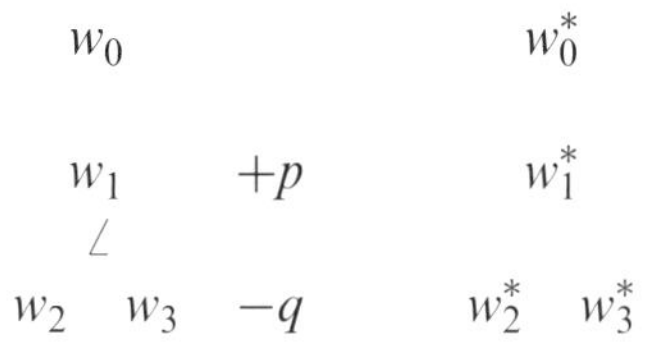

The configuration:

$$
\begin{array}{c}
a \\
\diagdown \\
b \quad c
\end{array}
$$

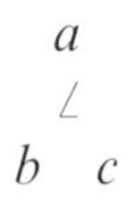

is a way of representing the relation $Rabc$. The accessibility relations involving w_0 have been omitted. These are taken for granted. Since all worlds except w_0 are non-normal, there is also no need to indicate non-normal worlds by putting them in boxes. In the depicted interpretation, $p \to q$ is true at w_2 (since it accesses nothing); hence, $(p \to q) \to q$ is false at w_1. But then, $p \to ((p \to q) \to q)$ is false at w_0.

10.3.5 The tableaux are sound and complete with respect to the semantics. This is proved in 10.8.1.

10.3.6 One may check that all formulas of the following form are logically valid in B:

(A1) $A \to A$

(A2) $A \to (A \vee B)$ (and $B \to (A \vee B)$)

(A3) $(A \wedge B) \to A$ (and $(A \wedge B) \to B$)

(A4) $A \wedge (B \vee C) \to ((A \wedge B) \vee (A \wedge C))$

(A5) $((A \to B) \wedge (A \to C)) \to (A \to (B \wedge C))$

(A6) $((A \to C) \wedge (B \to C)) \to ((A \vee B) \to C)$

(A7) $\neg\neg A \to A$

And that the following also hold in B:

(R1) $A, A \to B \vdash B$

(R2) $A, B \vdash A \wedge B$

(R3) $A \to B \vdash (C \to A) \to (C \to B)$

(R4) $A \to B \vdash (B \to C) \to (A \to C)$

(R5) $A \to \neg B \vdash B \to \neg A$

R4 is verified in 10.3.2. Details of the others are left as an exercise. All save A5, A6, R3 and R4 hold in N_*. (Again, details are left as an exercise.) Hence, the logic B is a proper extension of N_*. It is, in fact, R3 (*prefixing*) and R4 (*suffixing*) that are most distinctive about B. Together, these are referred to as *affixing*. Hence, the family of logics that we are currently concerned with are sometimes called *affixing relevant logics*.

10.3.7 The most common proof-theoretic treatment of the affixing logics in the literature is not tableau-theoretic, but axiomatic. An axiom system for B is obtained by taking every formula of the form of A1–A7 as an axiom, and every inference of the form R1–R5 as a rule.

10.3.8 In an axiom system, $\vdash$ is defined differently from the way in which it is defined in a tableau system. Specifically, $\Sigma \vdash A$ iff there is a sequence of formulas, $A_1, ..., A_n$ such that A is A_n, and every formula in the sequence is either an axiom, or a member of Σ, or follows from some prior members of the sequence by one of the rules. Such a sequence is called a *deduction.*

10.3.9 Here, for example, is a deduction of $C \to \neg\neg C$ in B (which is why this half of double negation is not needed as an axiom). The justification for each step is explained in the righthand column. Line numbers in the lefthand column assist this.

(1)	$\neg C \to \neg C$	A1
(2)	$C \to \neg\neg C$	(1) and R5

Note that (1) is an instance of A1, since $\neg C \to \neg C$ is of the form $A \to A$. Similarly, $\neg C \to \neg C \vdash C \to \neg\neg C$ is an instance of R5, since it is of the form $A \to \neg B \vdash B \to \neg A$. Here is another example to establish that $A \to B, B \to C \models_B A \to C$ (*transitivity*).

(1)	$A \to B$	assumption
(2)	$B \to C$	assumption
(3)	$(B \to C) \to (A \to C)$	(1) and R4
(4)	$A \to C$	(2), (3) and R1

10.4 Extensions of *B*

10.4.1 As with the modal logic K and its extensions, stronger relevant logics can be obtained by adding constraints on the relation R (which constraints may also involve $*$).

10.4.2 Now, there are many constraints that one might impose on the ternary R. But the most significant ones are much more complex than those in modal logic. We will have a look at five of the more notable ones here. The diagram attached to each condition may make it easier to visualise. The odd numbering will make more sense in a moment. In each case, the condition is for all worlds in W (normal *and* non-normal), a, b, c, d:

(C8) If $Rabc$ then Rac^*b^*

$$\begin{array}{ccc} & a & \\ & \angle & \\ b & & c \end{array} \quad \Rightarrow \quad \begin{array}{ccc} & a & \\ & \angle & \\ c^* & & b^* \end{array}$$

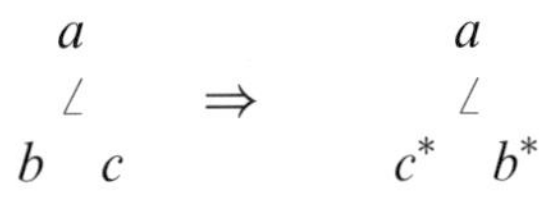

(C9) If there is an $x \in W$ such that $Rabx$ and $Rxcd$, then there is a $y \in W$ such that $Racy$ and $Rbyd$

$$\begin{array}{cccc} & a & & \\ & \angle & & \\ b & & x & \\ & & \angle & \\ & c & & d \end{array} \quad \Rightarrow \quad \begin{array}{ccccc} & a & & b & \\ & \angle & & \angle & \\ c & & y & & d \end{array}$$

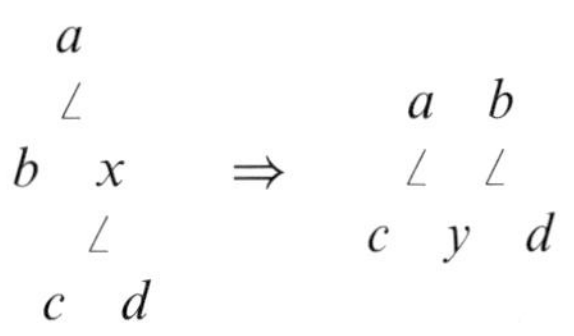

(C10) If there is an $x \in W$ such that $Rabx$ and $Rxcd$, then there is a $y \in W$ such that $Rbcy$ and $Rayd$

$$\begin{array}{cccc} & a & & \\ & \angle & & \\ b & & x & \\ & & \angle & \\ & c & & d \end{array} \quad \Rightarrow \quad \begin{array}{ccccc} & b & & a & \\ & \angle & & \angle & \\ c & & y & & d \end{array}$$

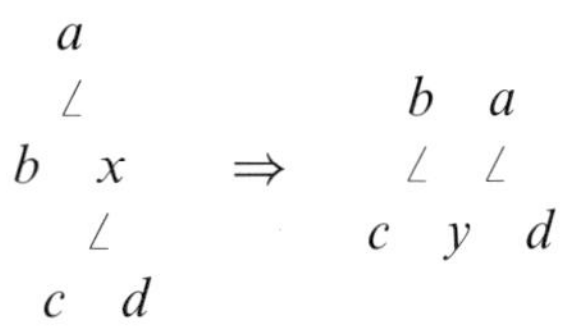

(C11) If $Rabc$ then $Rbac$

$$\begin{array}{ccc} & a & \\ & \angle & \\ b & & c \end{array} \quad \Rightarrow \quad \begin{array}{ccc} & b & \\ & \angle & \\ a & & c \end{array}$$

(C12) If $Rabc$ then for some $x \in W$, $Rabx$ and $Rxbc$

$$\begin{array}{ccc} & a & \\ & \angle & \\ b & & c \end{array} \quad \Rightarrow \quad \begin{array}{cccc} & a & & \\ & \angle & & \\ b & & x & \\ & & \angle & \\ & b & & c \end{array}$$

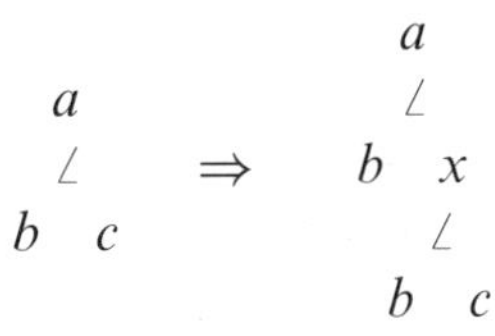

10.4.3 The tableau rules corresponding to the above conditions are not difficult to guess. They are, respectively, as follows, where j is always new to the branch (recall that if x is i, $\bar{x}$ is $i^{\#}$, and if x is $i^{\#}$, $\bar{x}$ is i):

(T8)

$$\begin{array}{c} rxyz \\ \downarrow \\ rx\bar{z}\,\bar{y} \end{array}$$

(T9)

$$\begin{array}{c} rxyz \\ rzuv \\ \downarrow \\ rxuj, ryjv \end{array}$$

(T10)

$$\begin{array}{c} rxyz \\ rzuv \\ \downarrow \\ ryuj, rxjv \end{array}$$

(T11)

$$\begin{array}{c} rxyz \\ \downarrow \\ ryxz \end{array}$$

(T12)

$$\begin{array}{c} rxyz \\ \downarrow \\ rxyj, rjyz \end{array}$$

10.4.4 The addition of the new rules adds a further complication. Because of the normality condition, we need to ensure that whenever $r0xy$ occurs on a branch, x and y are 'the same'. (This was not necessary before, since the only rules that introduced information of the form $r0xy$ required x and y to be identical. But this need no longer be the case.) The easiest way to achieve this is to allow lines on the tableau to have an additional form, $x = y$ (where x and y are of the form i or $i^{\#}$), and to add the identity rules:

$$\begin{array}{ccc} \cdot & i^{\#} = j^{\#} & x = y \\ \downarrow & \downarrow & \alpha(x) \\ x = x & i = j & \downarrow \\ & & \alpha(y) \end{array}$$

where $\alpha(x)$ is any node on the branch containing x, and $\alpha(y)$ is the same with some occurrences of x replaced by y, cancelling out any double occurrences of #. The normality condition can now be effected by the rule:

$$\begin{array}{c} r0xy \\ \downarrow \\ x = y \end{array}$$

10.4.5 The tableaux for extensions of B, though sound and complete (as is proved in 10.8.2) are very unwieldy, and, in any but the simplest cases, are too complex to be reasonably done by humans (though they can be mechanised easily enough). To make matters worse, open tableaux are normally infinite (because of the existential quantifiers in many of the conditions on R). In practice, other techniques for establishing validity and invalidity may be more viable, as we will see in a moment.

10.4.6 Each of the constraints on R is sufficient to make formulas of a certain form, which are not valid in B, logically valid. These are as follows (where the numbers correspond):

(A8) $(A \to \neg B) \to (B \to \neg A)$

(A9) $(A \to B) \to ((B \to C) \to (A \to C))$

(A10) $(A \to B) \to ((C \to A) \to (C \to B))$

(A11) $A \to ((A \to B) \to B)$

(A12) $(A \to (A \to B)) \to (A \to B)$

We will show this for A12. The others are left as an exercise.

10.4.7 The tableau in B for A12 is infinite, and it is easier to give a counter-model directly. The following will do:

$$\begin{array}{cccccccc} & & w_0 & & & & w_0^* & \\ & & w_1 & & & & w_1^* & \\ & & \angle & & & & & \\ +p & w_2 & & w_3 & -q & w_2^* & & w_3^* \end{array}$$

w_3 accesses no worlds; hence, $p \to q$ holds at w_3. Thus, $p \to (p \to q)$ is true at w_1. But $p \to q$ is false at w_1. Hence, $(p \to (p \to q)) \to (p \to q)$ is false at w_0.

10.4.8 We establish the validity of A12 in *R* by the following argument. Consider any normal world of any interpretation, w_0. We need to show that if Rw_0xx, then if $A \to (A \to B)$ is true at x, $A \to B$ is true at x. To show the latter, we need to show that if $Rxyz$ and A is true at y, B is true at z. In diagrammatic form:

$$\begin{array}{ccccc} & & w_0 & & \\ A \to (A \to B) & & w_1 & & \\ & & \angle & & \\ A & w_2 & & w_3 & B? \end{array}$$

By C12, we know that there is an x such that Rw_1w_2x, and Rxw_2w_3. And by the truth conditions for $\to$ at w_1, $A \to B$ is true at x. In pictures:

$$\begin{array}{cccccc} & & w_0 & & & \\ A \to (A \to B) & & w_1 & & & \\ & & \angle & & & \\ A & w_2 & & x & & A \to B \\ & & & \angle & & \\ A & & w_2 & & w_3 & \end{array}$$

By the truth conditions of $\to$ at x, B is true at w_3, as required.

10.4.9 If we augment the axioms of *B* with any combination of A8–A12, we therefore obtain stronger logics. The axiom systems are sound and complete with respect to the corresponding combination of conditions on *R*, though we will not prove this here.

10.4.10 The stronger logics have no very systematic nomenclature. Some names to be found in the literature are:[3]

$DW = B$+A8
$TW = DW$+A9+A10
$RW = TW$+A11
$R = RW$+A12

10.4.11 Note that in the stronger systems, some of the axioms and rules of the weaker systems may be redundant. For example, A8 clearly makes R5 redundant, and A9 and A10 render R3 and R4 redundant. Not so obviously, given C11, A9 and A10 collapse into each other, because of permutation (10.5.2 below).

10.5 The system *R*

10.5.1 Perhaps the most important of the above extensions of B is R (not to be confused with the ternary accessibility relation!). It is certainly the best known of these. Establishing what is valid in R, and what is not, is often a very hard matter. (It is known that there is no decision procedure for the logic.)

10.5.2 Sometimes, semantic arguments are relatively straightforward. For example, in this way one may establish the validity of *permutation*: $A \to (B \to C) \models_R B \to (A \to C)$. (To grasp the following reasoning, it is helpful to draw a diagram as the argument proceeds, as in 10.4.8.) Suppose that in an interpretation $A \to (B \to C)$ is true at a normal world, w. We show that $B \to (A \to C)$ is true there. So

[3] Anderson and Belnap (1975) investigated two other systems, E and T. T is obtained from R by replacing A11 with $(A \to \neg A) \to \neg A$. E is obtained from T by adding $(A \to C) \to (((A \to C) \to B) \to B)$ (that is, the special case of A11 with A replaced by $A \to C$), and $(N(A) \wedge N(B)) \to N(A \wedge B)$, where $N(C)$ is $(C \to C) \to C$. E and T have ternary relation semantics, but of a more complex kind than those of this chapter.

suppose that $Rwxx$, and that B is true at x. We need to show that $A \to C$ is true at x. To this end, suppose that $Rxyz$, and A is true at y. We need to show that C is true at z. By C11, $Ryxz$. Since $Rwyy$, and A is true at w, $B \to C$ is true at y. Hence, since B is true at x, C is true at z, as required.

10.5.3 Sometimes it is easier to deduce things from others we already know to be valid. For example, *consequentia mirabilis*: $\models_R (A \to \neg A) \to \neg A$.

(1)	$(A \to \neg A) \to (A \to \neg A)$	A1
(2)	$A \to ((A \to \neg A) \to \neg A)$	(1), *permutation*
(3)	$((A \to \neg A) \to \neg A) \to (A \to \neg(A \to \neg A))$	A8
(4)	$(A \to ((A \to \neg A) \to \neg A)) \to$ $(A \to (A \to \neg(A \to \neg A)))$	(3), R3
(5)	$A \to (A \to \neg(A \to \neg A))$	(2), (4) and R1
(6)	$(A \to (A \to \neg(A \to \neg A))) \to (A \to \neg(A \to \neg A))$	A12
(7)	$A \to \neg(A \to \neg A)$	(5), (6) and R1
(8)	$(A \to \neg A) \to \neg A$	(7), R5

10.5.4 The following shows that the law of excluded middle also holds in R.

(1)	$A \to (A \vee \neg A)$	A2
(2)	$(A \vee \neg A) \to \neg\neg(A \vee \neg A)$	double negation (10.3.9)
(3)	$A \to \neg\neg(A \vee \neg A)$	(1), (2) and transitivity
(4)	$\neg(A \vee \neg A) \to \neg A$	(3), R5
(5)	$\neg A \to (A \vee \neg A)$	A2
(6)	$\neg(A \vee \neg A) \to (A \vee \neg A)$	(4), (5) and transitivity
(7)	$\neg(A \vee \neg A) \to \neg\neg(A \vee \neg A)$	(6), (2) and transitivity
(8)	$(\neg(A \vee \neg A) \to \neg\neg(A \vee \neg A)) \to$ $\neg\neg(A \vee \neg A)$	*consequentia mirabilis*
(9)	$\neg\neg(A \vee \neg A)$	(7), (8) andR1
(10)	$\neg\neg(A \vee \neg A) \to (A \vee \neg A)$	A7
(11)	$A \vee \neg A$	(9), (10) andR1

In fact, it can be shown that all classical tautologies are logically valid in R.[4]

10.5.5 Establishing that inferences are invalid in R is even harder, since some kind of counter-model must be constructed. A useful technique is to employ a suitable many-valued logic.[5] For example, it is laborious, but not difficult, to check that every axiom of R takes a designated value in the many-valued logic RM_3 of 7.4, and that the rules of R preserve that property. (Details are left as an exercise.) It follows that R is a sub-logic of RM_3. Hence, if something is not valid in RM_3, it is not valid in R. This suffices to establish some facts about invalidity in R. For example, as we saw in 7.5.2, RM_3 avoids the standard paradoxes of both the material conditional and the strict conditional. Hence, the same is true of R.

10.5.6 A more complex many-valued logic can be used to establish the relevance of R (and *a fortiori*, of any of the weaker systems that we have met in this chapter). The truth values of the logic are $\{1, 0, b, n, 1', 0', b', n'\}$. The designated values are those with the primes. To compute the negation of a value, add or take away the prime, as appropriate. To compute the truth value of conjunctions and disjunctions, consider the following diagram:

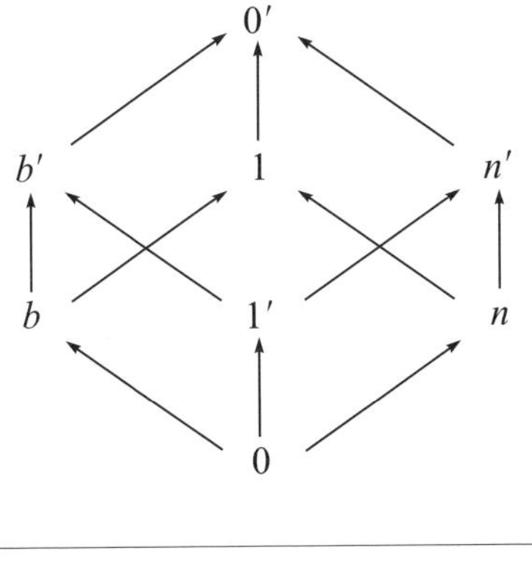

[4] The proof, in essence, is as follows. Let A be anything logically valid in classical logic, and let A' be its disjunctive normal form. In classical logic, this follows from the law of excluded middle by laws about conjunction, disjunction and negation, which also hold in R. Hence, A' holds in R. In classical logic, A' entails A by laws concerning conjunction, disjunction and negation, which also hold in R. Hence, A holds in R.

[5] Perhaps the most useful many-valued logic, in this context, is the one given in 10.11, problem 6.

Note that this is just the diamond lattice of 8.4.3, with an inverted copy pasted on top, and connected by vertical lines for corresponding elements. Conjunction is greatest lower bound; disjunction is least upper bound. Thus, for example, $b' \wedge n' = 1'$, $1 \wedge 1' = 0$, etc.[6] The truth function for $\rightarrow$ is as follows:

	$0'$	n'	b'	$1'$	1	b	n	0
$0'$	$0'$	0	0	0	0	0	0	0
n'	$0'$	n'	0	0	n	0	n	0
b'	$0'$	0	b'	0	b	b	0	0
$1'$	$0'$	n'	b'	$1'$	1	b	n	0
1	$0'$	0	0	0	$1'$	0	0	0
b	$0'$	0	b'	0	b'	b'	0	0
n	$0'$	n'	0	0	n'	0	n'	0
0	$0'$	$0'$	$0'$	$0'$	$0'$	$0'$	$0'$	$0'$

It is complex but mundane to check that all the axioms of R are valid in this logic, that the rules preserve this property, and hence that R is also a sub-logic of the logic. (Details are left as an exercise for masochists.)

10.5.7 Now, consider any formula of the form $B \rightarrow C$, where B and C share no parameter. Assign to every parameter in B the value b or b'; assign to every parameter in C the value n or n'. It is easy to check that B and C themselves have the same properties. But in that case, checking the table for $\rightarrow$ suffices to show that $B \rightarrow C$ has the value 0, and so is not logically valid in the many-valued logic, and so in R.

6 The structure is another example of a De Morgan lattice. Most mainstream relevant logics also have algebraic semantics based on such lattices.

10.6 The ternary relation

10.6.1 Let us now turn to some philosophical issues. In particular, what does the ternary relation mean, and why might it be reasonable to employ it in stating the truth conditions of a conditional?

10.6.2 It is difficult to give a satisfactory answer to this question. The most promising sort of answer seems to be to tie up the relation with the notion of information. Suppose, for example, that we think of a world as a state of information (as we did with intuitionist logic in 6.3.6). Then we may read $Rxyz$ as meaning that z contains all the information obtainable by pooling the information x and y. This makes sense of the truth conditions of $\rightarrow$. For if $A \rightarrow B$ holds in the information x, and A holds in the information y, we should certainly expect B to hold in the information obtained by pooling x and y. Conversely, if $A \rightarrow B$ does not hold in the information x, then it would certainly seem possible that we might add the information that A without thereby obtaining the information that B. Hence, there would seem to be a state of information, y, such that A holds in y, but B does not hold in the information obtained by pooling x and y.

10.6.3 The problem with this interpretation is that it seems to justify too much. For example, it justifies the claim that if $Rxyz$ and A is true at y it is also true at z. But if this were the case, $A \rightarrow A$ would be true at every world, and hence, for any B, $B \rightarrow (A \rightarrow A)$ would be logically valid, which it cannot be if the logic is to be relevant.

10.6.4 Another possibility for interpreting R is to suppose that worlds are not themselves states of information, but that they may act as conduits for information in some way. Thus, a situation that contains a fossilised footprint allows information to flow from the situation in which it was made, to the situation in which it is found. $Rxyz$ is now interpreted as saying that the information in y is carried to z by x. If we think of $A \rightarrow B$ as recording the information carried, this makes some sense of the ternary truth conditions. For if A is information at y, and x allows the flow of information $A \rightarrow B$ from y to z, then we would expect the information B to be available at z. Conversely, if x does not allow the information flow $A \rightarrow B$, then it must be possible for there to be situations, y and z, where A is available at y, but B is not available at z.

10.6.5 The problem now is to make sense of the metaphor of information flow – hardly a transparent one. Moreover, it is not at all clear that, when articulated, it will provide what is needed. For example, if a situation carries any information at all, it would appear to carry the information that there is some source from which information is coming. Call this statement S. If this is the case, then the inference from $A \rightarrow B$ to $A \rightarrow S$ would appear to be valid. But this would seem to give a violation of relevance, since A itself may have nothing to do with S.

10.6.6 The ternary relation semantics, and the study of information flow are both very new; and it may be the case that a satisfactory analysis of the two together will eventually arise. But if the ternary relation semantics is ultimately to provide anything more than a model-theoretic device for establishing various formal facts about various relevant logics, this is a task that must be discharged successfully. In particular, if the ternary relation semantics is to *justify* the fact that some inferences concerning conditionals are valid and some are not, then there must be some acceptable account of the connection between the meaning of the relation and the truth conditions of conditionals.

10.7 *Ceteris paribus* enthymemes

10.7.1 Setting this issue aside, let us return to the question of the conditional itself. Any relevant logic of the kind that we have met avoids the standard paradoxes of the material and strict conditionals, as we saw in 10.5.5. It also avoids the inferences of 1.9.1. (See 10.11, problem 7.) Hence, it is an excellent candidate for the conditional. A natural question at this point is whether it is possible to give an account of conditionals with a *ceteris paribus* clause in relevant logic. (The inferences of 5.2.1 are all valid in N_*, and *a* *fortiori*, all the relevant logics we have met. Details are left as an exercise.)

10.7.2 It is, and we will now see how. In fact, all we have to do is reproduce the techniques of chapter 5 in a relevant possible-world semantics. (Note that the connective $>$ of chapter 5 is not a relevant connective. For example, in all the logics of that chapter, $\models p > (q \vee \neg q)$; 5.12, problem 2(e).) We illustrate this with respect to the logic B, but it should be clear that it can be applied to any of the relevant logics that we have met.

10.7.3 Start by adding a new connective, $>$, to the language. Let $\mathcal{I}$ be an interpretation for B. To obtain a semantics for the extended language, we add the collection of accessibility relations, $\{R_A$; A is a formula of the language$\}$, to $\mathcal{I}$. Alternatively, and equivalently, we can add a set of selection functions, f_A. (See 5.3.5.)

10.7.4 The truth conditions for the old connectives are as for B. The conditions for $>$ are:[7]

$$v_w(A > B) = 1 \text{ iff } f_A(w) \subset [B]$$

10.7.5 Validity is defined in terms of truth preservation at all normal worlds. Let us call this system C_B. Tableaux for C_B can be obtained simply by adding the following rules to those of 10.3.1.

$$\begin{array}{cc} A > B, +x & A > B, -x \\ xr_A y & \downarrow \\ \downarrow & xr_A j \\ B, +y & B, -j \end{array}$$

In the second rule, j is a new number. Soundness and completeness proofs can be found in 10.8.3.

[7] In the case of the relational relevant logics, the natural conditions are:

$A > B\rho_w 1$ iff $f_A(w) \subseteq [B]$

$A > B\rho_w 0$ iff $f_A(w) \cap [\neg B] \neq \phi$

10.7.6 Extensions of C_B can be obtained by adding further conditions on f. Again, we simply illustrate this. Corresponding to the conditions for C^+, we have, for any $w \in N$:

(1) $f_A(w) \subseteq [A]$

(2) if $w \in [A]$ then $w \in f_A(w)$

(Why the conditions are for only normal w, we will come back to in a moment.) Call the system obtained in this way C_B^+. Tableaux for C_B^+ can be obtained by modifying the rule for false $>$, when (and only when) x is 0, to become:

$$\begin{array}{c} A > B, -0 \\ \downarrow \\ 0r_A j \\ A, +j \\ B, -j \end{array}$$

and adding the rule:

$$\begin{array}{ccc} & . & \\ & \swarrow \searrow & \\ A, -0 & & A, +0 \\ & & 0r_A 0 \end{array}$$

where A is the antecedent of any conditional or negated conditional on the branch. Soundness and completeness proofs are to be found in 10.8.4.

10.7.7 Here, for example, is a tableau to show that $\nvDash_{C_B^+} (p \wedge \neg p) > q$:

$$
\begin{array}{c}
(p \wedge \neg p) > q, -0 \\
0r_{p\wedge\neg p}1 \\
p \wedge \neg p, +1 \\
q, -1 \\
p, +1 \\
\neg p, +1 \\
p, -1^{\#} \\
\swarrow \qquad\qquad\qquad \searrow \\
\begin{array}{c}
p \wedge \neg p, -0 \\
\swarrow\searrow \\
\begin{array}{cc} p, -0 & \neg p, -0 \\ & p, +0^{\#} \\ & \end{array}
\end{array}
\qquad
\begin{array}{c}
p \wedge \neg p, +0 \\
0r_{p\wedge\neg p}0 \\
p, +0 \\
\neg p, +0 \\
p, -0^{\#}
\end{array}
\end{array}
$$

The counter-model determined by the lefthand branch may be depicted thus:

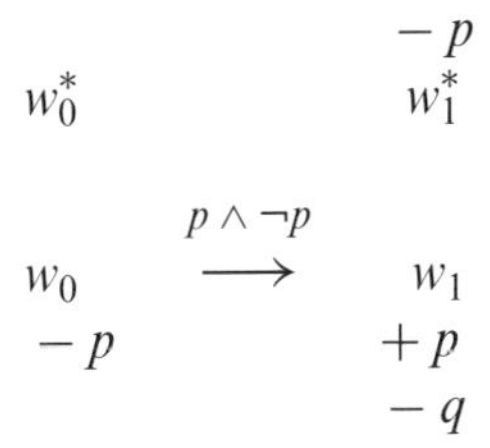

10.7.8 If we restrict our interpretations to those where $W = N$ and for all w, $w^* = w$, then we have, essentially, just interpretations for C^+. Hence C_B^+ is a sub-logic of C^+. In particular, all the inferences of 5.2.1 fail (5.12, problem 4).

10.7.9 On the other hand, if we consider interpretations where $W = N$ and $f_A(w) = [A]$ (which condition satisfies both (1) and (2)), then $>$ behaves just like $\rightarrow$ in K_*. In particular, for any inference involving $\rightarrow$ that fails in K_*, the corresponding inference for $>$ fails in C_B^+. Hence, C_B^+ is not subject to the standard paradoxes of strict implication. In fact, $>$ is a relevant connective. (For the proof of this, see 10.11, problem 10.)

10.7.10 Note, finally, that if condition (1) were not restricted to normal worlds, irrelevance would arise. For then, $A > A$ would be true at all worlds, and so $B > (A > A)$ would be valid.

10.7.11 Thus, the semantics of relevant logics can provide plausible candidates not only for the conditional, but also for *ceteris paribus* enthymemes.

10.8 *Proofs of theorems

10.8.1 THEOREM: The tableaux for B are sound and complete with respect to their semantics.

Proof:

The proofs are modifications of those for N_* (9.8.13). The definition of faithfulness is modified by the addition of the clause:

if $rxyz$ is on b, then $Rf(x)f(y)f(z)$ in $\mathcal{I}$

In the Soundness Lemma, we merely need to check the new rules. So suppose that we apply a rule to $A \to B, +x$ and $rxyz$. By assumption, $A \to B$ is true at $f(x)$, and $Rf(x)f(y)f(z)$. By the truth conditions of $\to$, either A is false at $f(y)$ or B is true at $f(z)$, as required. If, on the other hand, we apply the rule to $A \to B, -x$, then $A \to B$ is false at $f(x)$. Hence, there are worlds, u, v, such that the lines $Rf(x)uv$, A is true at u, and B is not true at v – and if x is 0, u is v, since $f(0) \in N$. Let f' be the same as f, except that $f'(j) = u$ and $f'(k) = v$. Then the result follows in the usual way. For the normality rule, since $f(0) \in N$, $Rf(0)f(x)f(x)$, by the normality condition, as required.

In the Completeness Lemma, the induced interpretation is defined as for N_* (so, in particular, only w_0 is normal), and $Rw_xw_yw_z$ iff $rxyz$ occurs at a node on b. The interpretation, so defined, is a B-interpretation. In particular, by the normality rule, for all x, $r0xx$ occurs on the tableau, so $Rw_0w_xw_x$. And if $r0xy$ occurs on the tableau, it must have got there by an application of either the normality rule or the rule for false $\to$s. In either case, x

is y. Hence, if $Rw_0w_xw_y$, $w_x = w_y$. It remains to check the clauses for $\rightarrow$ in the Completeness Lemma. So suppose that $A \rightarrow B, +x$ occurs on the branch. Then for all y and z such that $rxyz$ occurs on the branch, either $A, -y$ or $B, +z$ occurs on the branch. By induction hypothesis, for all worlds w_y, w_z such that $Rw_xw_yw_z$, if A is true at w_y, B is true at w_z. That is, $A \rightarrow B$ is true at w_x. Suppose, on the other hand, that $A \rightarrow B, -x$ occurs on the branch. Then for some j and k, $rxjk$, $A, +j$ and $B, -k$ occur on the branch. By induction hypothesis, for some worlds w_j, w_k, such that $Rw_xw_jw_k$, A is true at w_j and B is false at w_k. That is, $A \rightarrow B$ is false at w_x.

10.8.2 THEOREM: The tableaux for extensions of B are sound and complete with respect to their respective semantics.

Proof:

The proofs are extensions of those for B. The definition of faithfulness is now extended with the clause:

if $x = y$ occurs on b, then $f(x) = f(y)$

For the Soundness Lemma, we have to check the rules for identity, and the rules T8–T12. The three rules for identity proper are straightforward, any deletion of double #s being justified by the fact that $w = w^{**}$. For the fourth rule, suppose that $r0xy$ is on the branch; then, by assumption, $Rf(0)f(x)f(y)$. Since $f(0) \in N$, $f(x) = f(y)$, as required. It remains to check T8–T12. This is a routine matter, and is left as an exercise.

For completeness, the induced interpretation is defined slightly differently, employing standard techniques from the completeness proof for identity in first-order logic. The relation $x \sim y$, defined by the condition '$x = y$ is on b', can easily be checked to be an equivalence relation. Let $[x]$ be the equivalence class of x. The worlds of the interpretation are now $w_{[x]}$ for every x on the branch. $w^*_{[x]} = w_{[\overline{x}]}$. (This definition makes sense, since if $x = y$ is on b, so is $\overline{x} = \overline{y}$, as may easily be checked. And $w^{**} = w$, since $\overline{\overline{x}} = x$.) The rest of the definition is the same, with x replaced by $[x]$. (This makes sense, since any two members of an equivalence class behave in exactly the same way on a branch, by the substitutivity rules.) The Completeness Lemma is now reformulated as:

if $A, +x$ occurs on b, then A is true at $w_{[x]}$

if $A, -x$ occurs on b, then A is false at $w_{[x]}$

and its proof goes through essentially as usual. It remains to check that the induced interpretation has the appropriate properties. Since, for any x, $r0xx$ is on the branch, we have $Rw_{[0]}w_{[x]}w_{[x]}$. Moreover, suppose that $Rw_{[0]}w_{[x]}w_{[y]}$. Then $r0xy$ is on the branch. But then so is $x = y$. So $[x] = [y]$, and $w_{[x]} = w_{[y]}$. Thus, the normality condition is satisfied. Checking that each of the constraints C8–C12 is satisfied, given that the appropriate rule is in force, is routine, and details are left as an exercise.

10.8.3 THEOREM: The tableaux for C_B are sound and complete with respect to their semantics.

Proof:

The proof extends that for B. The definition of faithfulness is extended by the same clause as that required for C:

if xr_Ay is on b, then $f(x)R_Af(y)$ in $\mathcal{I}$

In the proof of the Soundness Lemma, we have to check only the rules for $>$; and these are as for C in 5.9.1, with appropriate modifications.

The induced interpretation is defined as for B, except that for each formula, A, R_A is defined as for C (5.9.1). The rest of the argument is then routine.

10.8.4 THEOREM: The tableaux for C_B^+ are sound and complete with respect to its semantics.

Proof:

The proof extends that for C_B. In the Soundness Lemma, we have to check the cases for the revised rules. The argument is as for C^+ (5.9.2), with the appropriate modifications.

In the Completeness Theorem, we have to check that the induced interpretation is a C_B^+-interpretation, and in particular, that w_0 satisfies conditions (1) and (2). The argument is as for C^+ (5.9.2).

10.9 History

The earliest known relevant logic is an axiomatisation of *R* by the Russian logician Orlov in 1928; see Došen (1992). This went largely unnoticed, however. After that, relevant logics or fragments thereof were published by Church in 1951 and Ackermann in 1956. The project was taken up and much developed in the 1960s by the US logicians Anderson and Belnap, together with a number of their students, including Meyer and Dunn (who developed the algebraic semantics for relevant logics). The result was Anderson and Belnap's *Entailment* (1975), which can also be consulted for a discussion of Church and Ackermann. Volume II of *Entailment* appeared later, as Anderson, Belnap, and Dunn (1992). The work of Anderson, Belnap and their school concentrated on the strong relevant logics, *T*, *R* and *E*, the last of these being their preferred logic. The model of *R* in 10.11, problem 6, is due to Meyer (1970).

The ternary relation semantics for relevant logics was developed by Routley (Sylvan) and Meyer (by that time in Australia), building on the earlier invention of the Routley $*$. The results appeared in a number of papers in the 1970s, starting with Routley and Meyer (1973). Further work by Routley, Meyer and their students, including Brady, was published in Routley, Plumwood, Meyer and Brady (1982). The second volume of this is currently in preparation by Brady. The semantics made it clear that the basic affixing relevant logic was *B*, and that there were many interesting logics between *B* and the strong American systems. Much of the work of the Australians concentrated on the weaker systems – especially those not containing *contraction* (A12) – which are much better for a number of applications, such as the theory of truth (see Priest 2000a, sect. 8). The Americans called the subject *relevance* logic, since they took themselves to be giving an analysis of (amongst other things) relevance. Routley argued that the logics did not really provide an analysis of relevance; though, in these logics, the antecedent is relevant to the consequent in logical truths of the form $A \rightarrow B$. He therefore preferred the name *relevant* logic, a usage that is followed by most Australian logicians.

The original Routley/Meyer ternary relation semantics was somewhat more complex than the ones used in this chapter. The simplified version employed here was given for B by Priest and Sylvan (1992), and extended to stronger systems by Restall (1993). These works can be consulted for the soundness and completeness proofs for the various systems of relevant logics formulated axiomatically.

The relevant logics based on relational semantics for negation are a somewhat different family of logics from the one considered in this chapter, though some of these can be given relational semantics by employing various devices. See Priest and Sylvan (1992), Routley (1984) and Restall (1995).

The suggestion of 10.6.2 to interpret the ternary relation in terms of information comes from Urquhart (1972), which contains a slightly different semantics for some relevant logics. Urquhart also proved the undecidability of the stronger relevant logics, including R. (The weaker members of the family are decidable.) The suggestion of 10.6.4, that the ternary relation can be thought of in terms of information flow, arose out of the similarities between relevant logic and situation semantics, and is due to Restall (1996) and Mares (1996). The debate on the question of whether the Routley/Meyer semantics has any philosophical significance has become quite heated at times. See Copeland (1979), Routley, Routley, Meyer and Martin (1982) and Copeland (1983).

The fact that the techniques of conditional logic could be applied just as well to relevant logics was first noted by Routley (1989a, sect. 8), and later by Mares and Fuhrmann (1995).

10.10 Further reading

Perhaps the gentlest introduction to mainstream relevant logic is Read (1988). Dunn (1986) is a good reference work for the stronger relevant systems (including their undecidability). For the more technical reader, Restall (2000b) is an excellent investigation of relevant logics, and the broader family of substructural logics to which they belong. There are many kinds of relevant logics outside the mainstream area. For an orientation, see Routley (1989b).

10.11 Problems

1. Fill in the details left as exercises in 10.3.6, 10.4.6, 10.5.5, 10.5.6 and 10.7.1.

2. Show that the following fail in B:

   (*a*) $(p \wedge q) \rightarrow r \vdash p \rightarrow (q \rightarrow r)$

   (*b*) $p \rightarrow (q \rightarrow r) \vdash (p \wedge q) \rightarrow r$

   (*c*) $\vdash ((p \rightarrow q) \wedge (q \rightarrow r)) \rightarrow (p \rightarrow r)$

   (*d*) $\vdash (p \rightarrow q) \rightarrow ((p \wedge r) \rightarrow (q \wedge r))$

   (*e*) $(p \wedge q) \rightarrow r \vdash (p \wedge \neg r) \rightarrow \neg q$

3. Show that $(p \wedge (p \rightarrow q)) \rightarrow q$ is not logically valid in B. Show that it is if we require every world, w, of every interpretation to satisfy the condition $Rwww$.

4. Give deductions for the following in R:

   (*a*) $\vdash \neg A \rightarrow \neg(A \wedge B)$

   (*b*) $\vdash \neg(A \wedge \neg A)$

   (*c*) $A \rightarrow B, A \rightarrow \neg B \vdash \neg A$

5. Show that if all worlds in an interpretation are normal, the constraints C8, C9, C10 and C12 hold. Infer that any logic obtained by extending B by adding some of these constraints

to interpretations is a sub-logic of K_*. Show that the same is not true of C11.

6. (Another exercise for masochists.) Show that all the axioms of R are valid in the following many-valued logic, and that all the rules of R preserve validity; hence, that R is a sub-logic of the logic. The values of the logic are the integers, together with a new object, ∞. All but 0 are designated. The logical operators are defined as follows:

$\neg 0 = \infty$; $\neg\infty = 0$; $\neg a = -a$ otherwise

$0 \wedge a = a \wedge 0 = 0$; $\infty \wedge a = a \wedge \infty = a$

$0 \vee a = a \vee 0 = a$; $\infty \vee a = a \vee \infty = \infty$

$0 \to a = a \to \infty = \infty$; if $a \neq 0$, $a \to 0 = 0$, if $a \neq \infty$, $\infty \to a = 0$

if a and b are positive integers, then:

if a divides b, $a \to b = b/a$; otherwise, $a \to b = 0$

$a \wedge b$ is the greatest common divisor of a and b

$a \vee b$ is the least common multiple of a and b

if a and b are negative integers, then:

$a \wedge b = -(-a \vee -b)$

$a \vee b = -(-a \wedge -b)$

$a \to b = -b \to -a$

if a is a negative integer and b is a positive integer, then:

$a \to b = 0$; $b \to a = b.a$

$a \wedge b = b \wedge a = b$

$a \vee b = b \vee a = a$

7. Use the result of the previous problem to show that the following do not hold in R:

   (*a*) $\models p \to (p \to p)$

   (*b*) $\models p \to (q \to (p \wedge q))$

   (*c*) $(p \wedge q) \to r \models (p \to r) \vee (q \to r)$

   (*d*) $(p \to q) \wedge (r \to s) \models (p \to s) \vee (r \to q)$

   (*e*) $\neg(p \to q) \models p$

8. Show that the following are valid in C_B^+:

   (*a*) $\vdash A > A$

   (*b*) $\vdash (A > \neg\neg A) \wedge (\neg\neg A > A)$

   (*c*) $\vdash (A \wedge B) > A$

   (*d*) $A > B, A > C \vdash A > (B \wedge C)$

   (*e*) $A, A > B \vdash B$

   (*f*) $A \to B \vdash A > B$

9. This exercise gives a proof of the relevance of the logic B.

   (*a*) Let $\perp$ and $\perp^*$ be a pair of non-normal worlds such that every propositional parameter is true at $\perp$ and false at $\perp^*$. Suppose that $R\perp\perp\perp$, $R\perp^*\perp\perp^*$, and that each world accesses no other worlds. Show that every formula is true at $\perp$ and false at $\perp^*$.

   (*b*) Let w and w^* be a pair of non-normal worlds such that $Rw\perp w$ and $Rw^*\perp w^*$. Using part (a), show that: (i) if every parameter in A is true at w and false at w^*, the same is true of A; (ii) if every parameter in B is false at w and true at w^*, the same is true of B.

   (*c*) Use this to show that if $\vdash_B A \to C$, A and C share a propositional parameter.

10. By defining suitable accessibility relations for $>$, modify the proof of the previous question to show the same for $>$ in C_B^+. (*Hint*: For every non-normal world, w, set $f_A(w) = \{w\}$.)

11. Let $D(n)$ be the disjunction of all formulas of the form $p_i \leftrightarrow p_j$ for all i and j, such that $0 \leq i < j \leq n$. Using the interpretation of problem 6, show that for all n, $D(n)$ is not logically valid in R. Hence, show that neither R nor any weaker relevant logic is finitely-many valued. (*Hint*: See the similar proofs for modal and intuitionist logics, 7.11.1–7.11.4.)

12. What is it to carry information? And what (ternary) properties does information flow have?

13. $*$ Check the details omitted in 10.8.2, 10.8.3 and 10.8.4.

11 Fuzzy logic

11.1 Introduction

11.1.1 In this chapter we look at fuzzy logic, that is, logic in which sentences can take as a truth value any number between 0 and 1.

11.1.2 We look at one of the major motivations for such a logic: vagueness. We also show some of the connections between fuzzy logic and relevant logics.

11.1.3 Finally, fuzzy logic gives a very distinctive account of the conditional, since *modus ponens* fails. The chapter examines what fuzzy conditionals are like.

11.2 Sorites paradoxes

11.2.1 Suppose that Mary is aged five, and hence is a child. If someone is a child, they are a child one second later: there is no second at which a person turns from a child to an adult. (We are talking about biological childhood here, not legal childhood. The latter does terminate at the instant someone turns eighteen, in many jurisdictions.) So in one second's time, Mary will still be a child. Hence, one second after that, she will still be a child; and one second after *that*; and one second after *that* ... Hence, Mary will be a child after any number of seconds have elapsed. But this is, of course, absurd. After an appropriate number of seconds have elapsed, so have thirty years, by which time Mary is thirty-five, and so certainly not a child.

11.2.2 The argument of 11.2.1 is known as a *sorites* paradox. It arises because the predicate 'is a child' is vague in a certain sense.

Specifically, very small changes to an object (in this case, a person) seem to have no effect on the applicability of the predicate.

11.2.3 In fact, most of the predicates we commonly use are vague in this sense: 'is tall', 'is drunk', 'is red', 'appears red', 'is a heap of sand' ('sorites' comes from the Greek *soros* meaning 'heap') – even 'is dead' (dying takes time: one nanosecond makes no difference). One can construct sorites arguments for all such predicates.

11.2.4 Sorites arguments can often be put in the form of a sequence of *modus ponens* inferences. Thus, if M_i is the sentence 'Mary is a child after i seconds', then the sorites of 11.2.1 is just:

$$\cfrac{\cfrac{M_0 \qquad M_0 \to M_1}{M_1} \qquad M_1 \to M_2}{M_2}$$

$$\ddots$$

$$\frac{M_{k-1} \qquad M_{k-1} \to M_k}{M_k}$$

where k is some very large number.

11.3 ... and responses to them

11.3.1 Various, very different, responses to the sorites paradox have been given. To see what some of these are, consider the sequence: $M_0, M_1, ..., M_k$. M_0 is definitely true; M_k is definitely false. What is one to say about what goes on in between?

11.3.2 If we suppose that every sentence is either simply true or simply false, and given that the change from child to adult is not reversible, then there must be a unique i such that M_i is true, and M_{i+1} is false. In this case, the conditional $M_i \to M_{i+1}$ is false, and the sorites argument is broken. The problem with this supposition is obvious, however: the discrete nature of the change (that is, the jump from truth to falsity) would seem to be incompatible with the relatively continuous nature of the change from being a child to being an adult.

11.3.3 Some have bitten the bullet, and accepted that there is, indeed, such a point. The most notable defence of this line (given by *epistemicists*) attempts to argue that we find the existence of the point counterintuitive because, as a matter of principle, we cannot know where it is; and we cannot know this for the following reason.

11.3.4 If you know something, this has to be on some evidential basis. Thus, if you know something about a situation, you must know the same thing about any situation that is evidentially the same. Now suppose that you know that M_i. Since, M_{i+i} is evidentially the same (you could not tell the difference), you would have to know M_{i+1} too. But you cannot, since M_{i+1} is false.

11.3.5 Whatever one makes of this argument itself, it cannot really serve to explain why we find the existence of a semantic discontinuity counterintuitive. For it is not just the fact that we do not *know* where the cut-off point is that is odd; it is the very possibility of a cut-off point at all: the changes involved in one second of a person's life just do not seem to be of the kind that could ground a difference between childhood and adulthood.

11.3.6 Some philosophers have suggested that vagueness requires us to reject a simple dichotomy between truth and falsity. In a sorites transition, there is a middle ground: some sentences in the middle of the transition are neither true nor false – or, perhaps, both true and false – something symmetric between truth and falsity, anyway.

11.3.7 Thus, a popular suggestion is that K_3 (7.3), possibly in conjunction with some supervaluation technique (7.10.3–7.10.5), is an appropriate logic for vagueness. In this case, there is some i, such that M_i is true and M_{i+1} is neither true nor false. Again, $M_i \rightarrow M_{i+1}$ is not true, and so the sorites argument fails.

11.3.8 The problem with any 3-valued approach is obvious, however. The existence, in a sorites progression, of a discrete boundary between truth and the middle value is just as counterintuitive as that of one between truth and falsity.

11.3.9 Moreover, the existence of relatively continuous change along a sorites progression would seem to be incompatible with any discrete boundaries. It is natural to suppose, therefore, that truth values must themselves change continuously. Thus, we must consider a logic in which truth comes in continuous degrees. This is fuzzy logic, and will concern us for the rest of this chapter.[1]

11.3.10 It should be noted, though, that even fuzzy logic is not entirely unproblematic. For if truth comes by degrees, there must be some point in a sorites transition where the truth value changes from *completely true* to *less than completely true*. The existence of such a point would itself seem to be intuitively problematic.

11.4 The continuum-valued logic Ł

11.4.1 A natural way to construct a fuzzy logic is as a many-valued logic with a continuum of truth values. Let the designated values, $\mathcal{D}$, be the set of real numbers (decimals) between 0 and 1, $\{x; 0 \leq x \leq 1\}$. This is often written as [0, 1]. 1 is completely true; 0 is completely false; 0.5 is half true; etc.

11.4.2 What are the semantic functions that correspond to the connectives $\wedge$, $\vee$, $\neg$ and $\rightarrow$? A standard answer is as follows:

$$f_{\neg}(x) = 1 - x$$

$$f_{\wedge}(x, y) = Min(x, y)$$

$$f_{\vee}(x, y) = Max(x, y)$$

[1] There are, in fact, sorites progressions where each step is clearly discrete: for example, the addition of a single grain of sand. So, in principle, one could use a finitely-many valued logic for these. But the continuum-valued semantics is more general, and can be applied to all sorites paradoxes, giving, what is clearly desirable, a uniform account.

$$f_{\rightarrow}(x, y) = x \ominus y$$

where *Min* means 'the minimum (lesser) of'; *Max* means 'the maximum (greater) of'; and $x \ominus y$ is a function defined as follows:

$$\text{if } x \leq y, \text{ then } x \ominus y = 1$$

$$\text{if } x > y, \text{ then } x \ominus y = 1 - (x - y) \quad (= 1 - x + y)$$

Note that we could say '$x \geq y$' instead of '$x > y$' in the second clause, since if $x = y$, $1 - (x - y) = 1$.

11.4.3 The truth functions for negation, conjunction and disjunction are fairly natural. As the truth value of 'Mary is a child' goes down, the truth value of 'Mary is not a child' would seem to go up coordinately. A conjunction would seem to be just as good as its least true conjunct; and a disjunction would seem to be just as good as its most true. The truth function for $\rightarrow$ is anything but obvious. Here is its rationale. Consider $A \rightarrow B$. If A is less true (or, better, no more true) than B, then the truth value of $A \rightarrow B$ is 1. That's how it works, after all, with the standard 2-valued material conditional. If A is more true than B, then there is something faulty about the conditional: its truth value must be less than 1. How much less? The amount that the truth value falls in going from A to B. In particular, if it falls all the way from 1 to 0, then the value of $A \rightarrow B$ is 0. All this is exactly what $\ominus$ means.

11.4.4 Note that:

$$\text{if } x \leq y, \text{ then } y \ominus z \leq x \ominus z$$

$$\text{if } x \leq y, \text{ then } z \ominus x \leq z \ominus y$$

For the first of these, suppose that $x \leq y$ (and so, that $-y \leq -x$): if $x \leq z$, then $x \ominus z = 1$, so the result follows. If $z < x \leq y$, then $y \ominus z = 1 - y + z \leq 1 - x + z = x \ominus z$. The second conditional is left as an exercise.

11.4.5 Notice that if we restrict ourselves to just the values 1 and 0, then the truth functions of 11.4.2 are exactly the same as those of classical truth tables. It is less obvious, but is easy to check, that if we restrict ourselves to just the values 1, 0.5 and 0, then the truth functions are exactly the same as those of $Ł_3$ (7.3.2 and 7.3.8), thinking of $\rightarrow$ as $\supset$, and 0.5 as *i*. In this sense, the logic is a generalisation of both classical propositional logic, and Łukasiewicz' 3-valued logic.

11.4.6 What of the designated values of the logic? In general, things do not have to be completely true to be acceptable. If I ask for a red apple, and you give me one with a very small patch of green (so that 'this is red' is, say, 0.95 true), that's probably good enough. *How* true something has to be to be acceptable will depend on the context. If you buy a new car, you expect it not to have been driven at all. (So 'this is a new car' needs to have truth value 1.) But you would still describe it as a new car to a friend, even if you had bought it and driven it around for a few weeks. (So in this context, 'this is a new car' need have truth value only 0.95, say.) But at any rate, if A is acceptable as true, and B is truer than A, then B is acceptable as true as well. What all this means is that any context will determine a number, ε, somewhere between 0 and 1, such that the things that are acceptable are exactly those things with truth value x, where $x \geq \varepsilon$.

11.4.7 Correspondingly, for every such ε, taking the set of designated values, $\mathcal{D}_\varepsilon$, to be $\{x; x \geq \varepsilon\}$, will define a notion of validity. Thus $\Sigma \models_\varepsilon A$ iff for all interpretations, ν, if $\nu(B) \geq \varepsilon$ for all $B \in \Sigma$, then $\nu(A) \geq \varepsilon$.

11.4.8 Each logic defined in this way is a perfectly good many-valued logic. But in logic, it makes sense to abstract from context and consider a notion of validity that is context-independent. Hence, it is natural to define the central notion of logical consequence as follows:

$$\Sigma \models A \text{ iff for all } \varepsilon, \text{ where } 0 \leq \varepsilon \leq 1, \Sigma \models_\varepsilon A$$

We will call this logic $Ł$.

11.4.9 A set of truth values, X, may have no least member. (Consider, for example, $\{0.41, 0.401, 0.4001, 0.40001, ...\}$.) But there will always be a greatest number that is less than or equal to every number in the set. (In this case, the number is 0.4.) This is called the *greatest lower bound* of X ($Glb(X)$). If the set is finite, then the Glb of the set is, of course, its least member. Notice that, by definition, if $x \in X$, $x \geq Glb(X)$; and if for all $x \in X$, $x \geq y$, then $Glb(X) \geq y$.

11.4.10 $\models$ has, in fact, a very simple characterisation. If Σ is a set of formulas, let $\nu[\Sigma]$ be $\{\nu(B); B \in \Sigma\}$. Then:

$$\Sigma \models A \text{ iff for all } \nu, Glb(\nu[\Sigma]) \leq \nu(A)$$

Proof:

Suppose that $\Sigma \not\models A$. Then there is some ε, such that $\Sigma \not\models_\varepsilon A$. That is, for some ν, and for all $B \in \Sigma$, $\nu(B) \geq \varepsilon$, and $\nu(A) < \varepsilon$. But if every member of $\nu[\Sigma]$ is $\geq \varepsilon$, $Glb(\nu[\Sigma]) \geq \varepsilon$. Hence, for this ν, it is not the case that $Glb(\nu[\Sigma]) \leq \nu(A)$. Conversely, suppose that for some ν, $Glb(\nu[\Sigma]) > \nu(A)$. Let $\varepsilon = Glb(\nu[\Sigma])$. Then for all $B \in \Sigma$, $\nu(B) \geq \varepsilon$, but $\nu(A) < \varepsilon$. That is, $\Sigma \not\models_\varepsilon A$. Hence, $\Sigma \not\models A$.

11.4.11 For a finite set, the Glb is its minimum. So if $\Sigma = \{B_1, ..., B_n\}$, then $\Sigma \models A$ iff for all ν, $Min(\nu(B_1), ..., \nu(B_n)) \leq \nu(A)$ iff $\nu(B_1 \wedge ... \wedge B_n) \leq \nu(A)$. A little thought concerning $\ominus$ suffices to show that $\nu(C) \leq \nu(A)$ iff $\nu(C \to A) = 1$. Hence:

$$\{B_1, ..., B_n\} \models A \text{ iff for all } \nu, \nu((B_1 \wedge ... \wedge B_n) \to A) = 1$$

Thus (for a finite number of premises), validity amounts to the logical truth of the appropriate conditional when the set of designated values is just $\{1\}$, that is, the logical truth of the conditional in $\models_1$. The logic with just 1 as a designated value is usually written as $Ł_\aleph$, and called Łukasiewicz' continuum-valued logic. Hence, to investigate $Ł$ further, we may investigate $Ł_\aleph$.[2]

[2] $\aleph$ is the Hebrew letter *aleph*, and, following Cantor, is used by logicians to denote a size of infinity.

11.5 Axioms for $Ł_{\aleph}$

11.5.1 There is, as far as I am aware, no tableau system for $Ł_{\aleph}$. Hence, we will use a suitable axiomatic notion of proof. The best-known axiom system has the sole rule of inference *modus ponens*, and the following axioms:[3]

$$(A \to B) \to ((B \to C) \to (A \to C))$$
$$A \to (B \to A)$$
$$(A \to \neg B) \to (B \to \neg A)$$
$$((A \to B) \to B) \to ((B \to A) \to A)$$
$$((A \to B) \to B) \leftrightarrow (A \vee B)$$
$$(A \wedge B) \leftrightarrow \neg(\neg A \vee \neg B)$$

The axiom system is hardly perspicuous. This is reflected in the fact that the two known completeness proofs for it are both very hard mathematically. We will not go into them here.

11.5.2 Something which is at least a little more perspicuous can be obtained from the logic *RW* of 10.4.10 – which is sometimes, in this context, called *C* (not to be confused with the basic classical conditional logic). Here, as a reminder, is an axiom system for it (with the numbers used in chapter 10). (A10 is redundant, as we observed in 10.4.11.)

(A1) $A \to A$

(A2) $A \to (A \vee B)$ (and $B \to (A \vee B)$)

(A3) $(A \wedge B) \to A$ (and $(A \wedge B) \to B$)

(A4) $A \wedge (B \vee C) \to ((A \wedge B) \vee (A \wedge C))$

(A5) $((A \to B) \wedge (A \to C)) \to (A \to (B \wedge C))$

(A6) $((A \to C) \wedge (B \to C)) \to ((A \vee B) \to C)$

(A7) $\neg\neg A \to A$

---

[3] Often, only the first four axioms are given, and $A \vee B$ and $A \wedge B$ are *defined* as $(A \to B) \to B$ and $\neg(\neg A \vee \neg B)$, respectively.

(A8) $(A \to \neg B) \to (B \to \neg A)$

(A9) $(A \to B) \to ((B \to C) \to (A \to C))$

(A11) $A \to ((A \to B) \to B)$

(R1) $A, A \to B \vdash B$

(R2) $A, B \vdash A \wedge B$

11.5.3 C is a sub-logic of $Ł_{\aleph}$. We can show this by showing that in every interpretation, each axiom takes the value 1, and that the rules preserve this property. It then follows that everything provable (that is, deducible from the empty set of assumptions) takes the value 1. The proofs of some of these facts are elementary. For example, since $\nu(A) \leq \nu(A \vee B)$, $\nu(A \to (A \vee B)) = 1$, giving A2. And if $\nu(A \to B) = 1$, $\nu(A) \leq \nu(B)$; so if $\nu(A) = 1$, as well, $\nu(B) = 1$, giving R1. Others require more detailed argument. In the next two sections, we do a couple of the harder ones, A5 and A9. The others are left as exercises. One piece of notation will be convenient: we write $\nu(A)$ as a, $\nu(B)$ as b, etc.

11.5.4 For A5: suppose that $b \leq c$. (The other possibility, that $b \geq c$, is similar.) Then, $a \ominus b \leq a \ominus c$, by 11.4.4. Moreover, $Min(b, c) = b$, so $a \ominus Min(b, c) = a \ominus b = Min(a \ominus b, a \ominus c)$; that is, $\nu((A \to B) \wedge (A \to C)) = \nu(A \to (B \wedge C))$. So A5 takes the value 1.

11.5.5 For A9: suppose that $a \leq b$. Then, by 11.4.4, $b \ominus c \leq a \ominus c$, so $(B \to C) \to (A \to C)$ takes the value 1, as, then, does the whole formula. So suppose that $a > b$. If $c \geq a$, then $A \to C$ takes the value 1, as, then, does the whole formula. So suppose that $c < a$. There are now two cases: $a > c \geq b$ and $a > b \geq c$. The value of the consequent is $(b \ominus c) \ominus (a \ominus c)$. In the first case, this is $1 - 1 + a \ominus c = 1 - a + c \geq 1 - a + b$, which is the value of the antecedent. In the second case, $(b \ominus c) \ominus (a \ominus c) = 1 - (1 - b + c) + (1 - a + c) = 1 - a + b$, which is the value of the antecedent. Hence, in both cases, the result follows.

11.5.6 Notice that the other axiom of R, A12 – $(A \rightarrow (A \rightarrow B)) \rightarrow (A \rightarrow B)$ – is not valid in these semantics. (Hence, $Ł_{\aleph}$ is not a sub-logic of R.) To see this, let $\nu(A) = 0.9$ and $\nu(B) = 0.6$. Then $\nu(A \rightarrow B) = \nu(A) \ominus \nu(B) = 0.7$. But $\nu(A \rightarrow (A \rightarrow B)) = 0.9 \ominus 0.7 = 0.8$. Hence, $\nu(A \rightarrow (A \rightarrow B)) > \nu(A \rightarrow B)$. For similar reasons, $\not\models (A \wedge (A \rightarrow B)) \rightarrow B$. Given the same ν, this formula evaluates to 0.9.

11.5.7 A logic sometimes known as CK (which is clearly not a relevant logic) is obtained by adding the following axiom to C.

(A13) $\quad A \rightarrow (B \rightarrow A)$

CK is also a sub-logic of $Ł_{\aleph}$, since this axiom, too, takes the value 1 in any interpretation. To show this, we argue by *reductio*. Suppose, for some ν, that $A \rightarrow (B \rightarrow A)$ does not take the value 1. Then $a > b \ominus a$. It must therefore be the case that $b > a$. But then $a > 1 - b + a$. That is, $b > 1$, which is impossible.

11.5.8 CK is nearly $Ł_{\aleph}$, but not quite. To obtain $Ł_{\aleph}$, we have to add one further axiom – the rather odd-looking:

(A14) $\quad ((A \rightarrow B) \rightarrow B) \rightarrow (A \vee B)$

This axiom is also valid in $Ł_{\aleph}$. For if $a \leq b$, $(a \ominus b) \ominus b = 1 - 1 + b = b \leq Max(a, b)$; and if $a > b$, $a \ominus b = 1 - a + b$. This is greater than b. Hence, $(a \ominus b) \ominus b = 1 - (1 - a + b) + b = a \leq Max(a, b)$.

11.5.9 Hence, this axiom system is sound. To show that it is complete, it suffices to show that it can prove all the axioms of 11.5.1. Since these are complete, we know that every logical truth can be proved from them (using R1). The first three axioms and the last are easy. If we can prove the fifth, the fourth follows from $(A \vee B) \rightarrow (B \vee A)$, which is easily proved. This leaves the fifth. From left to right, this is obvious. From right to left, this is left as an exercise.

11.6 Conditionals in Ł

11.6.1 The most distinctive feature of the conditional in Ł is the failure of *modus ponens*. It is true that $A, A \rightarrow B \models_1 B$. What this means is that whenever the premises take value 1, so does the conclusion. But recall (11.4.11) that $A, A \rightarrow B \models B$ iff $\models_1 (A \wedge (A \rightarrow B)) \rightarrow B$. And this, as we saw (11.5.6), fails.

11.6.2 Given that a sorites argument is simply a sequence of *modus ponens* inferences, the failure of *modus ponens* is hardly surprising. Suppose, for example, that the truth values of a sorites sequence, $M_0, M_1, ..., M_9$, are as follows:

M_0	M_1	M_2	M_3	M_4	M_5	M_6	M_7	M_8	M_9
1	1	1	0.8	0.6	0.4	0.2	0	0	0

Then the value of every conditional $M_i \rightarrow M_{i+1}$ is greater than or equal to 0.8. Hence, it is possible to make every conditional acceptable by setting the level of acceptability as 0.8. Since all the premises of the sorites are then acceptable, and the conclusion is not, *modus ponens* must fail.

11.6.3 The failure of *modus ponens* may still be thought counterintuitive. It should be remembered, however, that the inference is truth-preserving as long as all the formulas involved are completely true or false. It fails only when we trespass into the fuzzy.

11.6.4 Turning to other properties of the conditional in Ł, it is easy to see that $\not\models_1 (A \wedge \neg A) \rightarrow B$, i.e., $A \wedge \neg A \not\models B$ (set $\nu(A) = 0.5$, and $\nu(B) = 0$). Hence, $\models$ is paraconsistent. For similar reasons, $\not\models A \rightarrow (B \vee \neg B)$.

11.6.5 However, Ł is not a relevant logic. It has virtually all of the problematic features of the material conditional. In particular, all of the following hold:

$$A \models B \rightarrow A$$

$$\neg A \models A \to B$$

$$(A \wedge B) \to C \models (A \to C) \vee (B \to C)$$

$$(A \to B) \wedge (C \to D) \models (A \to D) \vee (C \to B)$$

$$\neg(A \to B) \models A$$

Most of these are easy to check. We will do the hardest, the fourth of these, with the others being left as an exercise. If $a \leq d$ or $c \leq b$, then the conclusion takes the value 1. So suppose that $a > d$ and $c > b$. If $a \leq b$, then we have $c > b \geq a > d$, and the first conjunct of the premise takes the value 1. Hence, if the inference fails, the value of the second conjunct must be greater than those of both disjuncts of the conclusion. In particular, because of the first disjunct, we must have $1 - c + d = c \ominus d > a \ominus d = 1 - a + d$, i.e., $a > c$, which it is not. If $c \leq d$, the argument is similar. The only other combination is $a > b$ and $c > d$. In this case, both conjuncts of the premise must have value greater than both disjuncts of the conclusion. In particular, because of the first conjunct, we must have $1 - a + b = a \ominus b > a \ominus d = 1 - a + d$ and $1 - a + b = a \ominus b > c \ominus b = 1 - c + b$, i.e., $b > d$ and $c > a$. Hence, we have $c > a > b > d$. But, by the second conjunct of the premise, we must also have $1 - c + d = c \ominus d > a \ominus d = 1 - a + d$ and $1 - c + d = c \ominus d > c \ominus b = 1 - c + b$, i.e., $a > c$ and $d > b$, both of which are impossible.

11.7 Fuzzy relevant logic

11.7.1 Although *Ł* is not a relevant logic, we can construct a relevant fuzzy logic by combining the techniques of relevant logic and of *Ł*. I will explain how to 'fuzzify' the relevant logic *B*. It should be clear that exactly the same technique will work for other relevant logics.

11.7.2 A fuzzy-*B* interpretation is a structure $\langle W, N, R, *, \nu \rangle$, where W, R, N and $*$ are as in *B* (10.2.4) – and we assume that R has been defined at normal worlds (10.2.8). For every $w \in W$, and every propositional parameter, p, $\nu_w(p) \in [0, 1]$. Truth conditions for the connectives are:

$$\nu_w(\neg A) = 1 - \nu_{w^*}(A)$$

$$\nu_w(A \wedge B) = Min(\nu_w(A), \nu_w(B))$$

$$\nu_w(A \vee B) = Max(\nu_w(A), \nu_w(B))$$

$$\nu_w(A \rightarrow B) = Glb\{\nu_x(A) \ominus \nu_y(B); Rwxy\}$$

Given the truth conditions of *B* and *Ł*, the truth conditions for negation, conjunction and disjunction speak for themselves. In the truth conditions for $\rightarrow$, the universal quantification over worlds, of *B*, has been replaced by a corresponding greatest lower bound. Notice that if all formulas have truth value 1 or 0, all these conditions just reduce to those for *B*. The least obvious is the case for $\rightarrow$. For this, note that when things are 2-valued, the value of a universally quantified sentence is, in effect, the minimum of those of its instances.

11.7.3 The definition of validity is also a natural generalisation of that for *Ł* (11.4.10). Specifically:

> $\Sigma \models A$ iff for every *normal* world, w, of every interpretation, $Glb(\nu_w[\Sigma]) \leq \nu_w(A)$

Notice, again, that if every truth value is either 1 or 0, this condition collapses into the definition of validity for *B*.

11.7.4 Call this logic *FB* (Fuzzy *B*). Since every *B*-interpretation is an *FB*-interpretation – namely, one where every formula takes either the value 1 or the value 0 at every world – *FB* is a sub-logic of *B*. That is, if $\Sigma \models_{FB} A$, then $\Sigma \models_B A$. In particular, then, if $\models_{FB} A$, then $\models_B A$; so *FB* is a relevant logic.

11.7.5 The relationship in the opposite direction is more complex. One may check that all the axioms of *B* (10.3.6) are logically true in *FB*, and all the rules of *B* preserve this property. It follows that if $\models_B A$ then $\models_{FB} A$. The next two sections verify some of the details; the others are left as an exercise. We write $\nu_w(A)$ as a_w, $\nu_w(A \vee B)$ as $(a \vee b)_w$, $\nu_w(A \rightarrow B)$ as $(a \rightarrow b)_w$, etc.

11.7.6 For A2: at any world of an interpretation, x, $a_x \leq (a \vee b)_x$; so $a_x \ominus (a \vee b)_x = 1$. So for every normal world, w, $Glb\{a_x \ominus (a \vee b)_x; Rwxx\} = 1$. For A5: suppose that in an interpretation, $Rxyz$. Suppose that $b_z \leq c_z$. Then, $a_y \ominus b_z \leq a_y, \ominus c_z$, by 11.4.4. Moreover, $(b \wedge c)_z = b_z$, so $a_y \ominus (b \wedge c)_z = a_y \ominus b_z = Min(a_y \ominus b_z, a_y \ominus c_z)$. If, on the other hand, $c_z \leq b_z$, the same result follows by a similar argument. Hence:[4]

$$\begin{aligned} ((a \rightarrow b) \wedge (a \rightarrow c))_x &= Min((a \rightarrow b)_x, (a \rightarrow c)_x) \\ &= Min(Glb\{a_y \ominus b_z; Rxyz\}, Glb\{a_y \ominus c_z; Rxyz\}) \\ &\leq Glb\{Min(a_y \ominus b_z, a_y \ominus c_z); Rxyz\} \\ &= Glb\{a_y \ominus (b \wedge c)_z; Rxyz\} \\ &= (a \rightarrow (b \wedge c))_x \end{aligned}$$

Hence, for normal w, $Glb\{((a \rightarrow b) \wedge (a \rightarrow c))_x \ominus (a \rightarrow (b \wedge c))_x; Rwxx\} = 1$, as required.

11.7.7 For R1: suppose that w is normal, and that a_w and $(a \rightarrow b)_w$ are both 1. Then, for all x such that $Rwxx$, $a_x \leq b_x$. Since $Rwww$, the result follows. For R4: suppose that w is normal, and $(a \rightarrow b)_w = 1$. Then, for all y, $a_y \leq b_y$. It follows that $b_y \ominus c_z \leq a_y \ominus c_z$ by 11.4.4. Hence, $Glb\{b_y \ominus c_z; Rxyz\} \leq Glb\{a_y \ominus c_z; Rxyz\}$. That is, $(b \rightarrow c)_x \leq (a \rightarrow c)_x$. Hence, $Glb\{(b \rightarrow c)_x \ominus (a \rightarrow c)_x; Rwxx\} = 1$, as required.

11.7.8 Although all logical truths of B are logical truths of FB, it is not the case that $\Sigma \models_B A$ entails $\Sigma \models_{FB} A$ for arbitrary Σ. *Modus ponens*, for example, fails, as is to be expected given the fuzzification. Thus, consider the interpretation where $W = N = \{w\}$, $Rwww$, $w^* = w$, $\nu_w(p) = 0.9$, $\nu_w(q) = 0.6$. Then $\nu_w(p \rightarrow q) = 0.7$, so $p, p \rightarrow q \not\models q$.

---

[4] For the third step, note that $Min(Glb\{x_i; i \in I\}, Glb\{y_i; i \in I\}) \leq Glb\{Min(x_i, y_i); i \in I\}$. *Proof*: Suppose that $m = Glb\{x_i; i \in I\} \leq Glb\{y_i; i \in I\}$. (The argument in the other case is similar.) Then, for all $i \in I$, $m \leq x_i, y_i$. Hence, for all $i \in I$, $m \leq Min(x_i, y_i)$. So $m \leq Glb\{Min(x_i, y_i); i \in I\}$.

11.7.9 A suitable proof theory (axiom system or tableau system) for the consequence relation of *FB* is, at the time of writing, an open question.

11.7.10 Finally, consider the inferences that we met in 5.2, in connection with the *ceteris paribus* clause:

$$p \to r \models (p \wedge q) \to r$$

$$p \to q, q \to r \models p \to r$$

$$p \to q \models \neg q \to \neg p$$

The second of these fails. (Just consider a model with one normal world, w, where $\nu_w(p) = 1$, $\nu_w(q) = 0.9$ and $\nu_w(r) = 0.8$.) The first and third hold, however. For the first: take any interpretation, and any world, x, of that interpretation. $(p \wedge q)_x \leq p_x$; hence, by 11.4.4, $p_x \ominus r_x \leq (p \wedge q)_x \ominus r_x$; hence, at all normal worlds, w, $\nu_w((p \wedge q) \to r) \geq \nu_w(p \to r)$. The third is left as an exercise.

11.7.11 One may construct a theory of enthymematic fuzzy relevant conditionals by adding a selection function to the semantics, and giving the appropriate truth conditionals, in exactly the same way that this was done for the non-fuzzy relevant conditional in 10.7. The details are complex, but involve no novelties, and are left to the reader.

11.8 History

The sorites paradox goes back to the Megarian logician Eubulides. After that, the problem of vagueness was largely neglected historically. It has become something of a growth area in the last thirty years, however. Epistemicism has been defended, most notably by Williamson (1994). A supervaluational account has been defended by many, including Fine (1975). The possibility of a 3-valued account, where the middle value is *both true and false* is defended in Hyde (1997). A fuzzy account of vagueness has been defended by many, including Machina (1976).

Continuum-valued logics were first proposed by Łukasiewicz and Tarski in 1930, though not with the application of vagueness in mind. The truth conditions of 11.4.2 are also due to them. The axiom system of 11.5.1 was proved complete by Wajsberg, though the proof was lost and never published, owing to the Second World War. The first published completeness proof was given by Rose and Rosser (1958). This was a combinatorial number-theoretic proof. The second was given by Chang (1959). This was an algebraic proof. There is a readable summary of the whole situation in Rosser (1960). The world semantics for *CK* of 11.10, problem 8, are due to Routley and Meyer (see Routley, Plumwood, Meyer and Brady, 1982). The version given here is taken from Restall (1993). Fuzzy relevant logic is developed in Priest (2000b).

11.9 Further reading

Good short introductions to the problem of vagueness are chapter 7 of Read (1994) and chapter 2 of Sainsbury (1995). Williamson (1994) is a more extended account, and Keefe and Smith (1996) is an excellent collection of readings in the area. A brief technical discussion of continuum-valued logic can be found in Rescher (1969); a longer one is given in Urquhart (1972). A survey of results concerning continuum-valued logic with different sets of designated values can be found in Chang (1963). An account of continuum-valued logic and its connection with fuzzy-set theory, with an eye on the application of both, is given in Klir and Yuan (1995).

11.10 Problems

1. Construct a sorites argument for each of the predicates mentioned in 11.2.3.
2. Check the details omitted in 11.4.4, 11.4.5, 11.5.3, 11.5.9, 11.6.5, 11.7.5 and 11.7.10.

3. Show the following in $Ł_{\aleph}$ (either by giving a proof or by showing that the formula takes the value 1 in all interpretations):

   (*a*) $\models (A \to B) \vee (B \to A)$

   (*b*) $\models (A \to (B \to C)) \to (B \to (A \to C))$

   (*c*) $A \to B \models (A \wedge C) \to B$

   (*d*) $A \to B \models \neg B \to \neg A$

4. By constructing appropriate counter-models, show the following in $Ł_{\aleph}$:

   (*a*) $\not\models p \vee \neg p$

   (*b*) $\not\models (p \wedge (\neg p \vee q)) \to q$

   (*c*) $\not\models ((p \to q) \to q) \to q$

   (*d*) $p \to q, q \to r \not\models p \to r$

   (*e*) $\not\models (p \to \neg p) \to \neg p$

5. Show the following in *FB*:

   (*a*) $A \to B, A \to C \models A \to (B \wedge C)$

   (*b*) $A \to C, B \to C \models (A \vee B) \to C$

   (*c*) $p \to q, q \to r \not\models p \to r$

6. Give the semantics of the *ceteris paribus* clause for fuzzy relevant logic (see 11.7.11), and investigate the properties of enthymematic conditionals.

7. Discuss the problem raised in 11.3.10.

8. Take a ternary relation semantics for *C*. If x and y are worlds, write $x \preceq y$ to mean that for all propositional parameters, p, if $v_x(p) = 1$, then $v_y(p) = 1$. Now consider the condition:

if $Rxyz$ then (i) $x \preceq z$
(ii) $z^* \preceq x^*$
(iii) if $Rzuv$, then $Rxuv$

(This is a ternary version of the heredity condition of the semantics for intuitionist logic (6.3.3).) Prove that if this condition holds in an interpretation for C, then for all A, if $\nu_x(A) = 1$, then $\nu_z(A) = 1$, and if $\nu_{z^*}(A) = 1$, then $\nu_{x^*}(A) = 1$. (*Hint*: Start by showing that if $Rxyz$, Rz^*yx^*; then prove the result by induction over the complexity of formulas.)

9. Show that an interpretation for C that also satisfies the constraint of the previous question verifies axiom A13.

10. *Adding the constraint gives us, in fact, a semantics for CK. To obtain tableaux for CK, we add the obvious tableau rules:

$$\begin{array}{ccc} rxyz & rxyz & rxyz \\ p, +x & p, +\overline{z} & rzuv \\ \downarrow & \downarrow & \downarrow \\ p, +z & p, +\overline{x} & rxuv \end{array}$$

Prove that these are sound and complete with respect to the semantics.

12 Conclusion: an historical perspective

The last chapters of the book have explored, in various ways, a relevant account of conditionals. Such an account seems to me to be better than any of the other accounts that we have traversed in the course of the book. This is, naturally, a contentious view. Logic *is* a contentious subject, and the conditional has been particularly so since the earliest years of the discipline. It was the Stoic logicians who first discussed conditionals explicitly, and they had at least four competing accounts. These accounts survived – one way or another – and others were added throughout the Middle Ages. Consensus might have been reached locally, but only locally.[1]

The changes in logic at the beginning of the twentieth century were revolutionary. The power of the mathematical techniques employed by the founders of modern logic made anything before obsolete. (Which is not to say that there is not now a good deal to be learned from it – just that whatever is of value in it must be seen through radically new eyes.) It is perhaps not surprising, then, that their work established a very general consensus over the conditional. The view of the conditional as material became highly orthodox – though never universal, as C. I. Lewis bears witness.

Digesting the results of the revolution occupied logicians in the first half of the century. But the second half was quite different. It has become clear that the mathematical machinery deployed by Frege and Russell is of a relatively simple kind, and that there is much more sophisticated machinery available, which can be used to do many exciting things. This has made it possible to challenge many of the assumptions built into 'classical logic'. In particular, the machinery has made it possible to construct a galaxy of 'non-standard' logics;

---

[1] For an excellent discussion of all this, see Sylvan (2000).

and I think it fair to say that there is less consensus now over many questions in logic than there has been for a very long time.

One of these questions is surely that of the conditional. In the light of the new developments, the account of the conditional as material must appear a crude one; and the consensus of the earlier part of the twentieth century concerning it, would seem to be entirely an artifact of the limited logical technology then available.

The relevant account of conditionality draws on many of the most notable developments in logic in the second half of the century, and would not have been possible without them: possible worlds, impossible worlds, truth-value gaps and gluts, *ceteris paribus* clauses, degrees of truth. What will happen to this account in the future, and what consensus, if any, will emerge in the twenty-first century, only time will tell.

References

Adams, E. W. (1970), 'Subjunctive and Indicative Conditionals', *Foundations of Language* 6: 89–94.

Anderson, A. and Belnap, N. D. (1975), *Entailment: The Logic of Relevance and Necessity* (Princeton: Princeton University Press), vol. I.

Anderson, A., Belnap, N. D. and Dunn, J. M. (1992), *Entailment: The Logic of Relevance and Necessity* (Princeton: Princeton University Press), vol. II.

Bennett, J. (1969), 'Entailment', *Philosophical Review* 78: 197–236.

Blamey, S. (1986), 'Partial Logic', in Gabbay and Guenthner (1986), ch. 1.

Brown, B. (1993), 'Old Quantum Theory: A Paraconsistent Approach', *Proceedings of the Philosophy of Science Association* 2: 397–441.

Burgess, J. (1983), 'Common Sense and Relevance', *Notre Dame Journal of Formal Logic* 24: 41–53.

Bynum, T. W. (1972), ed., *Conceptual Notation and Related Articles* (Oxford: Clarendon Press).

Chang, C. C. (1959), 'A New Proof of the Completeness Theorem of the Łukasiewicz Axioms', *Transactions of the American Mathematical Society* 93: 74–80.

(1963), 'Logic with Positive and Negative Truth Values', *Acta Philosophica Fennica* 14: 19–39.

Chellas, B. (1975), 'Basic Conditional Logic', *Journal of Philosophical Logic* 4: 133–53.

(1980), *Modal Logic: An Introduction* (Cambridge: Cambridge University Press).

Chomsky, N. (1971), 'Recent Contributions to the Theory of Innate Ideas', in J. R. Searle, ed., *The Philosophy of Language* (Oxford: Oxford University Press), pp. 121–9.

Cooper, W. S. (1968), 'The Propositional Logic of Ordinary Discourse', *Inquiry* 11: 295–320.

Copeland, B. J. (1979), 'On When a Semantics is Not a Semantics; Some Reasons for Disliking the Routley–Meyer Semantics for Relevance Logic', *Journal of Philosophical Logic* 8: 399–413.

(1983), 'Pure and Applied Semantics', *Topoi* 2: 197–204.

(1996), 'Prior's Life and Legacy', in B. J. Copeland, ed., *Logic and Reality: Essays on the Legacy of Arthur Prior* (Oxford: Clarendon Press), pp. 1–40.

Cresswell, M. (1967), 'The Interpretation of Some Lewis Systems of Modal Logic', *Australasian Journal of Philosophy* 45: 198–205.

(1995), '*S1* is not so Simple', in *Modality, Morality and Belief* (Cambridge: Cambridge University Press).

da Costa, N. C. A. (1974), 'On the Theory of Inconsistent Formal Systems', *Notre Dame Journal of Formal Logic* 15: 497–510.

de Swart, H. C. M. (1983), 'A Gentyzen- or Beth-Type System, a Practical Decision Procedure and a Constructive Completeness Proof for the Counterfactual Logics *VC* and *VCS*', *Journal of Symbolic Logic* 48: 1–20.

Došen, K. (1992), 'The First Axiomatization of Relevant Logic', *Journal of Philosophical Logic* 21: 339–56.

Dugunji, J. (1940), 'Note on a Property of Matrices for Lewis and Langford's Calculi of Propositions', *Journal of Symbolic Logic* 5: 150–1.

Dummett, M. (1976), 'What is a Theory of Meaning? (II)', in G. Evans and J. McDowell, eds., *Truth and Meaning* (Oxford: Clarendon Press), ch. 4.

(1977), *Elements of Intuitionism* (Oxford: Oxford University Press).

(1978), 'The Philosophical Basis of Intuitionist Logic', in *Truth and Other Enigmas* (London: Duckworth).

Dunn, J. M. (1986), 'Relevance Logic and Entailment', in Gabbay and Guenthner (1986), ch. 3.

Faris, J. A. (1968), 'Interderivability of "⊃" and "If"', in G. Iseminger, ed., *Logic and Philosophy: Selected Readings* (New York: Appleton-Century-Crofts), ch. 17.

Fine, K. (1975), 'Vagueness, Truth and Logic', *Synthese* 30: 265–300 (reprinted in Keefe and Smith (1996), ch. 9).

Fitting, M. and Mendelsohn, R. (1999), *First Order Modal Logic* (Dordrecht: Kluwer).

Fodor, J. (1975), *The Language of Thought* (New York: Cromwell).

Fraenkel, A., Bar-Hillel, Y. and Levy, A. (1973), eds., *Foundations of Set Theory* (Amsterdam: North-Holland).

Frege, G. (1970), 'On Sense and Reference', in P. Geach and M. Black, eds., *Translations from the Philosophical Writings of Gottlob Frege* (Oxford: Basil Blackwell), pp. 56–78.

Gabbay, D. and Guenthner, F. (1984), eds., *Handbook of Philosophical Logic*, Vol. II: *Extensions of Classical Logic* (Dordrecht: Kluwer).

(1986), eds., *Handbook of Philosophical Logic*, Vol. III: *Alternatives to Classical Logic* (Dordrecht: Kluwer).

Gent, I. P. (1992), 'A Sequent- or Tableau-Style System for Lewis's Counterfactual Logic *VC*', *Notre Dame Journal of Formal Logic* 33: 369–82.

Girle, R. (2000), *Elementary Modal Logic* (London: Acumen).

Gödel, K. (1933a), 'Eine Interpretation des intuitionistischen Aussagenkalküls', *Ergebnisse eines mathematischen Kolloquiums* 4: 39–40 (translated into English in J. Hintikka, ed., *The Philosophy of Mathematics* (Oxford: Oxford University Press), ch. 7.

(1933b), 'Zum intuitionistischen Aussagenkalküls', *Ergebnisse eines mathematischen Kolloquiums* 4: 40.

Gowans, C. (1987), ed., *Moral Dilemmas* (Oxford: Oxford University Press).

Grice, P. (1989), *Studies in the Way of Words* (Cambridge, MA: Harvard University Press).

Haack, S. (1974), *Deviant Logic* (Cambridge: Cambridge University Press).
(1979), *Philosophy of Logics* (Cambridge: Cambridge University Press).
Harper, W. L., Stalnaker, R. and Pearce, G. (1981), eds., *Ifs* (Dordrecht: Reidel).
Hilpinen, R. (1981), ed., *Deontic Logic: Introductory and Systematic Readings*, 2nd edn. (Dordrecht: Reidel).
Hintikka, J. (1962), *Knowledge and Belief: An Introduction to the Logic of the Two Notions* (Ithaca: Cornell University Press).
Howson, C. (1997), *Logic with Trees* (London: Routledge).
Hughes, G. and Cresswell, M. (1996), *A New Introduction to Modal Logic* (London: Routledge).
Hyde, D. (1997), 'From Heaps and Gaps to Heaps of Gluts', *Mind* 106: 641–60.
Hyde, D. and Priest, G. (2000), eds., *Sociative Logics and their Applications: Essays by the Late Richard Sylvan* (Aldershot: Ashgate).
Jackson, F. (1991), ed., *Conditionals* (Oxford: Oxford University Press).
Jaśkowski, S. (1969), 'Propositional Calculus for Contradictory Deductive Systems', *Studia Logica* 24: 143–57.
Jeffrey, R. (1991), *Formal Logic: Its Scope and its Limits*, 3rd edn (New York: McGraw-Hill).
Keefe, R. and Smith, P. (1996), *Vagueness: A Reader* (Cambridge, MA: MIT Press).
Kleene, S. C. (1952), *Introduction to Metamathematics* (Amsterdam: North-Holland).
Klir, G. L. and Yuan, B. (1995), *Fuzzy Sets and Fuzzy Logic: Theory and Applications* (Upper Saddle River, NJ: Prentice Hall).
Kneale, W. and Kneale, M. (1975), *The Development of Logic*, 2nd edn (Oxford: Clarendon Press).
Knuuttila. S. (1982), 'Modal Logic', in N. Kretzmann, A. Kenny, J. Pinborg and E. Stump, eds., *The Cambridge History of Later Medieval Philosophy* (Cambridge: Cambridge University Press), ch. 17.
Kripke. S. (1963), 'Semantical Analysis of Modal Logic, I: Normal Propositional Calculi', *Zeitschrift für Mathematische Logik und Grundlagen der Mathematik* 8:113–16.
(1965a), 'Semantical Analysis of Modal Logic, II: Non-Normal Modal Propositional Calculi', in J. W. Addison, L. Henkin and A. Tarski, eds., *The Theory of Models* (Amsterdam: North-Holland), pp. 202–20.
(1965b), 'Semantical Analysis of Intuitionistic Logic, I', in J. Crossley and M. Dummett, eds., *Formal Systems and Recursive Functions* (Amsterdam: North-Holland).
(1975), 'Outline of a Theory of Truth', *Journal of Philosophy* 72: 690–716.
(1977), 'Identity and Necessity', in S. P. Schwartz, ed., *Naming, Necessity and Natural Kinds* (Ithaca: Cornell University Press), ch. 2.
(1980), *Naming and Necessity* (Cambridge, MA: Harvard University Press).
Lemmon, E. J. (1957), 'New Foundations for the Lewis Modal Systems', *Journal of Symbolic Logic* 22: 176–86.
(1959), 'Is There Only One Correct System of Modal Logic?', *Proceedings of the Aristotelian Society, Supplementary Volume* 33: 23–40.
Lewis, C. I. and Langford, C. H. (1931), *Symbolic Logic* (New York: Dover).

Lewis, D. (1971), 'Completeness and Decidability of Three Logics of Counterfactuals', *Theoria* 37: 74–85.

(1973a), 'Counterfactuals and Comparative Possibility', *Journal of Philosophical Logic* 2: 418–46 (reprinted in Harper, Stalnaker and Pearce (1981), pp. 57–85).

(1973b), *Counterfactuals* (Oxford: Basil Blackwell).

(1979), 'Counterfactual Dependence and Time's Arrow', *Noûs* 13, 455–76.

(1986), *On the Plurality of Worlds* (Oxford: Basil Blackwell).

Loux, M. J. (1979), ed., *The Possible and the Actual* (Ithaca: Cornell University Press).

Łukasiewicz, J. (1967), 'Philosophical Remarks on Many-Valued Systems of Propositional Logic', in S. McCall, ed., *Polish Logic, 1920–1939* (Oxford: Clarendon Press), ch. 3.

Machina, K. (1976), 'Truth, Belief and Vagueness', *Journal of Philosophical Logic* 5: 47–78 (reprinted in Keefe and Smith (1996), ch. 11).

Mares, E. (1996), 'Relevant Logic and the Theory of Information', *Synthese* 109: 345–60.

Mares, E. and Fuhrmann, A. (1995), 'A Relevant Theory of Conditionals', *Journal of Philosophical Logic* 24: 645–65.

Martin, C. (1985), 'William's Machine', *Journal of Philosophy* 83: 564–72.

Meyer, R. K. (1970), 'R_I – the Bounds of Finitude', *Zeitschrift für Mathematische Logik und Grundlagen der Mathematik* 16: 385–7.

(1971), 'Entailment', *Journal of Philosophy* 68: 808–18.

Mortensen, C. (1983), 'The Validity of the Disjunctive Syllogism is not so Easily Proven', *Notre Dame Journal of Formal Logic* 24: 35–40.

Norman, J. and Sylvan, R. (1989), eds., *Directions in Relevant Logic* (Dordrecht: Kluwer).

Nute, D. (1980), *Conditional Logic* (Dordrecht: Reidel).

(1984), 'Conditional Logic', in Gabbay and Guenthner (1984), ch. 8.

Post, E. (1921), 'Introduction to the General Theory of Elementary Propositions', *American Journal of Mathematics* 43: 163–85 (reprinted in J. van Heijenoort, ed., *From Frege to Gödel: A Source Book in Mathematical Logic, 1879–1931* (Cambridge, MA: Harvard University Press), pp. 264–83).

Priest, G. (1979), 'Logic of Paradox', *Journal of Philosophical Logic* 8: 219–41.

(1987), *In Contradiction; A Study of the Transconsistent* (The Hague: Martinus Nijhoff).

(1992), 'What is a Non-Normal World?', *Logique et Analyse* 35: 291–302.

(1993), 'Can Contradictions be True?, II', *Proceedings of the Aristotelian Society, Supplementary Volume* 68: 35–54.

(1996), 'Logic, Nonstandard', in D. M. Borchert, ed., *The Encyclopedia of Philosophy, Supplement* (New York: Macmillan).

(1997a), 'Sylvan's Box: A Short Story and Ten Morals', in Priest (1997b), pp. 573–82.

(1997b), guest ed., *Notre Dame Journal of Formal Logic* 38, no. 4 (Special Issue on Impossible Worlds).

(1998), 'Dialetheism', *Stanford Internet Encyclopedia of Philosophy*, http://plato.stanford.edu/entries/dialetheism/

(2000a), 'Paraconsistent Logic', in D. Gabbay and F. Guenthner, eds., *Handbook of Philosophical Logic*, 2nd edn (Dordrecht: Kluwer).

(2000b), 'Fuzzy Relevant Logic', paper to the 2nd World Congress on Paraconsistency, São Paulo, Brazil.

Priest, G. and Routley, R. (1989a), 'Applications of Paraconsistent Logic', in Priest, Routley and Norman (1989), ch. 13.

(1989b), 'The Philosophical Significance and Inevitability of Paraconsistency', in Priest, Routley and Norman (1989), ch. 18.

Priest, G., Routley, R. and Norman, J. (1989), eds., *Paraconsistent Logic: Essays on the Inconsistent* (Munich: Philosophia Verlag).

Priest, G. and Sylvan, R. (1992), 'Simplified Semantics for Basic Relevant Logics', *Journal of Philosophical Logic* 21: 217–32.

Prior, A. (1957), *Time and Modality* (Oxford: Clarendon Press).

Quine, W. V. O. (1963), *From a Logical Point of View* (New York: Harper and Row).

Read, S. (1988), *Relevant Logic* (Oxford: Basil Blackwell).

(1994), *Thinking About Logic: An Introduction to the Philosophy of Logic* (Oxford: Oxford University Press).

Rescher, N. (1969), *Many-Valued Logic* (New York: McGraw-Hill).

Restall, G. (1993), 'Simplified Semantics for Relevant Logics (and Some of Their Rivals)', *Journal of Philosophical Logic* 22: 481–511.

(1995), 'Four-Valued Semantics for Relevant Logics (and Some of Their Rivals)', *Journal of Philosophical Logic*: 24: 139–60.

(1996), 'Information Flow and Relevant Logic', in J.Seligman and D. Westerståhl, eds., *Logic, Language and Computation* (Stanford: CSLI Publications), vol. I.

(1999), 'Negation in Relevant Logics (How I Stopped Worrying and Learned to Love the Routley Star)', in D. Gabbay and H. Wansing, eds., *What is Negation?* (Dordrecht: Kluwer), pp. 53–76.

(2000a), *Logic; The Fundamentals of Philosophy* (London: University College London Publications).

(2000b), *Consequences: An Introduction to Substructural Logics* (London: Routledge).

Robinson, J. O. (1972), *The Psychology of Visual Illusion* (London: Hutchinson).

Rose, R. and Rosser, J. B. (1958), 'Fragments of Many Valued Statement Calculi', *Transactions of the American Mathematical Society* 87: 1–53.

Rosser, J. B. (1960), 'Axiomatization of Infinite Valued Logics', *Logique et Analyse* 3: 137–53.

Routley, R. (1980), *Exploring Meinong's Jungle and Beyond*, Departmental Monograph, no. 3, Philosophy Department, Australian National University, Canberra.

(1984) 'The American Plan Completed: Alternative Classical Style Semantics, without Stars, for Relevant and Paraconsistent Logics', *Studia Logica* 43: 131–58.

(1989a), 'Philosophical and Linguistic Inroads: Multiply Intensional Relevant Logics', in Norman and Sylvan (1989), ch. 19.

(1989b), 'Routes in Relevant Logic', in Norman and Sylvan (1989), ch. 19.

Routley, R. and Loparić, A. (1978), 'Semantical Analysis of Arruda-da Costa *P* Systems and Adjacent Non-Replacement Relevant Systems', *Studia Logica* 37: 301–22.

Routley, R. and Meyer, R. K. (1973), 'The Semantics of Entailment', in H. Leblanc, ed., *Truth, Syntax and Modality* (Amsterdam: North-Holland).

Routley, R., Plumwood, V., Meyer, R. K. and Brady, R. (1982), *Relevant Logics and their Rivals* (Atascadero, CA: Ridgeview), vol. I.

Routley, R. and Routley, V. (1972), 'The Semantics of First Degree Entailment', *Noûs* 6: 335–95.

(1985), 'Negation and Contradiction', *Rivista Columbiana de Matemáticas* 19: 201–31.

Routley, R., Routley, V., Meyer, R. K. and Martin, E. (1982), 'On the Philosophical Bases of Relevant Logic Semantics', *Journal of Non-Classical Logic* 1: 71–102.

Russell, B. (1903), *The Principles of Mathematics* (Cambridge: Cambridge University Press).

(1905), 'On Denoting', *Mind* 14: 479–93.

Sainsbury, M. (1995), *Paradoxes*, 2nd edn (Cambridge: Cambridge University Press).

Sanford, D. (1989), *If P then Q: Conditionals and the Foundations of Reasoning* (London: Routledge).

Segerberg, K. (1989), 'Notes on Conditional Logic', *Studia Logica* 48: 157–68.

Smullyan, R. (1968), *First Order Logic* (Berlin: Springer Verlag).

Stalnaker, R. (1968), 'A Theory of Conditionals', in *Studies in Logical Theory*, American Philosophical Quarterly Monograph Series, no. 2 (Oxford: Basil Blackwell) (reprinted in Harper, Stalnaker and Pearce (1981), pp. 41–55).

(1996), 'Impossibilities', *Philosophical Topics* 24: 193–204.

Strawson, P. (1950), 'On Referring', *Mind* 59: 320–44.

Sylvan, R. (2000), 'A Preliminary Western History of Sociative Logics', in Hyde and Priest (2000), ch. 5.

Urquhart, A. (1972), 'Semantics for Relevant Logics', *Journal of Symbolic Logic* 37: 159–69.

(1986), 'Many-Valued Logic', in Gabbay and Guenthner (1986), ch. 2.

van Fraassen, B. (1969), 'Presuppositions, Supervaluations and Free Logic', in K. Lambert, ed., *The Logical Way of Doing Things* (New Haven: Yale University Press).

Von Wright, G. H. (1951), *An Essay in Modal Logic* (Amsterdam: North-Holland).

(1957), 'Deontic Logic', *Logical Studies* (London: Routledge & Kegan Paul), ch. 4.

Williamson, T. (1994), *Vagueness* (London: Routledge).

Wittgenstein, L. (1953), *Philosophical Investigations* (Oxford: Basil Blackwell).

Wright, C. (1987), 'Anti-Realism and Revisionism', in *Realism, Meaning and Truth* (Oxford: Basil Blackwell), ch. 10.

Yagisawa, T. (1988), 'Beyond Possible Worlds', *Philosophical Studies* 53: 175–204.

Index of names

Index of subjects

Unless otherwise indicated, references in this index are to pages. An italicised page number indicates a section (not a subsection) a substantial part of which deals with the indexed topic. A reference to a whole chapter dealing substantially with the indexed topic is indicated by 'ch.'.